MW00768042

1925 Exeter Road
Germantown, TN 38138

JUN 0 7 2010

A
HISTORY
of
GHOSTS

A
HISTORY
of
GHOSTS

THE TRUE STORY
OF SÉANCES, MEDIUMS,
GHOSTS, AND GHOSTBUSTERS

---

by Peter H. Aykroyd with Angela Narth

Foreword by Dan Aykroyd

RODALE

© 2009 by Peter H. Aykroyd

Rodale books may be purchased for business or promotional use or for special sales. For information, please write to:

Special Markets Department, Rodale Inc., 733 Third Avenue, New York, NY 10017

Printed in the United States of America

Rodale Inc. makes every effort to use acid-free ⊖, recycled paper ◎.

Photo insert, pages 1, 2, and 3: Courtesy of the Aykroyd family; page 4: *top row*: Reprinted with permission of Fortean Picture Library; *bottom row (left)*: Courtesy of University of Manitoba Archives and Special Collections; *(right)* Reprinted with permission of Fortean Picture Library; page 5, *top row (left to right)*: Reprinted with permission of Getty Images; Courtesy of Library of Congress; *bottom row (left)*: Courtesy of University of Manitoba Archives and Special Collections; *(right)* Courtesy of Time Life Books; page 6: Courtesy of the Lily Dale Assembly 2007; page 7: Courtesy of University of Manitoba Archives and Special Collections; page 8:*(trumpet)*: Courtesy of the Aykroyd family; *(hand cast)*: Reprinted with permission of Fortean Picture Library; *(slates)*: Courtesy of the Aykroyd family

Book design by Christina Gaugler

Library of Congress Cataloging-in-Publication Data

Aykroyd, Peter.
    A history of ghosts : the true story of séances, mediums, ghosts, and ghostbusters / by Peter Aykroyd, with Angela Narth ; introduction by Dan Aykroyd.
        p.   cm.
    Includes bibliographical references and index.
    ISBN-13   978–1–60529–875–7   hardcover
    1. Spiritualism—History. 2. Ghosts—history. I. Narth, Angela. II. Title.
    BF1241.A95 2009
    133.109—dc22   2009018360

Distributed to the trade by Macmillan

2 4 6 8 10 9 7 5 3 1   hardcover

RODALE
LIVE YOUR WHOLE LIFE™

We inspire and enable people to improve their lives and the world around them
For more of our products visit **rodalestore.com** or call 800-848-4735

This book is dedicated to my grandfather,
Samuel Augustus Aykroyd, DDS (1855–1933), pioneer,
dentist, philosopher, ethical humanist, and foot soldier
in the Spiritualist movement.

CONTENTS

FOREWORD

People often ask me how I came to write *Ghostbusters*. The truth is that in the early 1900s my family was part of a worldwide cultural and social phenomenon driven by a wish to make contact with spirits of the dead whether the dead wanted it or not.

My great-grandfather, Samuel Augustus Aykroyd, DDS, presided over his own home circle, and the sitters had their very own medium, Walter Ashurst, whom they believed acted as a conduit to many and varied afterworld personalities. Whether one believes in this kind of thing or not, my family was then and is now not alone in such pursuits. Thousands of people in Western society regularly hold séances and support mediums.

Around the beginning of the 20th century, mediums and their subsequent investigators became big stars and spiritualism took on a distinct show-business aspect. Were there fakes? Hoaxes? Many, to be sure, and some would say they were all tricks. But Baron Albert von Schrenk-Notzing, the German ectoplasm hunter; Sir Arthur Conan Doyle, writer of the Sherlock Holmes detective series; and Sir Oliver Lodge, eminent scientist and philosopher, were men who held the hope that someday natural science might rationally encompass the supernatural as a proven fact.

Levitations; apports; apparitions; limbs, complete with hair, skin, and bones, instantly growing out of living people; plasmic material molded into real-tissue impressions of faces and bodies—these things were seen by many witnesses, skeptics and believers alike. Were these mere spectacles achieved by artificial devices, or are some of them simply part of a reality that exists beyond our own sensible understanding?

Part of *Ghostbusters'* appeal derives from the cold, rational, acceptance-of-the-fantastic-as-routine tone that Bill Murray, Harold Ramis, director Ivan Reitman, and I were able to sustain in the movie.

This element originated from my great-grandfather's interest in the subject and from the books he collected. He bequeathed these to his son, my grandfather, Maurice, the Bell Telephone engineer who actually queried his colleagues about the possibility of constructing a high-vibration crystal radio as a mechanical method for contacting the spiritual world. His son, my father, as a child witnessed séances and kept the family books on the subject. My brother Peter and I read them avidly and became lifelong supporters of the American Society for Psychical Research, and from all this *Ghostbusters* got made.

My daughters are now up on the subject, and one of them, we have found, seems to affect photographs. Glops of light and other shapes attend her when pictures are taken in and around the old family farmhouse.

The children will have to make their own decisions about the verity and value of psychic studies.

Their grandfather's book, *A History of Ghosts,* will surely assist them. It is as objective as any serious seeker of the truth about alleged paranormal activities could wish.

Both believers and nonbelievers will, first, be highly entertained and then surprisingly enlightened by these stories of real empiricists chasing ghosts.

Dan Aykroyd
Los Angeles, California
February 2009

PREFACE

$\mathbf{I}$n families, we often find instances of succeeding generations of schoolteachers, military personnel, and lawyers. Traditions are like dynasties, often the lengthened shadow of a single person.

In our family, this person is my grandfather, Samuel Augustus Aykroyd, DDS, and the tradition he bequeathed to us was experimentation in psychic phenomena. One hundred years ago, he started keeping journals, diaries, letters, and opinion pieces on the subjects of spiritualism and psychic phenomena, based primarily on séances held in his home using a full trance medium.

This was all familiar territory to his son, my father, Maurice J. Aykroyd, who was himself an experimenter and, like Dr. Aykroyd, an ethical humanist.

My brother Maurice Jr. and I sat in on many of the séances, and in a quiet way, we felt that we were privileged to be part of something larger than ourselves, but because spiritualism has little dogma, no liturgy, and no consistent public and easily accessible expression, no one knew of this influence upon our lives. It was not until we were young adults that other influences came to bear and settle for us some of the great questions of life. My sister, Judy Harvie, obtained the same quiet assurance, and all three of us could be characterized as ethical humanists.

In my sons, Dan and Peter Johnathan, the shadow lengthened dramatically, and in the electronic age it spread to all corners of the planet.

In the fifth generation, the penumbra is there, but much weaker. All dynasties eventually fade away, and so it is with family traditions. That brings me to this book.

When Dr. Aykroyd's diaries fell into my hands, they cried out to be put into a book and disseminated. I am certain that Dr. Aykroyd had hoped that somehow, some day, this would happen.

Here it is.

Although not providing the actual spine of the book, Dr. Aykroyd's material was its major determinant, propelling me into 6 years of research and writing.

Beyond the world that we can see and touch, there is an invisible world. Consider radio waves, television waves, and cell phone signals, each vibrating at its own frequency. Have we ever seen any of these waves? No. Only what they produce. Consider magnetism, electricity, and gravity. We cannot see any of them. We only experience what they produce.

Put this book down every now and then and quietly look around. The room is teeming with invisible forces and signals that we cannot see—and loaded and present along with all the things we cannot see are ghosts and spirits. They, too, are part of the invisible world.

This book thoroughly surveys the universe of historical spiritualism, psychic phenomena, and the invisible world.

Many hair-raisers and gasp-elicitors are to be found here, as is, would you believe, surprising stuff that will make you laugh.

On your way through, look for what you are inclined to believe is empirical evidence of an afterlife. The search for such evidence is a major theme of this narrative.

In this book, you have something to have and to hold, to lend and to refer to. You can make its substance part of you. You could become your own ghost whisperer.

This is a good book, if I do say so myself.

Good value.

I trust you will enjoy reading it.

February 10, 2009

PROLOGUE

May 12, 1929, Sydenham, Ontario

Four cars, all black, all polished for the trip from town, roll down the long lane to the farmhouse, the crunch of gravel beneath the tires momentarily silencing the birds. Dust settles on the gleaming finishes of the automobiles and they pull up beside the farmhouse, parking randomly on the grass: a Whippet, a Durant, a Willys-Knight, and a Dodge. The occupants alight. Four men in three-piece suits with well-shined shoes form a little knot. The women, four of them as well, all in black with stylish hats, form a companion group.

The faces are familiar. I have seen them all before. At church or in town, these people always have something friendly to say to me. But from here, in my hiding place among the newly budding lilac bushes, they appear unapproachable. Their minds are on something else.

I slip unobserved across the lawn to the back of the house and toward the outside cellar entrance. The cellar stairs are damp, and as I pull open one side of the heavy horizontal doors, I smell the rich, loamy scent of ripened apples. The rest of the family is puzzled by my favored mode of entry, but I am quite content entering the house this way. It gives me access to experiences I might otherwise miss. At age 7, I am as curious as they come.

I cross the cellar, which is dimly lit by the slanting sunlight entering through the outside door. I climb up the inside cellar stairs and kneel patiently on the top step, waiting. The cellar door is open a crack. From here I can see the kitchen in one direction and, in the other, the fireplace and the table in the parlor. I can hear the voice emanating from the Philco radio. It is crisp and clear as it delivers the news: A man named de Valera has just been sentenced to 1 month in prison in Northern Ireland, and a singer named Josephine Baker has been banned from the stage for something the newscaster calls "indecent behavior." He doesn't elaborate.

If I lean forward, I can see the front door and the verandah. I shift my position to see if anyone has entered yet, but apparently the people in the driveway are enjoying the last rays of the spring sun, the scent of lilacs, and the soft sounds of birdsong.

My grandfather is sitting in his usual chair by the fireplace, intent upon hearing every last word the newscaster has to say about world events: Mr. Trotsky is vowing to give up politics; the first in-flight movie has just been shown in the air between Chicago and St. Paul, Minnesota.

Grandpa grunts and snaps the radio's dial, silencing it.

"People these days can't seem to tolerate one moment without entertainment!" he mutters, almost to himself.

He stands and straightens his jacket, buttoning it formally across his lean frame, then glances at his pocket watch dangling from a sparkling gold fob. Moving toward the square table in the center of the cozy room, he adjusts the silk cloth in its center, then says something to the young, dark-haired man who is sitting there. Other than a slight wave of his hand, the young man gives little acknowledgment of having heard. His head is bowed and he seems unconcerned with his surroundings. Grandpa looks out the parlor window, then nods toward the kitchen, where I know my grandma is setting out the tea things.

"It's time, my dear," Grandpa says to her quietly.

He turns and walks out the front door and stands on the verandah, his hands clasped loosely behind his back. The mantle clock is ticking, and I can hear the young man's soft, rhythmic breathing as the grown-up scent of his cigarette drifts toward me. Waiting is pleasant, but I don't have to wait long.

The group, with Grandpa bringing up the rear, enters the farmhouse. They are chatting quietly. Once in the parlor, they are greeted by Grandma, a plump, smiling lady. I see that she is also dressed in black, as if for a funeral. As the fresh breeze wafts through the house, it brings another scent to me—the distinct aroma of freshly baked bread. And sure enough, through the crack by the doorjamb I can see *two pans of buns, glistening from the application of homemade butter, warming at the back of the woodstove in the kitchen.*

My mouth begins to water, but my attention is drawn away from my already full stomach. Grandpa has invited the guests to be seated and I must alter my position for a better view. I sense that it is important for me to see but remain unseen, for I am supposed to be in my bedroom preparing for bed.

The unlit coal-oil lamp stands on the sideboard waiting to do its part when dusk turns to dark. I wedge myself carefully between the wall and the inside of the cellar door, sliding silently to a seated position. Comfort will be crucial. It will be a long night.

The drapes are drawn, but there is still a faint light in the room. As the guests file into the parlor, they nod significantly to the seated man and take their places, leaving vacant the chairs on either side of the young man. Once the guests are seated, Grandma takes the chair to the young man's left. Grandpa follows and occupies the last chair, to the young man's right.

For the first time I notice that the young man is dressed differently from the others. His attire is far more casual: an open-collar work shirt and a cardigan sweater in a curious shade that makes me think of Absorbine Jr. Grandpa speaks.

"Please hold hands around the table. Try to think positive thoughts. Pray silently, if you wish."

The young man stubs out his Turret cigarette. He leans back, closes his eyes, and slips into a trance. In the deafening, pin-drop silence, it is as if some curtain is about to rise into some invisible arch in the ceiling. But the show is an unusual one. These guests have not traveled from town to see a play or hear a concert. This is a meeting of Dr. Aykroyd's Circle. A séance is about to begin, and the people present are here to engage in an unusual form of communication.

They have come from town to talk to the dead.

Ghosts at Home: The Home Circle

The sights and sounds of that childhood scene came tumbling back to me one mild winter afternoon more than 50 years later. My sister Judy and I had taken on the task of clearing out the family home in Toronto, the place where my grandfather, Samuel Augustus Aykroyd, DDS, had spent the last days of his life. The house at 9 Garfield Avenue had been sold, and Judy and I had taken a weekend out of our own busy schedules to decide who would get what, what would go to auction, and what would be donated to the Salvation Army. The rest would go to the dump.

We had kept the dark basement for last. Several items that were seen as childhood treasures had been located upstairs: memorabilia and photos, ancient jewelry, original artworks, and a few rare books. We were not terribly excited about what could possibly be lurking in the dark wasteland below stairs.

With the last drops of a Manhattan made from bonded stock rye warming our insides, we had already made several trips up and down the stairs. Next to the furnace, in a corner of what was once the coal storage bin, we came upon our last load. Most of what we found was destined for the landfill: old suitcases with jagged zippers and broken handles that proved they had been to more places than most people, empty cardboard boxes, a stained mattress from a twin bed. And in the back, against a wall, an old, blue metal trunk. With the dedication of two people who felt duty-bound to thoroughly examine everything in their care, Judy and I pried open the rusted metal clasp with a screwdriver. We had expected to find either junk or emptiness. Instead, we found history.

Inside were a photo album of black-and-white prints attached with triangular corner mounts and yellowed newspapers from decades back, saved for articles germane to the family. There was a scrapbook of recipes, and our father's sheepskin from Queen's University, Applied Science 1913, and a bundle of notebooks of the type that children used in school. They were bound together with kitchen twine.

We untied the bundle and began to read page after page of penciled handwriting. Not good handwriting. Very hard to read. With no anticipation of doing so, we had come across Grandpa's journals (83 of them, to be precise), written in his own hand from 1905 through 1931 and containing thoughts, observations, and conjectures that he clearly had hoped might someday be shared with others.

Within the now fragile pages were handwritten copies of letters to his family and friends and to the editors of local newspapers. The majority of the words he recorded are actual accounts of séances, most of which took place in the small farmhouse on the north shore of Loughborough Lake, near the village of Sydenham, Ontario. Other passages are his musings over what it's all about. The notes and letters aid my remembrances of the taciturn elderly gentleman who lived in that farmhouse, where I spent many gloriously happy days and nights.

In my mind's eye I can still see him in faded blue shirt and baggy tweed pants, sitting on the bank of Lake Loughborough with his feet over the edge of the dock, jotting his thoughts into a child's notebook with a Dixon HB pencil. My grandfather created in me a lifelong interest in the paranormal, an interest that has proved to be enormously engaging and fun. I have passed it on to my sons, Dan and Peter, and it also resulted in a television series and movies, which have been the most fun of all. In 1984, the year of *Ghostbusters'* release, it became the most successful comedy in film history (to date it has been seen by a billion people), and it was absolutely and directly derived from the blue trunk. I only hope Grandpa knows what fun he started!

SAMUEL A. AYKROYD
The Young Dr. Aykroyd

Dr. Samuel Augustus Aykroyd was born March 22, 1855, in Storrington Township, a rural area of eastern Ontario 20 miles north of Kingston. His parents, Daniel and Martha, must have had a sense of history, because Augustus is not now, nor was it at the time of his birth, a common name.

Samuel grew up the eldest of 14 children in a small farmhouse on a piece of prime Ontario land designated as Lot 8, a portion of approximately 150 acres of property abutting Lake Loughborough in Frontenac County, Ontario, which his great-grandfather had purchased from the Crown in 1826. Samuel attended public school at Kepler and, following graduation from Sydenham High School, moved to the town of Kingston, where he obtained his teaching certificate. He obtained a teaching position in the town of Emerald on Amherst Island in Lake Ontario. While he was there, he met Ellen Jane Wemp, the lovely young woman who was to become his wife in 1884 and the mother of their two children, Lillian in 1885 and Maurice James in 1891.

Teaching public school to children ages 5 to 12 in a drafty one-room schoolhouse on Amherst Island wasn't particularly rewarding. Samuel soon received an appointment at a bigger school in Kingston Township, and he was content for a while. But the salary of schoolteachers in those days was abysmally low, and the prospect of future increases was uncertain. Samuel hadn't fled the farm with its limited opportunities to look forward to a life of penury as a public school teacher. His ambitions reached beyond that.

The school curriculum of the day had evolved beyond the three Rs to include some history, geography, and science. It was the latter subject that interested him the most, and his curiosity coupled with his ambition led him to consider dentistry as a profession. There was certainly opportunity to develop a substantial practice in Kingston and its surrounding towns and villages. The area, which at the time had a combined population of some 22,000, had only two dentists, both of whom had been practicing for nearly 2 decades.

So Samuel, at the age of 34, with his young wife and their small daughter in tow, enrolled as a student at the University of Toronto's School of Dentistry of the Royal College of Dental Surgeons. He graduated with the degree of doctor of dental surgery in 1891, and in 1892, after the required period of internship, he opened his own practice in rooms over Hobart's Medical Hall at 92 Princess Street in Kingston.

By today's standards, dentistry in 1892 was still in a primitive state. There was no electricity to drive the flexible cable that powered the drill; it was operated instead by a foot pedal similar in function to the old Singer sewing machine treadle. The x-ray was not discovered by the German scientist Wilhelm Röntgen until 1895, and it would be many more years before x-ray machines were affordable enough for the average practitioner, so finding the exact location and extent of decay was difficult. A variety of alloys for fillings went through a trial-and-error process. Similarly, analgesic drugs would come and

Mesmerism

The mind-over-matter technique of mesmerism was introduced in Europe in the late 1700s by Franz Mesmer, an Austrian mystic and physician. Although Mesmer himself fell into obscurity in the last 20 years of his life, his ideas were carried on. One of his students, Count Maxime de Puységur, discovered that the therapeutic value of Mesmer's methods lay in the suggestibility induced by the trance state. This discovery set the stage for further experimentation in Britain and on the continent. In 1841, from ideas based on Mesmer's theories, James Braid, a British physician, began to use a self-induced altered state of consciousness with his patients to produce anesthesia. He referred to this phenomenon as hypnotism, a practice that was later adopted by a number of surgeons.

go, their use in practice not resulting from any scientific basis, but from their efficacy in clinical settings. One treatment for pain control that came into vogue during the 1890s was hypnosis, or mesmerism, as it was then known.

It is unlikely that Dr. Aykroyd ever used hypnotism on his own patients. Suffice it to say that this intelligent and exceedingly well-trained professional, whose formal training included hundreds of lectures on everything from Visceral Anatomy to Elements of Bacteriology, would have been, at the very least, intrigued enough to look into this alternative method. The mere presence of his journals suggests that he was a thinking man, a man who approached all subjects in his sphere of interest with the sobriety and seriousness that one would expect from a professional. And whether or not its availability led to its use in his practice, hypnotism was probably one of the things that sparked Dr. A.'s interest in a relatively new phenomenon called spiritualism.

The second half of the 19th century and the first half of the 20th ushered in an escalation in the popularity of what was generally known as spiritualism, and it would serve us well to begin our discussion with a few definitions.

My preferred definition of "spiritualism" is the belief that departed spirits communicate with and show themselves to the living, especially when they do so through mediums; it also includes the system of doctrines and practices founded on this belief.

A more formal definition is found in *The Encyclopedia of Ghosts and Spirits:*

A nineteenth century social and religious movement that derived its appeal from spirit communications and evidence in support of survival after death (Guiley 2000, 362).

Dr. A. was a follower of the movement known as spiritualism. He believed that the human personality survives after bodily death and accepted the idea that those with biological life have the ability to communicate with those who appear to be minds without bodies. The uncertainty about what happens to us when we die and, even more importantly, whether we here on earth can communicate with those who have passed on drew people together to pursue the mysteries of the supernatural spirit.

As time went on, the connotation of spiritualism expanded to include psychic phenomena in general, things that were considered paranormal, and, eventually, channeling.

Although there is ample evidence of prehistoric humans attempting to communicate with spirits, and later evidence cited from such reliable sources as the Bible, the spiritualist movement as we now know it is fairly recent, having its origins in the United States within the last 200 years. Its followers are many and include thousands of people whom we consider rational—people like Dr. A.

A learned man with an open mind, Dr. A. considered himself "a humble student seeking knowledge." His interests were many, his pursuits varied. He was a pure scientist, trained in medical science. He was also an applied scientist, putting his knowledge to practical use as he treated his patients in his dental parlor. He knew about the human body; he knew chemistry. He was also an intellectual in the dictionary sense, an enlightened person who was attracted to subjects requiring the exercise of intellect. Not a religious man per se, he was the product of an old orthodoxy passed down from his Methodist great-grandfather Aykroyd (also named Samuel), who was among the charter subscribing members of the Kingston Wesleyan Chapel, the first Methodist church in the Kingston area. Although Dr. A.'s interest in the paranormal undoubtedly began in the early 1900s, at least one author on the topic who made a profound impact on him predated the good dentist's birth by 2 centuries.

Early Influences
Emmanuel Swedenborg

Emmanuel Swedenborg (1688–1772) was a Swedish scientist, philosopher, and scholar who showed keen interest and talent in mathematics and the sciences, particularly astronomy and physics. Although he made substantial contributions to the sciences (among other things, he suggested the nebular hypothesis for the formation of planets and provided a detailed description of the nature of cerebrospinal fluid), his name is best known for his ideas in the fields of theology and spiritualism.

Despite showing some psychic ability as a child, he came to spiritualism rather late when, at age 56, he was beset by dreams and mystical visions. Swedenborg proceeded to write about his views of death and the afterlife, and about his unorthodox views of the spiritual world. Between 1744 and 1745, Swedenborg experienced a number of profoundly moving dreams and visions. One particular vision in April 1745, during which Swedenborg was asked to bring a new revelation to the world, became the catalyst for the mission he pursued for the remainder of his life.

Swedenborg was a "traveling clairvoyant," one whose soul leaves the body in order to travel to distant places to bring back information. One event, among the most frequently cited of Swedenborg's "performances," was his announcement to 16 fellow guests at a dinner party that a major fire was at that moment burning in Stockholm, 300 miles away. The event was investigated by philosopher Immanuel Kant, a contemporary of Swedenborg's, who declared it absolutely authentic. Some considered him to be a mystic and a medium, but he might be more accurately described as a scientific and philosophical investigator whose theological and exegetical works stemmed from divine revelation. His views included the idea that all creation has its origin in divine wisdom and love, and that, as a result, all things created in the material realm have a corresponding counterpart on the spiritual plane.

Believing in neither reincarnation nor redemption, Swedenborg maintained that upon biological death of the body, the spirit goes to an intermediate plane where it makes choices about its next transition. Depending on the spirit's wishes, it then proceeds, for the remainder of eternity, to either one of the heavens or one of the hells. In heaven it will carry on a life much like the earthly one, but it will share the collective objective of peace and harmony. If it chooses a hell, it is free to do anything it desires, but it must be willing to suffer severe punishment by other residents who maintain order.

In his later years, Swedenborg was considered quite insane by many of his contemporaries. They no doubt had difficulty relating to a man who claimed he was able to travel to distant planets and to converse

The Question of Reincarnation

The Swedenborgian nonrecycling view of the human spirit is a premise that seems to agree with those who have passed to the spirit world. Reincarnation tends to be dismissed by the vast majority of spirits contacted through mediums. At the same time, the Swedenborgian view creates a conundrum with the traditional views of the survival of human personality. The linear model adhered to in Judeo-Christian orthodoxy is one in which the life of the soul goes on in what is presumed to be some level of the space-time continuum. The circular model, which is at the heart of the Hindu religion and embedded in Buddhist teachings, suggests that when our present form expires, we return again and again in other forms in infinite circularity.

with the spirits of ancient philosophers such as Aristotle and Plato. Swedenborg continued to write, but lack of public interest in his ideas and criticism from religious leaders forced Swedenborg to personally finance publication of his theories about the afterlife. Although largely ignored during his lifetime, they still gained a dedicated following after his death in 1772.

The Swedenborgian view of the afterlife, focused as it was on communal responsibility, must surely have appealed to the social democratic leanings in the character of Dr. A., for he was a socialist as well as a spiritualist. In a 1915 letter to the editor of the *Kingston Whig-Standard,* he expressed strong views regarding the war—World War I—and the lessons to be learned from it.

> The war is proving two things that have been contended for by the advanced guard of the human family during recent years, namely Socialism and Spiritualism. If Socialism could be defined as political and economical co-operation, which in essence it is, then any household man who reads nothing but newspapers must

see that the war is teaching the absolute necessity of Socialism. To bring the war to a successful conclusion and to save the Empire, all must co-operate to the utmost of their ability. What magic is in that word "co-operation," for it is not a creed, nor a dogma, but it is a living, growing principle with unlimited possibilities. Indeed, we are just beginning to see what co-operating can do.

The Co-operative Commonwealth Federation, Canada's first national political party, was not formed until 1932. Before that there was no structure or process other than letters to the editor through which Dr. A. could employ his socialist economic and political convictions. Swedenborg provided for Dr. A. a way of thinking that was neither against his ethics nor contrary to his scientist's need for order in the natural world. As one of his journal entries states: "I do not feel myself bound to accept any teaching from spirits or mortals if it does not harmonize with natural laws."

Dr. A.'s support of socialism was prompted by his visions of the future and the world: a future in which people are equal, and a world in which any person with the will and the fortitude can succeed, despite a humble background. One spiritualist writer with just such a background who was a tremendous inspiration to Dr. A. was Andrew Jackson Davis.

Andrew Jackson Davis

Andrew Jackson Davis was born in Orange County, New York, in 1826. Although Davis was, as Sir Arthur Conan Doyle later wrote, a lad with few "natural advantages" (being the feeble-bodied, untutored son of a drunken cobbler and a superstitious, uneducated mother), he was, at the age of 20, the author of what Doyle considered "one of the most profound and original books of philosophy ever produced" (1926, 1:42).

Davis's psychic powers began when he was in his teens. They were initially just voices he heard, usually giving him good advice or encouragement. Soon he began to display clairvoyance, and a traveling showman specializing in mesmerism used him in an experiment. Not long after that, a man named William Levingston, seeing the boy's amazing talents, took him under his wing. Together, they began touring the state. At first the performances were simply amusements, with a blindfolded Davis reading letters or telling the time on hidden watches for the audience. But soon Davis was using his so-called spirit eyes to cure people of disease. He once described this vision as an ability to see the organs of the body as if the body itself were transparent.[1] He claimed that each organ stood out clearly with a brightness that diminished if the organ was diseased. Davis's amazing powers quickly earned him the nickname the Poughkeepsie Seer, and owing to the fact that neither he nor Levingston charged fees for the services, he established a reputation for both authenticity and altruism.

When Davis was 18, a curious incident occurred. Up until then, Davis had no memory of what transpired while he was in his trances, which were induced by Levingston's hypnosis. Then on March 6, 1844, he came out of what appeared to have been a self-induced or perhaps involuntary trance only to say that he had been to the Catskill Mountains, where he had met two "venerable persons" with whom he discussed many significant things. Davis later divulged that one of the people was none other than Emmanuel Swedenborg.

In today's information age, it would be no surprise at all to find that a young man interested in the supernatural and intent upon maintaining a certain celebrity in the field might consciously choose such a luminary as his spiritual mentor. That Swedenborg's ideas were just starting to take hold would make his mentorship even more desirable. The fact was, however, that Davis had probably never heard of Swedenborg.

A professor of Hebrew at New York University, Dr. George Bush (no known relationship to the former US presidents), admitted that he was impressed by the ability of the young man to answer questions on geology, mythology, and anthropology, and to quote accurately in Hebrew. Bush bore witness to several of Davis's recountings of his trance-induced foray into the mountains, and the professor's blatantly politically incorrect description makes it rather clear that Bush felt Davis could not have been making it all up.

The circumference of his head is unusually small. If size is the measure of power, then this youth's mental capacity is unusually limited. His lungs are weak and unexpanded. He had not dwelt amid refining influences—manners ungentle and awkward. He has not read a book save one [the Bible]. He knows nothing of grammar or the rules of language, nor associated with literary or scientific persons (Doyle 1926, 1:48).

One of the pioneers of early spiritualist teaching, Davis bridged the gap between mesmerism and its more modern version. His writings also provide us with an operational, albeit obscure, definition of spirit. In records included in his *Harmonial Philosophy* (sometimes listed as *Harmonical Philosophy*), published from 1847 through 1852 in several volumes that he dictated while in a trance state, Davis suggested that the soul is the life of the body while the spirit is the life of the soul, and that after death the soul of the material body becomes the form of the eternal spirit. Perhaps a trance state is necessary in order to fully grasp his meaning.

Nevertheless, Davis became a prolific author whose writings attracted the attention and admiration of no less a literary luminary than Edgar Allan Poe. There was, in addition, a practical side to his intellect. Over his lifetime, Davis predicted the creation of the typewriter, the automobile, the airplane, and the birth of spiritualism.

THE SPIRITUALIST MOVEMENT
The Beginnings

It is generally agreed that spiritualism as a definable movement began in Hydesville, near Rochester in upper New York State, in an event that was foretold by Andrew Jackson Davis in the following cryptic message written in the early hours of March 31, 1848:

About daylight this morning a warm breathing passed over my face and I heard a voice, tender and strong, saying, 'Brother, the good work has begun—behold, a living demonstration is born' (Doyle 1926, 1:57).

Maggie Fox was 14 and her sister Kate 11 when they came to public attention due to a series of rappings and thumpings that occurred in their modest frame home. Little is recorded about the early lives of the two girls, the youngest of six children born to John Fox, a blacksmith, and his wife Margaret, both staunch Methodists. It is known that they were born to their American parents at Consecon, Ontario, a small village near Belleville on the Canadian side, across Lake Ontario from New York State, their parents' original home. In the late 1840s, presumably after a lack of financial success in Canada, the Fox family, minus an older daughter, Elizabeth, who had married a Canadian, returned to New York State.

At first the Fox family seemed somewhat bemused by the mysterious occurrences, and neighbors made the assumption that the two young girls, the elder of whom was described as somewhat cheeky, had created the noises themselves in an attention-seeking gesture. But as weeks went by, the Fox parents, who could also clearly hear the noises, became increasingly unnerved. They investigated all possible sources of the sounds, but could find nothing.

Shortly after eight o'clock on the evening of Friday, March 31, 1848, the girls' father appeared at the door of their neighbors' home begging them to come immediately. Mr. Fox was a man not given to histrionics or nonsense, but the noises in his house were so loud and so upsetting that he and his wife wanted someone else to hear. The neighbor, Mrs. Mary Redfield, a woman with sufficient cheek herself to suggest that if it was indeed a ghost she might have a set-to with it, assumed that it was an early and elaborate April Fools' joke. She followed her neighbor home and was astonished at what she saw and heard. The Fox women were huddled together in fright in the girls' dimly lit bedroom, and loud knocking sounds were coming from the walls.

Kate, who had begun calling the noisemaker Mr. Splitfoot, began clapping out sounds in a particular rhythm, which were then repeated. On gentle urging from Mrs. Redfield, Mrs. Fox said she felt the rappings were coming from the ghost of a murdered man whose remains she believed were still in the house. In order to test her theory, she began asking the entity to produce specific numbers of knocks. Then Mrs. Fox asked it to tap out her children's ages. The entity complied accurately to both requests.

"Count five . . . ," said Mrs. Fox. Five knocks were produced.

"Now count 12 . . . "

They all heard 12 knocks.

"Tell us how old Mary Redfield is," instructed Mrs. Fox, and the entity answered with 33 clear knocks, the astonished Mrs. Redfield's exact age.

Through continued questioning and answered rappings, the spirit made himself known as a 31-year-old peddler murdered with a butcher knife by a former occupant of the house during a robbery attempt. He claimed to have been buried under 10 feet of soil in the cellar. After receiving the spirit's permission to invite others to hear, Mrs. Fox brought in several more neighbors to witness the goings-on. For hours, the neighbors listened to rappings and knockings.

The following day, Mrs. Redfield and the others vouched publicly that the mysterious rappings could not have been made by anyone present, and in no time at all the town was bursting with tellings and retellings of the incident. Excavations were done in the Fox cellar, producing human hair and bones, but no skeleton. The following evening, 300 people crowded into the house.

In the days following the public rappings, the house's previous tenants revealed they had moved because of the strange noises. Dr. A.'s notes indicate that a girl named Lucretia Pulver, who was employed by tenant John Bell during 1883 and 1884, reported that she had heard knockings in the bedroom and unaccountable footsteps about the house at night. She also told of a mysterious peddler who had disappeared after visiting the house. A later tenant by the name of Michael Weekman claimed that he had heard tappings on the outer door, but could never find anyone at the door or about the premises. He claimed that once in the night his little girl, a child of 8, felt a "cold and clammy hand" pass over her face.

The stories bubbling up about past tenancies and past noises proved too much for the Fox family. Mrs. Fox was so unnerved by the happenings at Hydesville that her hair turned white in just a few days. To avoid the noises and publicity, Kate was sent to live with her brother David. Maggie was sent to stay in Rochester with her older sister Leah. But the phenomenon of the rapping sounds followed the girls and became increasingly frightening; they claimed they were terrorized by invisible forces whenever they were in their bedrooms. Ghosts stuck the girls with pins and hurled blocks of wood at them whenever they were in their rooms. It was not until the Fox sisters decided to resume their communication with the spirit that things settled back into a more placid routine.

In November of 1849, the three sisters were tested by a panel of people who had come together to investigate them. No fraud was detected, but many present were not satisfied and demanded a second panel be struck. The second group's findings were consistent with the first, and interest in the phenomenon grew.

Soon, the frenzy the Fox girls had started with their rappings took on a life of its own. Sitters at séances from one end of the country to the other were witnessing people levitate. Messages written by spirits appeared. Vases of flowers materialized. Tables tilted, spun, and rotated without any apparent assistance from those present. It was all very entertaining.

Séances soon became the new highlight of the social scene, and Victorian-era middle-class women were particularly vulnerable to their spell. At that time, married women whose husbands were not financially well-off spent their days (and nights) taking care of home, husband, and children with little or no compensation or status. Most unmarried women were little more than servants or unpaid workers in the homes of their male relatives. Whether married or not, every action was circumscribed by a rigid set of social expectations that limited their activity, their dress, and their circle of friends. It was no wonder they flocked to the innocent little gatherings, where they could talk to their dear departed Aunt Julia in the comfort of someone's well-appointed drawing room while sipping a cup of imported Ceylon tea from a Limoges cup! It was all very genteel—for a while.

Spiritualist Vocabulary

Medium: one who is able to facilitate communication between this world and the next

Clairvoyant: from the French meaning "clear seer," a medium with special powers to see and describe departed spirits

Séance: from the French for "sitting" or "showing" (and later, to refer to cinematic "performances"), the gathering at which a group of people come together in an attempt to communicate with spirits

Sitters: séance guests, usually numbering anywhere from 4 to 12, who sit in an alternating male-female configuration

Levitation: the raising into the air of physical objects without visible means and contrary to the laws of gravity

Materialization: the appearance of something in physical form and made evident to the senses

Back in New York . . .

The sisters went on tour with Leah along as a medium. She was, in fact, the first professional medium on record. A clever woman with an eye for the exploitability of her sisters' skills, Leah was soon controlling Maggie and Kate's touring schedule. In 1852, Maggie married the Arctic explorer Dr. Elisha Kane, and Leah married David Underhill, her third husband. On her own for several months while her sisters adjusted to their married lives, Kate (later Mrs. Fox-Jencken) traveled to Europe, where she allowed herself to be examined by a number of notable psychic researchers. Again, no evidence of fraud was detected.

Interesting as it is that two young girls from an unknown village could create such a stir, it was perhaps no accident. The area around

Hydesville, New York, had already established for itself a reputation as a center for some rather unusual activity. In the early 1840s, evangelist Charles Grandison Finney, finding "no fuel left to burn" (i.e., no one left to convert) in western New York, dubbed the region the Burned-Over District. And it was no wonder.

The hub of activity of the United Society of Believers in Christ's Second Coming, a splinter group of the Quakers commonly known as Shakers, and the birthplace of Joseph Smith Jr., who started the Mormon religion in Palmyra in 1830 after a visitation from the angel Moroni, western New York State in the late 1830s through the mid-1840s was a hotbed of religious and pseudoreligious enthusiasm. During that time, the area also housed the Perfectionist Oneida Society, one of the first group-marriage communes, and was home to the followers of Jemima Wilkinson, who claimed to be Christ's female reincarnation. The area was also the center of operations for William Miller, whose "Millerites" were waiting for his prediction to come true that the end of time and the second appearance of Jesus would arrive in October 1843.

In addition to the religious groups, the region also had its share of social reformers, among them Elizabeth Cady Stanton, a feminist and a leader in the women's suffrage movement, and the Fourierist utopian socialist movement, both of which were extremely active in the early 1840s. That the spiritualist movement should have started in western New York was no surprise at all to the thousands of people already on the verge of some religious or social awakening.

The Victorian era was bringing a great many changes to the lives of ordinary people in New York and around the globe. The invention of the telegraph, the discovery of electricity and all the mysterious possibilities that came with it, and the building of rails to carry the great iron horse galloping across the landscape gave people the sense that they were on the threshold of a new world order.

Charles Darwin published *On the Origin of Species* in 1859, challenging all previous theories and belief systems about what it meant to be human. Simultaneously, the possibilities opened up by a movement that purported to put people in touch with a pantheon of illustrious leaders who had gone before them to the great beyond seemed to be the answer to the prayers of many. Forget established religion. Here was the ultimate guidance, and just when they needed it!

By 1853, there were more than 30,000 mediums in the United States alone, and paranormal fever was rapidly spreading to Britain and the continent. Within months, mediums were everywhere, and, sadly but not surprisingly, charlatans entered the picture.

Many of the mediums were fakes and hucksters out to profit from the trend. And as each fraudulent psychic was exposed, a barrage of skepticism directed toward the Fox sisters seemed to follow. At one point it was suggested that the girls produced the knockings by cracking their knee and toe joints. One woman, a Fox relative named Mrs. Culver, supported this suggestion by claiming that Kate had confessed to her that knee and toe cracking was precisely how they performed their "tricks."

The accusations certainly harmed the Fox girls' reputations, but they continued to exhibit many astonishing displays of their powers at numerous venues across the United States and eventually in Europe, where Leah managed to present her sisters in the homes of the rich and powerful people of the time, who were wide open to this new fad known as spiritualism.

Lily Dale, New York

While the Fox girls were stretching their wings in England and on the continent, an expansion of paranormal activity began. The religious and quasi-religious fervor seen in the Burned-Over District gave way to a complete and utter transformation in upper New York State. It became a haven for spiritualists, and in 1879, Lily Dale came into existence.

Along the shores of lily-covered Lake Cassadaga, a village was established as a summer camp for people who firmly believed in the phenomenon of spirit communication. In no time at all, the place became a mecca of sorts. One of the first areas in New York State to have electricity, Lily Dale was nicknamed the City of Light in the early years of the 20th century.

Although referred to by unbelievers as Spooksville and Silly Dale (Wicker 2003, 13), the town had its share of supporters. By 1893, it had more than 200 cottages for rent and was home to some 40 full-time families. By the turn of the century, hotels and restaurants were in abundance for those who were willing to travel for a psychic experience. But there were others in North America who experienced phenomena of the paranormal in the comfort of their own parlors in small groups that came to be called home circles.

Dr. A.'s journey into spiritualism was undoubtedly fostered through his readings of Swedenborg and others, and through correspondence with other spiritualists. But the fact that he lived 50 miles as the crow flies across Lake Ontario from the very birthplace of spiritualism may have been the fuel that kept the flames of his interest burning. It must be made clear here, however, that although Dr. A. was thoughtful on the subject in the early part of the 20th century, he was not yet a confirmed believer in spiritualism. That epiphany, so to speak, occurred gradually. And it likely began some time after his first visit to Lily Dale, about the middle of August 1908.

During this visit, at one or more séances, Dr. A. and his wife had

Spiritualist Camps

Cassadaga, New York, is not to be confused with Cassadaga, Florida, the latter of which is a small, unincorporated community in central Florida and home to the Southern Cassadaga Spiritualist Camp Meeting Association. Chartered in 1894, the Florida community is home to a large number of mediums and is sometimes referred to as the Psychic Center of the World. But it was not the only psychic camp setting. The July 14, 1928, issue of *The Progressive Thinker,* the major publication of the spiritualist movement during the height of the movement's popularity, contained advertisements for upcoming meetings for no fewer than 16 spiritualist camps from New England to California. Of the camps listed as active in 1928, only those at Cassadaga in Florida, Lily Dale in New York, Wonewoc in Wisconsin, and Chesterfield in Indiana are still in operation to this day.

their initial firsthand experience with spirit communication and with materialization and slate writing.[2] Precisely how many séances there were and with whom is unclear, although we do know from later writings that one group he was a part of had a séance with a materializing medium named Mrs. Moss, who was attended by a spirit assistant identified only as "her little Indian maid." At another séance with a medium named Mr. P. A. Keeler, Dr. A. and his wife witnessed the manifestation of independent slate writing. Dr. A.'s reason for mentioning these people in later writings is remarkable: He met them again during a spirit visit 14 years later!

A Séance with Mrs. Etta Wriedt

On January 16, 1922, Dr. A. traveled to Montreal to attend a séance with the famous Detroit medium Mrs. Etta Wriedt.[3] The séance was held in a private home at 5:00 p.m. and was attended by Dr. A. and his wife as well as by a Mr. P. B. Motley and a Mr. Walter A. Scott. One of the first voice manifestations was an Indian girl who identified herself as Pansy, along with Mrs. Moss, who had apparently passed to the spirit side some years before. Dr. A. was amazed:

> To our great surprise, Mrs. Moss, and her little Indian maid, came here this afternoon, and asked if we did not remember our séances with them at Lily Dale? Which, of course, we surely did, and never shall forget, for they were among the most wonderful experiences of our lives, and time can never erase them from our memories. But why they should come now and not some of our spirit friends, who materialized for us then, and spoke to us at trumpet séances,[4] and wrote on closed slates, is somewhat of a mystery.

No sooner had Dr. A. and his small group gotten over the shock of hearing from Mrs. Moss and Pansy than another surprise guest spirit spoke to them. This time the message that came through the medium was delivered in a rather lighthearted way, preceded by a bit of jolly whistling. The voice identified himself simply as Christie. Dr. A. noted that the sitters were, like himself, primarily interested in hearing from their departed loved ones, and no one immediately claimed any recognition at all of the owner of the voice. But the spirit visitor was persistent.

"Christie!" he repeated, very distinctly, then waited.

Still no one responded. The room remained hushed, everyone listening intently. The spirit was clearly playing a guessing game with them.

"Don't you remember me and the message on the slates?" the spirit asked brightly. "You have the slates even yet."

It was then that Dr. A. remembered. "You were P. A. Keeler's guide[5]?" he asked in astonishment.

"Yes, yes!" answered the spirit. "You remember? I told you I would speak to you sometime, when I got the chance. And here I am."

They continued to talk for some time, discussing various issues that seemed of importance to the sitters. When someone in the room remarked on the spirit's showy manner, he told them that in life he had been a theatrical man. It came as no surprise, as it was clear to all present that he was enjoying his performance. Toward the end of Christie's communication with the group, he addressed a question directly to Dr. A.

"Well, what do you know now, doctor?" he asked in the same bright manner he had displayed throughout. Dr. A.'s response reflected his continued ambivalence toward the entire process.

"Sometimes I thought I knew quite a lot," he answered. "And then again I thought I did not know anything."

This answer seemed to satisfy the spirit. "It is well not to know too much," he said somewhat teasingly. "Then you will not get into trouble."

And he was gone. During that same séance, the sitters were also visited by a number of other spirit voices, including relatives of Mr. Motley's and a Reverend Dr. Barnes, who gave a talk "of rather sermon character" that the group thought quite appropriate since, in life, the man had been a Unitarian preacher in Montreal.

Their success encouraged them to hold another séance, a trumpet séance, after dinner later that same evening, in another house in the Montreal suburb of Westmount: the home of the Aykroyds' son Maurice, my father. Although the séance began well enough, it lasted only 1 hour,[6] ending rather abruptly by purely earthly means. The trumpet was floating in the air and someone from the spirit world was attempting to communicate with Mr. Scott when suddenly my late brother Maurice Jr., who was 4 at the time, pushed open the door to the séance room, letting in a little light. The trumpet crashed to the floor and contact was gone. The door was closed again and the sitters tried to resume the atmosphere with no success.

There is little on record about the first séance of Dr. A.'s circle, which presumably took place at some point in 1920. A letter dated simply 1920, written by Dr. A. to a Mr. S. Burnette in White Plains, Saskatchewan, describes a séance at which a spirit by the name of Carol Andrew was present. Since the letter does not specify, Dr. A.'s reference to having held the séance (as opposed to simply having attended) seems to clarify that he had acted as host.

The International Survivalist Society gives the following brief description of a typical séance:

> A group of people sit themselves in a dark room. They join hands: after a few minutes or more one of their number passes into a sleep-like state. This is the trance. It [the spirit entity] may display various automatisms, such as writing or visions, or speech. This latter occurs when the medium's own voice is used by a trance personality whose speech habits and voice timbre generally differ quite considerably from those of the medium in a normal waking state (Hamilton 1942, Section 2).

Home circle séances were sometimes set up as regular weekly or biweekly meetings. They were typically by invitation only, and there was a reason for this. Most spiritualists agree that a certain level of trust and comfort is required among the sitters in order to summon the spirits, which is, of course, the raison d'être of the exercise. The most successful séances seem to be those at which there is a body of "regulars," people who meet on a consistent basis over an extended period of time. As one spirit communicator advised Dr. A.'s circle, "If you want to make progress and get good results, you want to limit the members of your circle to a chosen few and not keep on letting new ones in."

The sitters at Dr. A.'s séances were presumably a fairly homogeneous group. Most of them were likely members of Dr. and Mrs. A.'s social group, although their exact identities have been lost over time. One entry in 1923 lists a group of people whose names appear frequently and who may have been his "chosen few." They included Dr. A. and his wife Ellen Jane, whom he refers to as "EJ"; Mr. William Guild, who often took notes; Mrs. Annie Worrell of Toronto (Dr. A.'s sister); Mr. and Mrs. Shurtleff; Mrs. George Nobes; Mrs. Francis Moloney; and the medium Walter Ashurst, whom you have already met. It is important to note that Dr. A. was merely the host or facilitator of his séances—not a medium. To this list should be added my father, Maurice; my mother, Marjorie; and sometimes my brother Maurice Jr. and myself.

At a séance in 1929, the chosen few had gathered around the table and Walter the medium was sitting at his usual place with his head bowed, oblivious to the room around him. So was I. I was the 7-year-old secretly perched on the stairs waiting for the séance to begin. However, having been in my hiding spot for a little longer than usual as the result of a miscalculation in time, I was very cramped. The sitters had begun their meeting, as was their habit, with a prayer. They were holding hands silently around the table when I was seized with an overwhelming itch. But in moving to achieve an effective scratching position, my foot bumped a broom that someone had leaned against the wall.

As I squeezed my eyes shut in horrible anticipation, the broom fell, its handle hitting a basket of metal canning lids that were sent clattering down the cellar stairs in a terrible din that could alone have wakened the dead. And thus, my brilliant spy world crashed to an end.

When the clatter subsided, Walter's somewhat bemused voice called out in Bela Lugosi–style theatrical eeriness, "Would the young gentleman in the cellarway care to join this circle?"

From that evening on, whenever I was "in residence" at my grandparents' farmhouse, the sitters permitted me to be part of the circle. During these wonderful experiences, I got to know Walter, and I felt that he was special. I grew to like and admire him as I know Dr. A. did. And how Dr. A. first came into contact with Walter was every bit as unusual as Walter himself.

WALTER, THE AYKROYD FAMILY MEDIUM

One afternoon in early 1917, as Dr. A. walked along Princess Street in Kingston, a 27-year-old man who introduced himself as Walter Ashurst intercepted him and proclaimed that he thought he was a medium. He wondered if Dr. A. could help him find out. For the next 4 years, Walter's gifts as a trance medium evolved under the guidance of an experienced local medium who assisted his development. During this developmental period, Walter was "adopted" by Dr. A. and became a fixture in the household. In 1921, Walter became the sole, very reliable, medium for Dr. A.'s circle.

As far as we can ascertain, Walter was born on September 15, 1890, in Newark, New Jersey. At the time of his first meeting with Dr. A., he was a machine operator working at the Kingston Locomotive Works. It is unclear precisely when Walter suspected that he had mediumistic gifts, but it must have been early on. When he was a boy, Walter's father used to whip him for telling about the visions he was having, and he tried to badger his son into believing he was just having nightmares. Walter had only what Dr. A. referred to as a "common school education," and he read little save for pulp magazines, his favorites being *Detective Fiction Weekly* and *The Shadow*. He reportedly did not have any interest in spiritualist literature.

Walter's early séance experiences as a medium were extremely unpleasant for him. For the first 20 minutes or so, he would see various spirits and describe them. But the descriptions were usually accompanied by physical side effects such as pains and aches and the sensation of having crushed or broken bones, which the sitters assumed represented the diseases or accidents of the spirits just before or at the time of their passing. Following this, he assumed a passive state that normally lasted for 1 to 1½ hours, during which he was entranced (see "Altered States of Consciousness" on page 24) and completely unaware of his surroundings and his own utterances. After recovering his awareness, which in itself apparently was not an easy process, he coughed considerably (possibly a side effect of the copious amounts of Turret cigarette smoke he inhaled) and "in other ways seemed quite distressed." According to Dr. A.'s notes, he came back from the trance state very tired and his first request was always for a cigarette.

During those early months, the sitters were visited, through an entranced Walter, by the voice (and sometimes clairvoyant manifestation discernible only by Walter) of one or another of a small group of regular spirit visitors (see Comments, Chapter 1, i), including Lee Long, who said he lived in China during the Ming Dynasty and would become one of Walter's controls, and Blue Light, who at first would not reveal his identity but later informed the group that he was a prince from ancient Egypt. There was Mike Whalen, an Irishman, and three men listed in the notes as Indians who identified themselves as Blackhawk, Broken Arrow, and Black Feather. Carol Andrew, the name his counterparts gave one spirit whom they referred to as a

Altered States of Consciousness

The trance state is not unconsciousness, but rather an altered state of consciousness (ASC) during which the medium has, through relaxation, meditation, or other technique, changed the pattern of continuous brain waves. There are four basic brain-wave patterns that constitute the various levels of ASC: beta, which is wide-awake consciousness; alpha, which is associated with a light trance and occurs during mild hypnosis, meditation, biofeedback, or daydreaming; theta, a deep trance state in which the individual is unaware of the surroundings, as in a light sleep; and, lastly, delta, which occurs when a person is sleeping soundly. Mediums tend to operate in either the alpha or theta state, both of which allow the medium to experience sensations that would normally be unavailable to the fully conscious mind. Walter typically operated in the theta state.

Moor, also appeared. He was one of the first spirits to make his presence at the séances known. He was also one of the first to "de-exist."[7]

Despite the challenges of the early séances, and in particular the misery that the sittings caused Walter, Dr. A. and his group persisted. In many ways the persistence had to do with what they as a group considered to be a successful séance. In the early days of Dr. A.'s circle, they were quite content to view the exercise as successful if any contact was made: voice, clairvoyance, or table tipping. Later on, as Walter's skills developed, it seemed that Dr. A.'s goals and those of the group grew loftier. They were no longer satisfied with voices; they were hoping to produce a materialization. But their journey was to prove difficult.

Dr. A.'s notes record in detail no fewer than 80 séances held between early spring 1921 and fall 1933 for the express purpose of producing a materialized spirit. Along the way, he and his sitters received a number of positive signs that encouraged them to continue their quest.

We sat in the dark most of the time. Sometimes we were requested to light the lamp for a period of five minutes or so while the medium rested and to also relax the tension of the sitters. During this rest, the medium would remain in the trance state in a stiff and upright position as if he were a piece of statuary. We had some remarkable developments and striking phenomena, considering the circumstances and the comparatively short time we have been sitting for materialization.

A number of lights appeared in different parts of the room and in the vicinity of some of the sitters. Some of these lights were small and some were quite large. One light of considerable size seemed to be in a square frame with a dark bar across it. These lights would come and go, some lasting for quite a space of time and some only a second or two. They seemed to be "self-contained," that is they didn't light up the room or make it perceptibly lighter. There was no possibility of these lights being produced by artificial means or of their coming into the room from any outside source. All the members of the circle were perfectly sure of this by examination and experiments. Nothing like them could be produced in the room where we sat, and so we concluded they must have been of spirit origin.

Then we also had some "whistling" and what seemed to be independent voices close to the medium, right by the side of his neck and shoulder. These were distinctly heard by all the sitters and were considered very wonderful and convincing.

For the next several years, there were many séances with little more than the appearance of lights and some automatic writing to add hope that they would achieve a materialization. Although most of the séances with Walter as medium were held at Sydenham,[8] some took place at Dr. and Mrs. A.'s home at 333 Earle Street in Kingston, while a few others were held in Toronto. Lee Long and the other regular spirit visitors maintained contact and continued to encourage the group to persist, telling them that they had the ability to produce a materialization and should continue in their efforts. According to the spirits, the sitters just had to be patient and remain in the right frame of mind. Blue Light's visits ceased for a number of years after 1926, and then on January 30, 1931, he appeared again, and for the next several months the Aykroyd circle séances took quite a different turn.

Dire Predictions

In these séances of ours, we seem to be on the borderland of some very wonderful things which are quite new to this materialistic age but which were not unknown but believed in, in past ages, as recorded in history, both sacred and profane (Dr. A., early 1923).

On the evening on which Blue Light appeared after the nearly 5-year absence, he made the first of several predictions. He said that a great earthquake would hit the continent in a short time and that a city would be destroyed and many lives lost. In response to sitters' questions about the city, they received only the initials *M* and *N*. On March 12, 1931, Blue Light appeared again and once more predicted that the earthquake would take place. This time he said it would occur "within the week." On March 31, an earthquake was registered in Nicaragua, where the city of Managua was destroyed, with a loss of 2,000 lives. Although his timing was off by a little more than 1 week, the sitters believed absolutely that Blue Light had predicted the Nicaragua earthquake.

Over the next few months, Blue Light appeared repeatedly and made a number of predictions, some of which came to pass, some of which did not. He predicted that one of earth's empires would fall within 6 months and that one-half of its great population would be wiped out. He also predicted that "in the first three months of the fourth year from the present time" (which would have been January through March 1935), a great spiritual movement would sweep over the world from revelations made from the spirit world. The revelations would have a profound effect on all religions. On May 9, 1932, he predicted that within 12 months the United States would go off the gold standard, which it did—11 months later.

In addition to providing Blue Light's predictions, the séances during this 1-year period furnished additional encouragement that the circle would accomplish a materialization. On February 24, 1931, it had a visit from "an interesting character, abrupt in speech, emphatic and decisive, with short, crisp statements, and obviously accustomed to having his own way in life." It wasn't long before the spirit was identified as Dr. A.'s great-grandfather, Samuel Aykroyd, who had left this world nearly 100 years before, in 1832. He informed the group that he was doing his best to materialize for them and assured them they would eventually be successful. That evening, some of the group who were considered to be clairvoyant said they could see his face and even described his clothes, a double-breasted waistcoat. Unfortunately, not all the sitters were able to see the manifestation.

Three days later, another strange and new phenomenon occurred. Dr. A. wrote:

> We sat again for materialization. The medium went into a trance, then we put the lights out. He left his chair and went around to a sitter on the opposite side of the table, standing at his back and placing his hands at the back of the sitter's neck and taking one of the sitter's hands in one of his hands. Soon the sitter felt strong vibrations as if he were holding an electric battery and then dense waves of light of whitish appearance are formed right in front of him. The waves flowed up and down and formed rings with a dark band around the rings. One of the sitters saw the outline of a face forming in one of the rings of the whitish substance floating in front of this particular sitter.

At that moment, the sitter in front of whom the "whitish substance" had appeared began to complain that his eyes were watering and sore. The medium immediately dropped his hands limply to his sides and another control took possession of him. This control explained that they had stopped "operating" on the first sitter because they were afraid they would injure him.

Just a little more than a week later, they had another astounding sitting. On April 5, 1931, the following entry in the journals suggests that "something" was about to happen:

> We had the most interesting séance tonight. The hand conducting the séance started to build up some forms, but did not proceed with the work for any great length of time because one

of the sitters drawn upon was suffering pain in her shoulder, neck and teeth. The control explained to us that the extraction of the so-called ectoplasm caused this pain.

They had not yet achieved a materialization, but it seems that Dr. A.'s circle had successfully managed to produce ectoplasm, "a white, fluidic substance said to emanate from the bodily orifices of a medium that is molded by spirits to assume phantom physical shapes" (Guiley 1991, 178).

Ectoplasm is a fascinating thing. Ectoplasm has never been proven to exist beyond the reports of witnesses and photos that have been taken of it. The substance does not appear to be subject to physical capture and analysis, at least not to the knowledge of this writer. It can be seen in darkness or semidarkness, but has never been seen in full light. It has no substance, yet it has a form—which usually takes the shape of spiritual entities who, according to scholar Stan McMullin, are making a purposeful attempt to contact the living (2004, Chapter 10).

The first published description of ectoplasm was written by Emmanuel Swedenborg in 1744. He saw "a kind of vapour steaming from the pores of my body. It was a most visible watery vapour and fell downwards to the ground upon the carpet" (Doyle 1926, 16).

Even though not all the Aykroyd circle sitters present had seen the ectoplasm, the group was encouraged and its séances continued into 1933. Having enlisted the help of spirits who continued to tell them that they would eventually be successful, the sitters were exceedingly careful to follow their directions. But they became more and more frustrated at their inability to achieve a materialization. Their failure was often the topic of discussion during séances, and the sitters put forward a number of theories for their failure, which the encouraging spirits tended to downplay.

One suggestion was that a medium's cabinet might be necessary.[9] But the spirit guides told them that that was not the problem, and that they could and would achieve a materialization without one. Walter's inexperience was suggested by some of the sitters. However, by this time, Walter had been a trance medium for more than 12 years and the spirits, particularly Blue Light, assured them that

Walter was not the impediment. The spirits suggested that it was just a matter of time and attitude.

The sitters found comfort in the words of Alfred Russel Wallace, spiritualist and author of *On Miracles and Modern Spiritualism*: "It is an indubitable fact that the manifestations which take place at séances depend more upon the nature, disposition, and state of mind of those present, than on the psychical development of any medium; and that where incredulity, and especially scoffing, is felt, the spirits will not, or cannot, manifest themselves or demonstrate" (Moore 1913, 162)

So the group turned inward, questioning its own reasons for being there. Over the next several months they began to be more selective about who attended the sittings. But it is not always possible to judge someone else's motives, and the question hung unvoiced in the air: Were there skeptics, even scoffers, among the Aykroyd circle's chosen few whose negative attitudes were weakening the ambiance?

While Dr. A. and his group continued working with their frustrating and inexplicable inability to produce a materialization, the spiritualist fever that had caught on in that little New York town had been sweeping the planet for at least 3 decades, and other home circles across North America were striving for similar goals. One of them, at least, was extremely successful.

Ectoplasm

Considered by spiritualists to be the basis of all physical phenomena, ectoplasm is referred to in some texts as teleplasm. In other writings it is referred to as ideoplasm (a term coined by Swedenborg) because it takes the shape impressed on it by spirits. Materialization séances are held in semi- or full darkness because light is said to destroy ectoplasm. An apport is any item that has been dematerialized somewhere else and then materialized in the séance room by the spirit (typically gemstones, flowers, or even small live animals).

OTHER HOME CIRCLES
Dr. Glen Hamilton

Considered even today to be one of the most distinguished researchers of psychical phenomena Canada has ever produced, Dr. Thomas Glendenning Hamilton[10] (1873–1935) of Winnipeg, Manitoba, compiled an astounding collection of psychic data during his lifetime.

Born in Agincourt, Ontario, Hamilton moved with his parents to Saskatchewan at the age of 10, and then at age 18, just months after the death of his father, he moved to Manitoba. Hamilton put himself through medical school, completing his internship at the Winnipeg General Hospital in 1904. In 1905, he set up practice in the Winnipeg district of Elmwood, where he continued to work until the end of his memorable and varied career. On the surgical staff of the Winnipeg General Hospital, he lectured for a number of years in clinical surgery and medical jurisprudence at the University of Manitoba Medical School.

Among his most memorable accomplishments, and one that garnered him international recognition, was his reputation as a psychic investigator, an interest that led him to personal contacts with experts internationally known in the area of psychic phenomena, including Sir Oliver Lodge, Sir Arthur and Lady Conan Doyle, and Alexander Fleming. His interest began with his observation and documentation of the phenomenon of telekinesis,[11] but he gradually moved into the areas of clairvoyance, trance writing, visions, and, ultimately, teleplasmic manifestations. His first subject was the medium Elizabeth M., and records indicate that the investigations started as early as 1918 (coincidentally, around the same period that Dr. A.'s home circles were starting). After little more than a year of attending séances with Elizabeth M., Dr. Hamilton was sufficiently impressed by her ability to achieve telekinesis as well as other manifestations of a psychic nature that he was forced to abandon his previously held skeptical views. He came to believe that one should not reject psychic phenomena without first observing them with an open mind.

Beginning in 1922, Hamilton made an extensive study of Elizabeth M., observing and documenting her activities at regular séances held in the parlor of his gray frame home in Winnipeg. Hamilton's wife, Lillian, often acted as recorder during these sessions and kept close track of the evidence being documented. During this 4-year experimentation period, Elizabeth M. developed as a medium, and by 1923 she was displaying an ability to enter into a state of spontaneous deep trance.[12] The fact that his subject was in a deep trance made Dr. Hamilton's experiments all the more significant and gave him an opportunity to document many of the manifestations the trance state produced.

Dr. Hamilton presented his findings publicly for the first time in April of 1926, when he shared his research with colleagues at a meeting of the Winnipeg Medical Society. Although his work did not at first receive overwhelming support, he managed to pique the interest of a number of fascinated colleagues who, after expressing interest in observing Elizabeth M. at work, participated in some of the séances. But the events that led to Dr. Hamilton's greatest contribution to the world of psychic research did not begin until 2 years later.

Around 1928, Mary Marshall, one of the sitters sometimes present at Dr. Hamilton's séances, began to exhibit talent at clairvoyance. Mrs. Marshall had emigrated from Scotland after World War I with her husband and their three children. Although she had some experience at being "controlled" by various communicators at previously attended séances, the full development of her ability as a medium did not begin until she joined Dr. Hamilton's circle.

According to International Survivalist Society information, Mary Marshall became a regular member of Dr. Hamilton's group in 1928, and both she and Elizabeth M. were soon visited by a trance personality,[13] an entity both of them could see and hear. Fair-haired, blue-eyed, with a mischievous personality, he became known as FYM (the Fair Young Man) because he repeatedly refused to identity himself. FYM became a frequent visitor at their séances.

By early March 1928, activity at the séances was starting to focus less on Elizabeth M. and more on Mary Marshall as the main medium. She was usually listed in the reports as Mary M., but sometimes as Dawn, one of her trance personalities, and the séances became quite entertaining. But Dr. Hamilton, of a background similar to that of Dr. A., was not an easy audience. A medical man whose orthodox background made it difficult for him to accept a psychic explanation for what he originally felt could be ascertained scientifically, he was soon to have his own convictions profoundly shaken. But it was not without ammunition that he entered the psychic investigation arena, and in this he had the full support of those in the spirit world.

The first to enlist Dr. Hamilton's cooperation was FYM, who later identified himself as Walter King.[14] In mid-March 1928, while he was still appearing clairvoyantly to Mary and Elizabeth, Walter asked, through Mary, that a bell device be set up so he could prove his presence by ringing it at a specified time. Agreeing to go along with the directions, Dr. Hamilton built a lidded wooden bell box and had it mounted in their medium's cabinet.[15] The box contained two dry-cell batteries wired to a small bell. Applying a pressure of anything more than a third of an ounce to the lid caused the circuit to close and the bell to ring.

At first Walter did not specify where the box should be mounted, but within a couple of weeks he became increasingly insistent that the box be placed high up on a shelf, well out of reach of the sitters and mediums. On April 25, the bell rang several times, as Walter predicted it would. Unfortunately, Dr. Hamilton was absent that day, but the bell ringing occurred several more times, and he managed not only to witness the phenomenon but also to photograph it. Following explicit directions given by Walter, Dr. Hamilton set up several cameras of various specific uses, including one wide-angle lens camera and two stereoscopic cameras. High-speed electrically fired flashbulbs completed the setup. In addition to the professional photography equipment, Dr. Hamilton gave sitters and mediums the option of bringing their own cameras.

The photographing of the bell box began in early June 1928 and continued, after a brief break in sittings, into August. Soon after that, the séances began to include a phenomenon that would have most of those present, as well as those who read the reports, react in utter amazement. Photographs taken in the dark on August 5, 1928, showed, along with the bell box and the cabinet that surrounded it, an unusual white mass hanging from the nostrils of the entranced medium. To their astonishment, the sitters realized that Mary M. had managed, while in their presence, to produce ectoplasm. Dr. Hamilton's séance had produced the substance considered to be essential to materialization. Even better, they had photographs to prove it! (See photo insert.)

Some time before the first appearance of the ectoplasm, Dr. Hamilton's real-life situation caused him to question whether he should continue as an investigator of the paranormal.

As the new "religion" of spirituality made more and more headlines, Hamilton worried that his involvement with it would undermine his credibility as a serious physician. As such, for a brief period at the dawning of his most successful séances, he took a brief hiatus from communion with the spirit world. But his sojourn from séances was not long-lived. The members of his circle had come to depend on his guidance as group leader and chief investigator, and his colleagues, particularly those who had shown interest in his extracurricular endeavors, joined with his patients to encourage him to continue his investigatory work. So, assured that his patients were still happy to have him care for them, Hamilton's work with his circle resumed.

Having been warned by Walter and the other spirits that light would damage ectoplasm,[16] the Hamilton circle always held its séances in absolute darkness, although dim red light was sometimes used when necessary for the adjustment of photographic equipment. But the specter of fraud was a constant companion in spiritualist circles. With little or no light with which to ensure there was no deception on the part of the mediums or others who might assist them, measures had to be undertaken. In addition to the sophisticated electronic equipment he had set up, Dr. Hamilton established a number of fraud-proof procedures for which he enlisted the help of several highly respected community members and regular sitters in his home circle.

Before a séance, Miss Ada Turner, a high school English department head, escorted Mary M. into a private room, where she helped her undress. She then sponged the medium's upper body with warm water, presumably to ensure that Mary M. had not concealed or smeared on her body any substance that could be construed as homemade ectoplasm. Once the séance began, Dr. James Hamilton, Dr. Glen Hamilton's brother, had the specific task of holding the medium's left hand while Mr. W. Cooper, a businessman, held her right. One of the regular members was assigned the task of taking notes from beginning to end, although it is not clear how these notes were taken in the absolute darkness that apparently was maintained throughout the sittings.

The séances at which materialization was scheduled to occur[17] were also attended by Isaac Pitblado, a prominent Winnipeg lawyer and later chairman of the Board of Governors of the University of Manitoba, who was asked to attend as an objective observer. Before the séance began, Pitblado examined the cabinet, the room, and the photographic equipment, then searched each of the guests. The doors to the room were locked from the inside and sealed with tape that Pitblado examined afterward to ensure that there had been no tampering. His detailed reports verified that he could find absolutely no evidence of anything having been interfered with.

Many more materializations were produced by Mary M. over the next few years. Among their spirit visitors were Sir Arthur Conan Doyle and explorer David Livingstone. Dr. Hamilton's careful research produced unassailable photographic and written records of materializations and other psychic phenomena. His work ended with his death in 1935, but the bulk of his documentation has been carefully stored and catalogued by Lillian and their daughter Margaret in the T. G. and Lillian Hamilton fonds in the University of Manitoba Libraries Archives and Special Collections. The Hamilton collection includes some of the most provocative evidence of spirit contact ever compiled.

Thomas Lacey

Although Dr. Hamilton's work may have been illuminating and included visits from some famous spirit characters, the cast of his performances was not the most star-studded. That distinction goes to another Canadian, Thomas Lacey, whose circle also managed to produce materialization.

Born in Derbyshire, England,[18] Lacey immigrated to Canada as a young man and first came to the attention of spiritualists at Lily Dale. In 1932, while attending a summer spiritualist camp, Lacey

Do-It-Yourself Ectoplasm

You can try this at home! Rosemary Guiley, in her *Encyclopedia of Mystical and Paranormal Experience* (1991, 178), provides us with two recipes for homemade ectoplasm: Soap, gelatin, and egg white mixed together and then blown into the air will shimmer and glow in forms that resemble bubbles. A less effective but simpler mixture, toothpaste and peroxide, will create a foaming substance that, in softened light, could resemble ectoplasm. These were among the mixtures commonly employed during the late 19th and early 20th centuries to fake the production of ectoplasm.

astonished visitors and practitioners alike with his seemingly effortless ability to produce automatic writing and drawing as well as voice contact with spirits. Lacey's success could be accounted for by the fact that he had perhaps one of the most reliable of all spirit controls—his own brother. Walter Lacey[19] had passed on at a young age and was his brother's constant spirit companion during his trances.

The Lacey circle séances began in the early 1930s, with some initial "casting about for focus" (McMullin 2004, 162). As with the Hamilton circle, the Lacey group set up photographic equipment to record the happenings. Sadly, no photographic records were kept, so it is impossible to say whether the efforts were successful. However, the séance during which equipment was first used seemed to have set off something of a stir in the next world, for that was the first of a long series of séances that featured the spirit of a famous person, an occurrence that became fairly characteristic of Lacey séances.

The record for a sitting held on September 12, 1931, indicates that after the cameras had been mounted and the séance was about to begin, "the illuminated trumpet was seen moving toward the cameras. Walter, the spirit guide, said that Mr. Stead[20] was examining them to see if everything was in order" (McMullin 2004, 163). Walter also indicated that Mr. Stead, who also regularly visited Dr. Hamilton's group, was receiving assistance in this task by none other than Arthur Conan Doyle, who had passed on a little more than a year before.

During later séances, the Lacey group was visited by more luminaries, including Archdeacon Colley, Thomas Alva Edison, and the Reverend George Vale Owen (see Comments, Chapter 1, iii). The prominence of this group among the documenters of psychic phenomena was not simply due to its star-status visitors, but to some of the astounding demonstrations it witnessed.

At one sitting in early 1932, the disembodied visitors gave a deafening 10-minute performance of spirited clog dancing on the séance table (the clogs were dancing, not the spirits). This performance was accompanied and perhaps enlivened by the earthly members' singing of some rousing Scottish Highland songs. Although the speaking trumpet was occasionally employed to enable the spirit voices to be heard, Thomas Lacey was often able to let the spirits speak using his own vocal cords. On several occasions, spirit voices spoke in French, German, or Italian, languages that Lacey did not know.

The séances also produced many physical manifestations. Both ingress and egress movements of flowers and fruits were typical, as were table tilting and other examples of telekinesis. The Lacey circle witnessed the production of ectoplasm as well as a phenomenon known as transfiguration, in which the medium took on the physical characteristics of the spirit who was communicating through him. The eyewitness accounts of these are significant for their apparent lucidity.

> The medium's face took on the features of Mr. Stead, while a beard could be seen forming which the entity stroked in a natural manner (McMullin 2004, 166).

And later, a note about the transfiguration of the medium for the entry of a Hindu spirit called Abdula Bay stated that "the turban could be noticed very distinctly on the medium."

The Lacey circle séances usually began at 9:00 p.m. and were opened with a prayer or sometimes by a hymn sung to the accompaniment of the organ. Many of the séances included long discussions of the afterlife, with Doyle and Stead providing most of the commentary and always with Walter Lacey as the spirit control. At some point in the early fall of 1932, Walter announced that he was going to enlist Mr. Stead's help in decreasing the number of spirit visitors they would be getting, suggesting that limiting the visitors would increase their chances of achieving a materialization.

In September 1932, the group members decided to follow more explicitly the spirits' directions for achieving full materialization, and they began holding their séances in either total darkness or in low red light. But contrary to the manner in which Dr. A. and his home circle proceeded, the Lacey group decided it might be more successful with a makeshift cabinet. By stretching a black curtain across one end of the room in which the séances were held, they created an energy-generating space from which the medium could work. And it proved to be most effective. Soon after erecting the cabinet, they had their first materialization: a "North American Indian" named Blue Snake who apparently permitted some of the sitters to touch him.

On October 8 of the same year, several new phenomena were observed. Some time after Thomas Lacey entered the cabinet, a halo of light suddenly appeared above the curtain. It was followed by bright flashes off to the right of the cabinet. Shortly thereafter, Walter's voice was heard explaining that he was working hard to prepare for visits from the "loved ones" of the sitters.

Within minutes, the sitters witnessed a series of lights moving around the room. In places, plasmic forms began to build, forms that gradually manifested themselves as fully embodied spirits: a small child named Violet, and Mr. W. T. Stead himself was walking around the room shaking hands with sitters. They were followed by the Indian Blue Snake and a priest who chanted in Latin. During that séance, the curtain was pulled aside by one of the spirits to reveal Mr. Lacey, seated inside the cabinet, calm and cool and apparently completely oblivious to the scene whose creation he had facilitated.

Further manifestations occurred in subsequent sittings, all carefully documented. At a number of sittings, several spirit voices, both male and female, could be heard coming from the cabinet at one time, even while one form or another was materializing. At one sitting a spirit materialized, which was, by now, not unusual. The unusual event happened a few minutes later, when the same spirit dematerialized before their eyes, evaporating into thin air as they watched; normally, spirits dematerialized by melting, sinking into the floor. There were also examples of spirit painting, one of which was a memorable sketch of the head of a woman done by a materialized Egyptian spirit.

In December 1932, an electronic device was used for the first time to allow the sitters to be aware throughout the séance of the medium's weight in his chair. McMullin (2004, 168) is quick to point out that this was not a function of a lack of confidence in the medium's integrity, but rather "to distinguish between transfiguration and materialization" that might be taking place inside the medium's cabinet. If Lacey stood and "took on" the physical characteristics of the spirit, the manifestation would be considered a transfiguration. If Lacey was lying back, allowing his body to produce ectoplasm, which in turn would develop into the manifesting spirit, it would be considered a materialization. It was the first time such a device was used in séances. Following publicity in the United States, Canada, and Britain after Lacey participated in a radio-aired séance, there was a spike in interest in his sittings, and general public interest in psychic phenomena soared.

The experiences of Thomas Lacey, Glen Hamilton, and Dr. A. paved the way for dozens of interested individuals to try their hands at private séances held in various Edwardian parlors. While many very successful séances were being conducted by home circles, the amazing phenomenon of spiritualism began sweeping beyond the bounds of small parlors. What had started as a small movement on North American soil was soon to take an international stage.

Chapter 2

Ghosts Abroad: The International Stage

> It came upon them like a smallpox, and the land was spotted with mediums before the wise and prudent had had time to lodge the first half-dozen in a madhouse.
>
> —*Augustus de Morgan,*
> *British journalist (De Morgan 1863, xi)*

Though public appearances for the psychic Fox sisters were to continue through the turn of the century and into the '20s, all was not well among the siblings. Kate and Maggie, kept on a tight leash and an even tighter budget by their ambitious older sister Leah, began to resent her control over their lives; but it was control that, sadly, they were losing. By the time they were in their mid-thirties, both younger sisters were confirmed alcoholics who had to rely on clever handlers in order to appear sober and capable in public.

But others had been picking up the slack, many in a transparent attempt to cash in on the fad. In North America and Europe, hordes of people calling themselves psychics took to the stage alongside actors, magicians, and mind readers or "mentalists" to present teacup readings and other demonstrations such as vanishing acts and ventriloquism. Audiences who attended these circuslike performances included both the well-bred and the barely literate, the true believers and the frankly bored, but they flocked to these public displays in droves.

The success of home circle séances was manifested in a more public type of séance: stage performances in which psychics and mediums purported to contact the spirits. Among the earliest and most charismatic of the "star" mediums was D. D. Home.

STAGE MEDIUMS
Daniel Dunglas Home

A scant 2 years after the Fox sisters first displayed their genuine abilities, a young Scottish-born Connecticut man discovered his. During a brief but stunning career, Daniel Dunglas Home (pronounced HUME) was able to levitate 100-pound tables, elongate and levitate his own body, and make spirits appear fully formed.

Daniel Home was born in 1833 in Currie, near Edinburgh, to a laborer and his wife. While still an infant, the somewhat sickly[1] Daniel was taken in by a childless aunt and her husband. The couple emigrated with their young charge to the Norwich, Connecticut, area 9 years later, where they joined Daniel's parents and sister. Daniel's skills began to develop, as is the case with many psychics, soon after the death of a loved one: in Daniel's case, his 12-year-old sister Mary Betsey. The phenomena were at first just visions of his sister and of a childhood friend of Daniel's who had died shortly after Mary. By the time he was 17, he was experiencing more than just visions. His presence began producing knockings and instances of mobile furniture that were not unlike the Fox manifestations. His aunt and uncle were not amused.

Fearing that their nephew had been possessed by the devil, the staunch Presbyterians promptly disowned him and turned him out to his own devices. His devices turned out to be most lucrative. Attractive, charming, and accomplished, albeit sickly, Daniel quickly wove a story around himself that was rarely questioned by those who were taken in by him, and who in turn took him in.

Tall and slender, with curly auburn hair and deep-set gray eyes, he looked like an aristocrat and played the role to its utmost. He maintained that his father was the illegitimate son of the 10th Earl of Home, and he adopted the name Dunglas, one of the aristocratic Home family names, in support of this claim. Although many people of the time believed the story and treated him accordingly, his aristocratic connection has never been supported by documentation.

His ability to play the piano and his quick and easy wit quickly established Home as one of Connecticut's most eligible bachelor guests. In those early days, his psychic work was confined to clairvoyance and healing. Soon, however, he was astounding people with his abilities, even confounding the likes of Professor David Wells of Harvard, who, with a team of colleagues, investigated Home during one particularly memorable table turning. Wells's investigative team eventually concluded that Home could not have performed the feats they witnessed without the assistance of some spiritual intelligence.

By 1852, Home had learned to levitate himself and was, on a few occasions, able to materialize full-size figures and phantom hands that sitters were able to touch. But the séances in Connecticut were nothing compared to the status he achieved 2 years later when he decided (on the advice of the spirits) to leave the United States and ply his trade in London, where spiritualism, promoted as it was by the rich and famous, had a certain cachet.

A serial houseguest, Home never felt the need to charge for his work. His hosts took care of his every need. And over the years they introduced him to a fabulous array of notable sitters, among them novelist William Makepeace Thackeray of *Vanity Fair* fame, Russian novelist Ivan Turgenev, and the poet Dante Gabriel Rossetti. Attending only one of the sittings was the celebrated poet Elizabeth Barrett Browning, along with her equally celebrated poet husband Robert Browning, who was, by all accounts, not as impressed as his good wife. One of the few who ever publicly denounced Home and his spirit skills, Browning began referring to him as Daniel "Dungball" Home and later penned his famous poem deriding spiritualism, which left little doubt of his feelings toward the freeloading table tipper.

"Mr. Sludge 'The Medium'" is considered to be one of Browning's most dramatically profound works, and it has been said that D. D. Home was the subject of the poem, a perception that may have been, at least in part, prompted by the following lines:

> Then, it's so cruel easy! Oh, those tricks
> That can't be tricks, those feats by sleight of hand,
> Clearly no common conjurer's!—no indeed!
> A conjurer? Choose me any craft i' the world
> A man puts hand to; and with six months' pains
> I'll play you twenty tricks miraculous
> To people untaught the trade

Even though Browning was obviously inspired by Home's blatantly sycophantic personality, it is more likely that the character Sludge is an exemplar of the frauds so prevalent at the time. It is unknown whether Browning's denunciation of Home was due to honest cynicism, jealousy over Home's obvious flirtation with Elizabeth, or rumors that the medium was homosexual. Whatever the case, Browning's public aspersions did little to quell the enthusiasm with which Home continued to be received in the great houses of Europe.

Home went off to Florence in 1855, where, less than 2 years later, he was set upon and injured by a group of fearful peasants who tried to murder him for practicing sorcery. Finding the Italian arrows even sharper (and more painful) than Mr. Browning's, he left for Paris in 1857, where he held séances for Emperor Napoleon III and Princess Eugénie. Although no records were kept of these séances, it is assumed that their novelty wore off after a year or so, for at about that time Home was unceremoniously escorted to prison. The charge was likely fraud or possibly homosexuality. While in prison, Home's ability to conjure in self-interest came in handy. He managed to dig up some proof about a homosexual scandal involving highly placed members of the court and threatened to expose it. It wasn't long before Home and his story were made to do a quiet disappearing act.

He turned up in Russia and was soon holding séances for Czar

Alexander II, where he quickly charmed the royal family, particularly one lovely member of the czar's court, Alexandrina de Kroll. In 1861 Alexandrina and Daniel were married, with Alexandre Dumas Sr. acting as best man and Count Alexei Tolstoy, a cousin of author Leo Tolstoy, as one of the witnesses. Sadly, the young Mrs. Home contracted tuberculosis and died the following year. Home, finding himself in financial trouble and having lost some of his contacts at court, returned to Britain.

In 1866, he began holding private séances with a 75-year-old widow, Mrs. Jane Lyon, and it was that alliance that nearly was his undoing. The husband's spirit, speaking through Home, informed the widow Lyon that Home was his spiritual son, and that she should adopt him *and* provide him with a regular retainer. All was well until the spirit appeared to get a little greedy. The spirit suggested that Mrs. Lyon set up a retainer of £700 a year, which Mrs. Lyon paid, followed by several ever-increasing payments amounting to more than £12,000 over the next few months—a veritable fortune in those days.

Mrs. Lyon's financial acumen trumped her spiritual beliefs when she realized she was being bilked. She dismissed Home and sued him for fraud, creating a scandal that was *the* hot news item for weeks in Britain and on the continent. But it did not all bode badly for Home. Mrs. Lyon, who had married well above her station, was seen by some as a vulgar parvenu of the worst kind, taking advantage of the gentle young "aristocrat's" connections in order to raise her own social level. And although Home was considered guilty by some of trying to swindle the poor old widow, he behaved like the aggrieved young sensitive who was powerless against the establishment. He managed to pull it off. Although the court found in Lyon's favor, several friends with whom Home had lost touch renewed their friendships, and it was as a result of one of these friendships that his most famous and most astonishing séance occurred.

On the night of December 16, 1868, D. D. Home was invited to hold a séance at Ashley House, the London flat of the young Lord Adare (later Lord Dunraven) that he shared. Also in attendance were James Ludovic Lindsay (later Lord Crawford) and Adare's cousin, Major Charles Bradstreet Wynne. All three young men had previously attended séances with Home and were quite aware of his ability to levitate and perform other feats of astounding skill. They looked forward to the evening as a bit more of the same, but they couldn't have been prepared for what they saw.

Shortly after the sitting began, they were visited by a number of spirits who came and went. Home paced the room. Soon his body began to elongate, then levitate. Home calmly told them not to be afraid and not, under any circumstances, to leave their seats. Then he went into the next room and shut the door between them. Lindsay heard a voice whisper in his ear, "He will go out one window and then enter by another."

The flat was on the third floor of the building, and Lindsay spent several seconds in alarm, wondering if his friend would be injured or killed in the attempt. He needn't have worried. They heard the sound of a window opening in the next room, then seconds later Home was hovering outside the window of the room where they sat. He opened the window from outside, then calmly stepped in and took his seat.

With one seemingly impossible feat, documented by three gentlemen of impeccable character, Home had managed to recover his reputation. He spent the rest of his life writing his memoirs and attempting to defame other mediums, most of whom, he claimed, were fakes.

Home died of tuberculosis in France in 1886 at the age of 53, no one ever having proved for certain whether or not he was a fraud,

Whom Are We to Believe?

The pedigrees of the three young men who witnessed D. D. Home's astounding feat of levitation may have been more perfect than their memories (or perhaps their sobriety). To this day there is controversy: about the date on which the Ashley House séance took place (was it December 13th? December 16th?), about whether the room was illuminated by full moonlight (the sitters said yes, the almanac says not a chance on either night), or whether in fact the séance was even held at Ashley House.

despite his having been investigated by some of the best. And like a real-life example of the stereotypical theatrical understudy waiting impatiently in the wings for some disaster to befall his principal, William Eglinton (see Comments, Chapter 2, i) took to the stage. But he never captured the public's or the scientific community's attention the way his predecessor had. The investigators were keeping busy elsewhere. Among the mediums who were examined and investigated repeatedly was a pair of American siblings who were as flamboyant about their talents as Home was cryptic about his.

The Davenports

The Davenport brothers, Ira and William, a Buffalo duo, did not claim to be spiritualists at all. In the late 1850s, while they were in their teens, they created what became their major claim to fame: a wooden cabinet that they used as a prop in their stage work as escape artists.

Six feet long and seven feet high, it was not unlike a church confessional box on the outside. It contained three compartments, each with its own door to the audience. The center compartment appeared to be inaccessible from each of the side compartments, and its door had a diamond-shaped hole carved at about head height. Onstage, Ira would sit in one of the side compartments, William in the other. In the compartment between them were placed a number of musical instruments. The brothers asked for volunteers from the audience to tie them up and close the doors of all three compartments. Within minutes, strains of music would come from the instruments within, and hands could be seen through the diamond-shaped window in the center door. When the music stopped, the doors were opened by another member of the audience. The instruments were once again silent, and Ira and William would be sitting, tied up as they had been before the performance.

Despite never claiming to be spiritualists, they recognized a good thing when they saw it. Taking advantage of the paranormal craze, they called their box invention a "medium's cabinet" referred to their performances as "séances," and proceeded to achieve fabulous fame and fortune. Between 1860 and William's death in 1877 at age 36, they appeared thousands of times in the United States, Great Britain, and Australia; in Russia before Czar Alexander II; and in Paris before Napoleon III and his Princess Eugénie. The Davenports, like many others in their profession, were tested again and again. No fraud was ever detected.

THE RISE OF PSYCHICAL INVESTIGATION

I never said it was possible. I only said it was true.
—Sir William Crookes (Flammarion 1907, 315)

The bandwagon was rolling and thousands were climbing on. Then one day, predictably, the wheels fell off. In an astonishing appearance one evening in the fall of 1888, 40 years after the Hydesville knockings, Maggie Fox, with her silent sister Kate by her side, appeared onstage at the New York Academy of Music and admitted publicly that it had all been a hoax. The women proceeded to demonstrate before the large, rather annoyed audience the unusual skill that had taken them all in. The girls who had begun the spiritualist craze had indeed done so by learning how to crack their knees and toes at will.

Many of the faithful did not believe the confession, and the spark the Fox girls ignited had already inflamed a host of others. Fraud, once only suspected and now publicly admitted, had created a knee-jerk response in all but the unshakably faithful. Fraud had already created a whole new science: psychic investigation.

The Medium's Cabinet

The wooden medium's cabinet made famous by the Davenports became a standard prop for mediums. Although spiritualists claimed that the cabinets were a requirement for successfully achieving communion with the spirits, debunkers and other critics suggested that all the cabinet did was hide from the audience the trickery mediums claimed was spirit activity.

Frederic William Henry Myers

In 1874, a little more than a decade before the Fox sisters' confession, Frederic W. H. Myers (1843–1901) began to take an interest in psychic phenomena after attending a séance with the British medium and theologian William Stainton Moses (see Comments, Chapter 2, ii). Following a brilliant early career in higher education and writing, Myers's later life was more and more devoted to the work of the Society for Psychical Research (SPR), which he founded in 1882.

A graduate and later a fellow of Trinity College Cambridge, Myers earned a reputation as a brilliant psychologist, erudite lecturer, versatile author, and energetic psychic explorer. His early writings spanned the genres from poetry to biography (on poet William Wordsworth in 1881) and essay. Some of his later works, which bridged the gap between psychology and the paranormal, were considered by William James, one of the founders of the US counterpart to the SPR, the American Society for Psychical Research (ASPR) (see Comments, Chapter 2, iii), to be "the first attempt to consider the phenomena of hallucination, hypnotism, automatism, double personality and mediumship, as connected parts of one whole subject" (Proudfoot 2004, 57).

The SPR's aim—to collect evidence of psychical phenomena and undertake scientifically controlled experiments—was focused almost exclusively on the science that had become known as parapsychology. Myers's quickness of mind and verbal adroitness enabled him to become the society's spokesman at a time when spiritualism fever was just waxing.

His ardent yet rational approach was a refreshing attitude in a discipline that had its share of scoffing, cynical skeptics on the one side and defensive, unquestioning believers on the other. With one foot in each camp, Myers was able to distinguish for the avid public the differences between theory and proof and between speculation and confirmation. He did so wisely, without entering into the argument of what was or was not possible. Interestingly, his own convictions appear to have had more to do with survival after bodily death than with communication from the spirit world. He fervently desired to believe in the former, but was most willing to remain skeptical about the latter, even after observing astounding feats of a psychical nature. His two-volume treatise *Human Personality and Its Survival of Bodily Death,* published in 1903, is considered to be a seminal landmark work.

Over the years, Myers recorded numerous cases where individuals displayed inexplicable knowledge of details. Labeling the power "telepathy," Myers maintained that its practitioners must have been engaging in a form of mind reading or thought transference. His views were supported by a French colleague, Charles Richet.

Charles Robert Richet

Charles Richet (1850–1935), a Frenchman, was a professor and researcher in physiology and an esteemed bacteriologist, psychologist, and pathologist. Among his many contributions to medicine were his discovery of the presence of hydrochloric acid in gastric juices and his research in the areas of serum therapy, respiration, and immunity. His work on hypersensitivity to previously encountered foreign proteins, which he named "anaphylaxis," earned him the Nobel Prize in Physiology or Medicine in 1913. He was also a poet, novelist, and playwright, and a tireless promoter of peace. In his spare time, he investigated occult phenomena.

In 1872, after a personal experience with what is now known as extrasensory perception, Richet began to investigate hypnotic states. He believed that parapsychology was "a science dealing with the mechanical or psychological phenomena due to forces that seem to be intelligent or to unknown powers latent in human intelligence" (Buckland 2006, 296). His original premise was that strange manifestations of the type he was witnessing during sittings were purely mentally or physiologically produced by the medium and/or sitters, and for 20-odd years, that conclusion was validated for him many times over.

In the early 1890s, Richet began to work with Myers and Baron Albert von Schrenck-Notzing, whose extraordinary career is dealt with later in this chapter. Together they pursued investigations of a number of people who claimed to be mediums. At about this time, another prominent figure was becoming interested in spiritualism.

Sir Arthur Conan Doyle

A British author, physician, lecturer, and historian, Arthur Conan Doyle (1859–1930) was the creator of the ultramethodical, cocaine-addicted detective Sherlock Holmes, who first appeared in print in 1887. After graduating from Edinburgh University, Doyle practiced medicine until 1891, when his first historical novel, *The White Company,* was published. Turning to writing and public affairs as dual pursuits, he produced several more works in addition to the Sherlock Holmes stories, among them a history of the Boer War published in 1900, several novels, and a play based on the Napoleonic wars.

The ingenious methods for crime detection with which he imbued his detective stories led to advances in criminology in Britain, and Doyle was admired as a logical and rational thinker. But he also had a side that many of his contemporaries felt never quite squared with his professional reputation. He dabbled in what was considered a highly irrational pursuit—spiritualism.

Three weeks after the death of his father in 1893, Doyle joined the SPR. It wasn't until several years later, in 1902, shortly after Doyle was conferred a knighthood,[2] that he began a long and significant relationship with a fellow peer of the realm and an avowed spiritualist, Sir Oliver Lodge, to whom Doyle in 1926 dedicated his best-known book on psychical matters, *The History of Spiritualism.*

Sir Oliver Joseph Lodge

Oliver Lodge (1851–1940) was born in Staffordshire and received his higher education at University College London. At 28, he became assistant professor of applied mathematics and was later called to the chair of physics at his former alma mater. He remained in that post until Birmingham University opened its doors in 1900 and he was selected as its first principal.

In 1883 he became interested in psychical research and began attending a few séances, but his early work was limited to experiments in thought transference. Like a number of his colleagues in the early years, Lodge did not yet entertain the question of spirit communication as a plausible explanation for the manifestations he witnessed. His investigations were little more than cursory until 1889, when he began to take an active role as an observer and reporter at séances. Even then, psychic investigation remained a sideline for him while he concentrated his intellectual efforts on academic pursuits.

His academic work centered on physics, most particularly the study of lightning and electricity, and he was responsible for a number of original pieces of investigation in related areas. Knighted in 1902 in recognition of his contributions to science, he went on to receive the Albert Medal of the Royal Society of Arts in 1919 for his pioneering work in wireless telegraphy. Applying his own theories led him to invent the Lodge spark plug and a method of tuning in radio waves.

In addition to his scientific research, Lodge was active in the SPR, serving as its president from 1901 to 1903 and its honorary president (jointly with Mrs. Eleanor Sidgwick[3]) in 1932. Lodge devoted a good deal of his time to writing on various topics ranging from physics to child rearing. His work developed quite a following, judging by the numerous references to his titles in the pages of *The Progressive Thinker*.[4] But his work most germane to the present context is his

Mediumship

Mediumship is the ability to communicate with spirits from the next world. Known variously throughout history as seers, prophets, priests, medicine men, oracles, wizards, and mystics, mediums are practitioners of an ancient and universal skill. Two main types are: (i) mental mediumship, in which the medium communicates automatic writing or speech through clairvoyance or clairaudience (in which the medium hears a voice from an unseen source), and (ii) physical mediumship, which is characterized by rapping, levitation, and other physical manifestations.

writing on psychic phenomena, which included *Man and the Universe* (1908), *The Survival of Man* (1909), *Continuity* (1914), *Raymond, or Life and Death* (1916), and *Past Years* (1931), his autobiography. For these, Lodge secured his reputation as one of the major philosophical thinkers of the spiritualist era.

PHYSICAL MEDIUMS AND THEIR INVESTIGATORS

The stage was set. These four gentlemen of science, Myers, Richet, Doyle, and Lodge, after reading about and investigating various mediums, found them wanting. The Davenports were clever, but did not seem worthy of their attention. D. D. Home was certainly skilled, but his was the skill of illusion and legerdemain rather than paranormal activity. Some of the other practitioners warranted being seen again, and the scientists were willing to continue their investigations where needed. But even when these investigations exhausted all possible avenues of approach, Doyle, Lodge, and others were unable to conclude that they were dealing with spiritual matters.

Believing in the hereafter and in the human personality's continued existence after bodily death, they felt sure that life of some sort existed beyond the grave. But they were still unclear as to whether these people calling themselves mediums were communing with spirits or simply manifesting physiological phenomena created by their own minds. They had almost despaired of ever finding an answer, and then they met Eusapia Palladino.

Eusapia Palladino

The Italian woman (some said she had Gypsy blood) who would become known as the Queen of the Cabinet was a short, heavyset young woman with charm of neither face nor personality. Orphaned early on, Eusapia (1854–1918) was taken in by several well-meaning families in Naples. She worked for some time as a household servant before being "discovered."

There were some incidents of poltergeist[5] when she was quite young: linens torn off her bed and table knockings. But she seemed neither perturbed by nor much interested in these phenomena until one day in the early 1870s, when one Signora Damiani, the English wife of an Italian spiritualist, showed up at her door offering to pay her to do a sitting. Signora Damiani's story was that the spirit named John King (see Comments, Chapter 1, i) had appeared at a séance that she and her husband had given, and King had told the Damianis about Eusapia and her talents.

Eusapia went along with the idea, but in the singular style that would become her trademark: apportation, the transference of objects. Whereas other mediums apported lovely items such as bouquets of flowers or pretty gemstones, Eusapia's apports were sometimes dead rodents and wilted flowers, particularly if she took a disliking to one or more of the sitters. Often, instead of bringing items into the séance room, she teleported them out.[6] Sitters could never be sure if their watches and jewelry would be returned to them, as Eusapia's "spirits" seemed quite fond of them. There was another feature that made Eusapia's séances unusual: sex.

Perhaps today's audiences, inured as they are to on-screen and public displays of wantonness, would not be scandalized. But this was, after all, the Victorian era. The mere hint of sexuality or whisper of naughty words sent women into fits of fainting and men into displays of undisguised horror and distaste. When the uncomely little Eusapia began flailing about the room in a seemingly uncontrollable spectacle of licentiousness, the sitters were understandably horrified.

Her séances continued, although for several years her fame remained fairly localized to the Naples area. Sitters, it seemed, forgave her overtly sexual behavior because of the entertainment she provided. And she certainly entertained—with apports, asports, table tippings, materializations of extra limbs,[7] and sexual advances to the male sitters that left nothing to the imagination.

Then in 1888, she began to be taken more seriously. A Professor Ercole Chiaia of Naples had witnessed one of her séances and was so impressed by what he saw that he wrote an article in a journal published in Rome in which he invited Cesare Lombroso,[8] an Italian criminologist and avowed skeptic, to investigate Eusapia for himself.

Lombroso complied, but not until 2 years later. By that time, Eusapia's fame had spread and Lombroso became curious enough to attend two of her sittings. At first convinced that she was suffering from a mental disorder that was out of her control, he was soon moved to rethink his diagnosis.

After the second sitting had taken place, during which nothing much out of the ordinary had occurred, all those present witnessed a small table moving on its own out of the curtained cabinet. Without touching the table in any way (her hands and feet were tied), Eusapia, who was sitting outside the cabinet with the other sitters, managed to bring the table to within inches of herself. An immediate and thorough examination of both the table and Eusapia confirmed that nothing was attached to either one that could have made it move in that way. That was all it took for Lombroso's complete and utter conversion. "I am filled with confusion and regret," he wrote, "that I combatted with so much persistence the possibility of the facts called Spiritualistic" (Doyle 1926, 2:13).

Beginning in March 1891, Lombroso subjected Eusapia to a number of tests, and over the next 20 years, he championed her cause. He subjected her to urine tests, x-ray imaging during séances, photographic samples, cardiographs, and other sophisticated measures, and time and again he reported that she was genuine. Lombroso's investigative sittings led to others. Then, in 1892, the Milan Commission was struck for the investigation of paranormal activity. Among the investigators for the series of 17 séances were eminent scientists from a number of European countries, including Frederic Myers and Dr. Charles Richet.

Myers and Richet entered the ring, and along with them were Lodge and Doyle, who were by then leading figures in the SPR. They and several other notable scientists took their turns at the perpetually disdainful and often downright incorrigible medium. She threw tantrums if things did not go her way. She refused to be seated when they wanted her to sit and insisted on sitting when they wanted her to stand. She constantly attempted to cheat at the "tests" they gave her, citing as an excuse boredom, fatigue, or the scientists' own lack of security measures. She was several times caught red-handed in blatant trickery, but the phenomena she produced when the investigators were certain there was no trickery astounded them all, and the documentation continued.

Despite the cheating, Myers and Lodge were by now in full support of her genuineness. Richet, however, was not yet ready to give his stamp of approval. After the Milan Commission's inquiries, numerous investigative ventures were undertaken: in France and in Italy, in Poland, at Cambridge, and in America. There were so many tests, in fact, that Sir Arthur Conan Doyle referred to Eusapia as the most investigated medium of all time. He was awestruck by her abilities:

> This woman rises in the air, no matter what bands tie her down. She seems to lie upon the empty air, as on a couch, contrary to the laws of gravity; she plays on musical instruments—organs, bells, tambourines—as if they had been touched by her hands or moved by the breath of invisible gnomes. . . . This woman at times can increase her stature by more than four inches (Doyle 1926, 2:16).

At first more skeptical than the others (he was the lone dissenter when the Milan Commission declared her genuine), Richet was curious. He invited a group including Myers, Mrs. Eleanor Sidgwick, Mr. Henry Sidgwick, and Sir Oliver Lodge to his villa near Toulon, France, for a sitting with Eusapia. It was a remarkable séance during which Eusapia managed to produce from nowhere a fresh melon, which was deposited on the table in front of the sitters. She also moved, by psychokinesis or telekinesis, a small wicker table high enough off the floor to place it upon the séance table. In his report on the Toulon séance to the SPR, Sir Oliver Lodge wrote:

> However the facts are to be explained, the possibility of the facts I am constrained to admit. There is no further room in my mind for doubt. Any person without invincible prejudice who had had the same experience would have come to the same broad conclusion, viz.: that things hitherto held impossible do actually occur. . . . The result of my experience is to convince me that certain phenomena usually considered abnormal do belong to the order of nature, and, as a corollary from this, that these

phenomena ought to be investigated in natural knowledge (Doyle 1926, 2:17).

Unfortunately, Dr. Richard Hodgson, a member of the Cambridge investigation committee, had been unable to attend the Toulon sittings. He flatly told the group they were being hoodwinked. They decided to hold another séance with Eusapia, this one at Myers's home in Cambridge in the early spring of 1895, with Hodgson as the only addition to the previous group. By the end of the sitting, which became known as the Cambridge Experiments, Richet was a convert. But due to an unfortunate turn of events, the same séance was nearly this medium's undoing.

Despite having everything set up according to her demanding specifications, Eusapia embarrassed everyone with her vulgarity and her lack of restraint. Her behavior was so bizarre that, had Lombroso been in attendance, he may have reverted to his original diagnosis of mental instability. The group blamed the outlandish behavior on her social insecurity. In any event, she was given a few rather blatantly obvious opportunities to cheat, which she took, without appearing to care who saw her. Everyone at the séance saw her cheat, and Hodgson and the mighty Sidgwicks were not at all impressed. Shortly after the séance, the SPR announced that it was done with her.

By this time, however, Eusapia's skills had earned the grudging acceptance of Charles Richet, although he never quite went so far as to say she was communicating with the next world. Nevertheless, he and Doyle, along with a host of other supporters, managed to pull Eusapia's only slightly tarnished reputation out of the flames of disaster. With the performance of a few more astonishing séances, she raised her profile to worldwide prominence, which endured until 1909, when she took a half-year-long American tour that effectively ended her career.

This time there were too many reports of fraud for her to live down, and the fantastic phenomena she produced were no match for the bad press she received. She returned to Naples, where she kept the books for her husband's business until her death in 1918.

Some time after Eusapia Palladino dematerialized from center stage, a medium emerged who would later be known by the mysterious alias Eva C.

Marthe Béraud, aka Eva Carrière or Eva C.

The daughter of a French garrison officer stationed in Algiers, Marthe Béraud, born about 1884, came to prominence at a somewhat more advanced age than had the teenaged Eusapia. In 1903, at the age of about 19, she was living with General Noel and his wife, a couple who would soon have been Marthe's in-laws had it not been for the untimely death the previous year of their son Maurice, Marthe's fiancé. Her mediumistic gifts had developed in the months since the young man's death, and Marthe had a firm place in the family as their live-in medium.

When Charles Richet got wind of the young woman, he lost no time in traveling to Algiers to see the phenomena for himself, and even he, the great cynic, was bewildered by what he witnessed. From the very first séances, Marthe Béraud produced a pasty substance from her mouth and her breasts that gradually developed into the materialized form of a man who called himself Bien Boa. The entity was purported to be an Indian Brahman who had passed from living form some 300 years before. Richet made public the reports of the experimental séances he held with Béraud at Villa Carmen in Algiers,

A Blip on the Screen

The spiritualist epidemic that had begun in the mid-19th century had, after a slight lull, a resurgence in the early part of the 20th. Interestingly, the resurgence was said to be largely due to the atmosphere of war that pervaded the world, but it may have been indirectly due to the very phenomena that had started it all. In 1904, nearly 6 decades after the first report of strange goings-on in Hydesville, a skeleton was found in the basement of the old Fox home, along with a peddler's tin box inscribed with the name Charles B. Rosna, a traveling peddler. The discovery was no surprise to those who had never doubted the Fox girls' claims of spirit communication.

describing in detail the substance he coined "ectoplasm."[9] But the reports were not well received. Doubt was cast on the results, and it was claimed that a costumed hired domestic was likely responsible for the appearance of the Brahman spirit.

It was Doyle's turn to snicker in vindictiveness for the first time since a parting of ways that occurred between the two investigators several years before. Throughout his later life, Doyle was often critical of SPR representatives, referring to their tactics as "thumb-screw methods" (Doyle 1926, 2:102). Some of the criticism was of Richet, since, although not strictly acting for the SPR, he often fed their skepticism with the poor positive results he obtained as a function of his tightly controlled experiments. Doyle felt that Richet believed everything that pointed to fraud and nothing that pointed to authenticity.

In a display of strong residual bias against Richet some 20 years after the publication of Richet's reports on such mediums as Eusapia Palladino, Doyle suggested: "It is only poetic justice that Professor Richet should have been subjected to this unfair and annoying criticism, for in his great book 'Thirty Years of Psychic Research,' he is most unfair to mediums" (Doyle 1926, 1:103).

Somewhat unworthy sour grapes, but it was no secret that these investigations could make or break a career. And while it may have been true that Richet treated most mediumistic phenomena with arrogant dismissal, Béraud's manifestations confounded him. Of Bien Boa he wrote:

> It walks, speaks, moves, and breathes like a human being . . . and there are reasons for resolutely setting aside every other supposition than one or the other of these two hypotheses: either that of a phantom having the attributes of life; or that of a living person playing the part of a phantom (Doyle 1926, 1:103).

But even in the seriousness of his pursuit, Richet was able to see the humor in some of the incidents he reported. One event in particular shows a clear sense of showmanship on the part of either the mediums or the spirits they claimed to be representing. Richet was hoping to collect some of the materialized Bien Boa's breath to test it for the presence of carbon dioxide. The entity complied and breathed into a flask of baryta water.[10] When the water turned white, indicating a positive result, the sitters erupted into calls of "Bravo!" Bien Boa promptly appeared three more times at the opening of the medium's cabinet, bowing and smiling after each round of applause. He was taking curtain calls!

Despite the lightness of tone of the foregoing, it is clear that Richet was serious about what he saw, and his reports illustrate the significance with which he felt the scientific community ought to deal with the phenomena:

> The materialisations given by Marthe Béraud are of the highest importance. They have presented numerous facts illustrating the general processus [sic] of materialisations, and supplied metapsychic science with entirely new and unforeseen data (Doyle 1926, 1:107).

But all of Richet's seriousness could not outweigh public opinion. A newspaper article published in February 1906, shortly after his reports were made public, had more impact in 1 week than his many years of successful experimentation. Sadly, the impact was totally negative. The article stated that an Arab coachman by the name of Areski who had previously worked for the Noels now admitted that he had been hired to play the part of Bien Boa. He claimed that he had made his appearances through a trapdoor conveniently placed in the floor of the medium's cabinet. The same article alleged that the medium herself had admitted to the fraud.

Richet adamantly refuted the allegations, citing as possible explanations for the former's claims the lack of character of the low-caste coachman and for the latter's alleged confession the medium's unstable temperament. He insisted that he had carefully examined the medium's cabinet for evidence of a trapdoor and vouched that there was none. But the denials were of little use as damage control. Although no proof was ever offered for either allegation, Marthe Béraud was disgraced.

Richet returned to a scant few more séances with her, but inexplicably, Bien Boa never materialized again. Richet promptly withdrew from investigation of mediums, perhaps reasoning that his reputation was not worth losing in the continuous battle between what was authenticated and what was acknowledged in the rigid world of scientific investigation.

The medium herself was never heard from again—at least not as Marthe Béraud. She managed to reappear 2 years later, still in Algiers and still in bodily form, but now going by the name of Eva Carrière. It seems that in the intervening years, Marthe/Eva had found herself a mentor in the person of a certain artist, Madame Juliette Bisson,[11] who took the young woman under her wing. Madame Bisson engaged the assistance of the German physician Baron Albert von Schrenck-Notzing, who bravely picked up where Richet had left off.

Albert von Schrenck-Notzing

A medical doctor with a degree from Munich University, Schrenck-Notzing (1862–1929) developed an interest in mediumship in a similar way to Dr. A.: It began with his study of hypnotism while in medical school. Schrenck-Notzing's interest increased after a meeting with Charles Richet in Paris in 1889, during which the two scientists had a fascinating discussion on telepathy. Two years later, Schrenck-Notzing published a German translation of Richet's reports of his experimentation in thought transference.

Schrenck-Notzing was involved to some extent in investigating mediums with Richet and Myers, but it was only after his introduction to Eva C. that he decided to devote most of his time to the field of parapsychology. He eventually set up his own laboratory for the investigation of mediums, with particular focus on their physical manifestations. In doing so, Schrenck-Notzing set himself up for a great deal of ridicule within and outside of the scientific community.

In 1909, Schrenck-Notzing began experimental sessions in Paris with Eva C., as she had become known. The first manifestations were sequels to Bien Boa's marvelous appearances, and although the new Bien Boa was also turbaned, he was beardless. Then, at sittings in November of the same year, Eva C.'s body began producing material that resembled masses of cloudy, veil-like fabric of a light gray color that, over the months, appeared to vary in form and density. By May of 1910, the masses seemed to resemble a smoky, filmy substance.

The production of these forms was always preceded by the sounds of deep, hoarse breathing and often appeared after "loud, convulsive coughing, muscular contractions in the arms, deep groaning and perspiration" (Schrenck-Notzing 1920, 3). The inchoate masses were often seen to be attached by some threadlike projection from Eva C.'s mouth or through whatever orifice the ectoplasm was exiting.[12]

One might suggest that the physical convulsions the medium went through are not dissimilar to those experienced by someone in the throes of regurgitation, and that the threadlike projections might well have been filament or fine string used for the express purpose of helping the medium to snag whatever it was she had swallowed (or inserted). Indeed, the problems with Eva C.'s emanations did not end with such elementary observations. But the difficulties were certainly not due to a lack of zeal on the part of her German investigator.

For all his apparent naïveté in the face of rather thin information, Schrenck-Notzing was nothing if not thorough. He put forward the theory that ectoplasm was composed of leukocytes, which are white or colorless blood corpuscles, and epithelium, a thin cellular tissue that performs the body's functions of protection, secretion, and assimilation. And he continued his study of his fascinating subject, observing her again and again in a long series of séances, making copious notes and observations.

There were interesting differences and similarities between the way Eva C. and her predecessor, Eusapia Palladino, proceeded in a séance. Whereas Eusapia most always went into a spontaneous trance, Eva C. required someone to hypnotize her, and it was usually Madame Bisson. Both mediums, however, were similar in requesting sitters to accompany the beginnings of materialization with song. In Eva C.'s case, it didn't much matter what they sang or how. As Schrenck-Notzing reported, "Hymns or slow chants are as welcome as '[La] Marseillaise' or tunes from *Carmen*. It is also immaterial whether or not the singing is in time or in tune" (Schrenck-Notzing 1920, 47).

Physical mediumship, the production of physical manifestations such as levitations, table tippings, and materializations, had always been viewed by investigators as the type most susceptible to fraud. The SPR, in fact, gave the impression that it felt physical mediumship was nothing more than a bizarre sideshow, and its members typically refused to have anything to do with it. Schrenck-Notzing was aware of the skepticism with which his work was viewed by many. In order to forestall criticism and, indeed, opportunities for fraud, Schrenck-Notzing employed some extreme measures. These measures included the requirement that mediums drink or eat foods such as bilberry or beet juice an hour or so before the séance. The idea was that the foods would line their insides, effectively tinting anything they might swallow to later regurgitate.

Hands were a problem. Schrenck-Notzing's notes indicate that when new observers were present, they frequently made comments about Eva's hands, which seemed to draw back inside the closed curtain anytime a form began to materialize. So, as with other investigations, Schrenck-Notzing included the holding of the medium's hands as a deterrent to fraud. There were many instances in the record, however, that indicate that Eva C.'s hands were not being held by someone throughout all séances. The medium's hands are described holding the curtain—"She now holds the curtain with crossed hands" (Schrenck-Notzing 1920, 223)—or resting on her knees—"Hands visible all the time on the knees" (Schrenck-Notzing 1920, 209).

Schrenck-Notzing also employed a number of dress requirements for mediums that included a séance costume: a tightly fitting full-length gown that left arms uncovered and often required the medium to be sewn into it. In some cases, Eva C. was nude during the experiments, but it appears that this occurred only when Madame Bisson was the sole sitter. Despite his insistence that the phenomena produced by Eva C. were real, and although he kept an open mind, Schrenck-Notzing stopped short of declaring that there was, as yet, enough evidence to accept a spiritual connection.[13] His friend and colleague Dr. Gerda Walther said after Schrenck-Notzing's sudden death at the age of 67 that he tended "to attribute psychic occurrences to the workings of the subconscious mind," but "in rare cases he did not entirely exclude the spiritualist theory" (Pleasants 1964, 287).

Despite the precautions, Schrenck-Notzing came under fire from both his colleagues and the public, but his perseverance was inexhaustible. Having seen the fraud engaged in by Eusapia, yet having observed enough of her skills to wonder at their origins, he was doubly passionate about learning as much about Eva C. as he could before her powers deserted her.[14] According to some critics, this seemed to happen quite early on in the investigations. By the autumn of 1911, Eva C. was beginning to create visible forms in the ectoplasm. She never again produced a moving, breathing entity such as Bien Boa and his successor, but forms such as hands, feet, and even whole limbs— and, later, faces—were produced.

The first faces produced formed on the back of the medium's head in a clot of ectoplasmic substance that was thought to have emanated from her ear or scalp. Sometime later they seemed to develop just outside the cabinet curtain while Eva C. was visible inside.[15] The forms usually appeared to be attached to the curtain and were described, even by the most trusting of sitters, as quite flat and immobile. Some witnesses even suggested they looked like magazine or paper cutouts. This observation may have been due to the folds that were sometimes visible on their surfaces. It may also have been a result of more obvious trickery.

In 1914, Madame Bisson wrote a book about Eva C. and had it published. The illustrative plates included one photograph that Schrenck-Notzing had developed from a camera placed inside the medium's cabinet. The photo showed a flat white disk apparently emerging from Eva's head. Parts of both sides of the disk could be seen at once: on one side was a face; on the other the letters "LE MIRO" could be clearly seen. It prompted more than one adroit observer to suggest that the two-dimensional face had been clipped from the French magazine *Le Miroir,* and faithful readers quickly scrambled through back issues until they found published photos to match a number of Eva C.'s photographed "spirits."

Schrenck-Notzing's rebuttal to this accusation showed as much inventiveness as it did gullibility. He suggested that Eva C. suffered from two rare conditions: hypermnesia, an extremely acute memory, and cryptomnesia, total recall of mental images. Together the conditions gave Eva C. the ability to materialize the memory of a photo seen in a magazine *exactly* as it had been recorded by her brain, including insignificant or extraneous data showing through from the verso.

After 4 years of observing Eva C., Schrenck-Notzing still admitted to some misgivings as he reported on the phenomena he had witnessed. In what could be seen as a disclaimer of sorts, Schrenck-Notzing prefaced *Phenomena of Materialisation* (1920), his major work on the manifestations observed and recorded during séances with Eva C., with the following words:

> Any dealings with the discredited so-called "spiritistic" phenomena are attended, even now, by certain disadvantages to the investigator. Not only are his powers of observation, his critical judgment and his credibility brought into question, not only is he exposed to ridicule by the reproach of charlatanism . . . but he even incurs the danger of being regarded as mentally deficient, or even as insane (Schrenck-Notzing 1920, v).

Despite the stated personal and professional risk he took, Schrenck-Notzing persisted, but it is with some skepticism that his work should be viewed. All other things being equal, the reported phenomena are astounding. Sadly, all other things were far from equal.

The majority of the experimental sessions with Eva C. were conducted in Paris. Although Schrenck-Notzing stood behind his experiments, it is interesting to note that he was at home in Germany and not present at many of the sessions on which his findings were based. Instead, Schrenck-Notzing left the quality control in his absence in the hands of Madame Bisson, who was often the only observer. Another curious aspect of the two volumes outlining his results is the photographic records, the majority of which indicate that they were retouched, ostensibly to preserve the modesty of the nude medium. But many of the plates in the collection appear to be more sketch than photograph, and Schrenck-Notzing admitted they were "reconstructed, according to the records, by the welcome assistance of the painter, Karl Gampenreider" (Schrenck-Notzing 1920, vii). Are they truly photographs then, or merely artist's renderings of events that the artist himself did not witness?

Furthermore, some of the phenomena (spontaneous pseudobirths, etc.) were produced only in the presence of Madame Bisson. Schrenck-Notzing rationalizes his unquestioning acceptance of Madame Bisson's reports with an assertion that the phenomena witnessed were made possible only because of the medium's close association, and presumably her comfort level, with the observer. Schrenck-Notzing contended that since the medium and the observer resided together, it was highly unlikely that the observer misrepresented the events. Quite the contrary may have been the case, and the question of observer objectivity needs to be taken into serious consideration.

Schrenck-Notzing would likely have continued working with Eva C. had it not been for the advent of World War I. At this point, his travel between Germany and Paris was severely curtailed, and it really is with regret that one is unable to add more of this researcher's work to the body of knowledge about physical mediums and, even more specifically, about materialization. Schrenck-Notzing is, in fact, considered by some to have been the foremost authority on materialization.[16]

With Schrenck-Notzing out of the picture, Gustave Géley took over the role of principal investigator of Eva C. beginning in September of 1916. A brief interruption in their work occurred in 1920, when the SPR relaxed its stance toward physical mediums and called Eva C. and Madame Bisson to London for 2 months of experimental sittings, which turned out to be an abject failure for the medium. Of the 40 séances held, half were entirely without manifestations; the remainder were extremely weak. During one sitting, a sample of ectoplasm was taken and laboratory tested. The resulting analysis: the "ectoplasm" was chewed-up paper. Although they grudgingly admitted that they had no idea *how* she had managed it, the SPR reverted to its original claim that the so-called ectoplasms were simply regurgitations. They dismissed Eva C. as a fraud.

Two years later, through their association with Dr. Géley, Eva C. and Madame Bisson were involved in experimental sessions at the Sorbonne University in Paris, a series that could go down in the history of spiritualism as the Sorbonne Fiascos. Out of 15 sittings, 13 produced no phenomena at all. Madame Bisson insisted that the conditions had been unfavorable for the medium and had compromised her abilities. But the harm had been done, and the fallout was predictable. In late 1922, Eva C. retired, no doubt realizing that her time in the spotlight was as good as over. Her demise virtually ended the popularity of physical mediums. A new, more modern kind of medium was emerging.

MENTAL MEDIUMS AND THEIR INVESTIGATORS

Physical mediums can be compared in the world of performance to slapstick comedians, who rely on sight gags and visually shocking images. Mental mediums,[17] on the other hand, depend on subtlety for the success of their performances. The prurient fad of watching young women with ectoplasmic body parts adhering to their torsos and strange substances leaking from orifices disappeared along with the Victorian era. Its fade-out between the two world wars permitted the new, more subtle, more sedate trance mediums to come into vogue. Among the most recognized of the trance mediums were two British women, Gladys Osborne Leonard and Eileen Garrett.

Gladys Osborne Leonard

Born in Lancashire, England, Gladys (1882–1968) was the eldest of the four children of a wealthy yachting entrepreneur and his wife. As with most mediums, she began to experience psychic phenomena early in life, having visions of very beautiful landscapes with peaceful-looking people walking through them. Gladys called these places Happy Valleys and was not at all disturbed by them. Some internal caution told her not to mention the visions to her down-to-earth parents, and so she kept her Happy Valleys to herself. One morning, however, she shared a particularly beautiful sight with her father, who immediately forbade her to speak such nonsense again.

When Gladys was in her teens, her father lost most of the family fortune and Gladys had to learn to take care of herself, which she did by making a living as a musical stage actress in both drama and comedy touring companies. When she was 24, Gladys became interested in spiritualism after she had a vision of her mother standing in a sunlit garden, looking like the picture of good health. Apparently at that very same moment, her mother died in a nearby town.

Gladys's entry into spiritualism began with table tipping. She tried out various techniques with two fellow actresses, but they were unsuccessful at first. Then one day an entity Gladys named Feda[18] communicated through table tipping. Feda claimed that she was a Hindu girl who had been the wife of one of Gladys's great-great-grandfathers. She communicated that she had been only 14 years old at the time of her death in childbirth in about the year 1800. There was no record of the existence of Feda, but a story of such a girl being married to William Hamilton, Gladys's great-great-grandfather, had circulated within the family for generations. In subsequent séances, Feda became Gladys's loyal attendant, acting as her spirit guide and as her control in the séance setting.

In March 1914, following up on messages from the spirits, Gladys became a professional medium. Feda made it clear that Gladys was to be a private medium, and that she was not to go onstage for dozens of people at a time. It was also made clear that her role was to help people through a terrible catastrophe that was about to happen. Many of the messages she received ended with these words: "Something big and awful is going to happen to the world. Feda must help many people through you" (Guiley 2000, 218). Not long after that, World War I erupted.

She was married by this time to a fellow actor named Frederick Leonard, who became her dedicated supporter and helper. Gladys successfully followed Feda's petition to remain a private medium, developing a reputation as a communicator with the spirits of the war dead. Then, in the autumn of 1915, Raymond Lodge, son of Sir Oliver Lodge, was killed in action in Flanders. Lady Lodge and her husband held numerous sittings with Mrs. Leonard, who accurately described details of a photograph for which Raymond, through Feda, reported having sat. Neither Mrs. Leonard nor the Lodges themselves had ever seen the photograph, which they later obtained through a comrade of Raymond's. It verified every detail reported by Mrs. Leonard.

In 1916, Sir Oliver published the account of the medium's contact with his deceased son in his book entitled *Raymond, or Life and Death*. The book created a sensation. Mrs. Leonard subsequently allowed herself to be investigated, but no fraud was ever hinted at. Mrs. Leonard also managed to confound investigators who felt she must have been using some sort of mental telepathy to read sitters' minds about details of their departeds' lives. She was not only able to carry out third-party proxy sittings,[19] but also to pass very stringent "book tests" in which material unknown to either Mrs. Leonard or the sitters was transferred through the medium from Feda. The material was later verified to be absolutely accurate. In later years, Mrs. Leonard's messages included some unusual direct-voice messages.

From time to time during Mrs. Leonard's séances, a whisper could be heard from the empty space a foot or two in front of her that would round out what Feda was passing on to her. Doyle describes Mrs. Leonard at these sittings at which he was present:

> The outstanding merit of her gift is that it is, as a rule, continuous. It is not broken up by long pauses or irrelevant intervals, but it flows on exactly as if the person alleged to be speaking were actually present. The usual procedure is that Mrs. Leonard, a pleasant, gentle, middle-aged, ladylike woman, sinks into slumber, upon which her voice changes entirely, and what comes through purports to be her little control, Feda. The control talks in rather broken English in a high voice with many little intimacies and pleasantries which give the impression of a sweet, amiable and intelligent child (Doyle 1926, 1:198).

Direct-Voice Mediumship

Direct-voice mediumship is a method of spirit communication in which the spirit speaks directly to the audience without using the medium's speech apparatus. In the early days of spiritualism, this was often accomplished via the voice trumpet. Some spiritualists believe the vocalization is made possible by spirits who use ectoplasm to construct an artificial larynx, then translate their thoughts into audible vibrations. As could be expected, this type of mediumship is quite amenable to fraud by skillful ventriloquists. Leslie Flint, whom you will meet later, was one of the best-known direct-voice mediums. Flint's spirits appeared to speak from a point slightly above and to the left of his shoulder.

Although she never produced physical manifestations such as ecto-plasm, materializations, or bouncing balls of light, Mrs. Leonard was considered by many to be one of the greatest psychics who ever lived. Indeed, Doyle referred to her in *The History of Spiritualism* as "the greatest trance medium with whom the author is acquainted" (Doyle 1926, 1:198).

Gladys Leonard died in 1968 at the age of 86, her psychic talents continuing to defy explanation by investigators. Although the SPR was careful not to admit that her case was evidence of life beyond the grave, it did acknowledge that Mrs. Leonard certainly provided evidence of some inexplicable psychic gifts. In the words of Mrs. Eleanor Sidgwick: "On the whole, I think that the evidence before us does constitute a reasonable prima facie case for belief" (Time-Life Books 1989c, 91). It was clarified that the SPR "belief" was in clairvoyance, not survival.

Eileen Jeanette Vancho Lyttle Garrett

The mediumship of Eileen Garrett (1893–1970) began during the rise of spiritualism that occurred following World War I. A truly gifted medium, she was born on St. Patrick's Day in the misty, folklore-rich countryside of County Meath, Ireland. Her early psychic experiences included visions of the dead, which neither frightened nor upset her, for she felt that her Celtic heritage had given her a healthy acceptance of death as part of life's cycle. She married young, to a British man 12 years her senior, and moved with him to London. The couple had four children, the first three of whom, all sons, died young, and the marriage ended in divorce before World War I erupted.

During the war, Garrett opened a hostel for wounded soldiers who were on leave before returning to the front. Many times she would sit with them and tell them that all would be well when they returned to battle, although there were several whose deaths she foresaw, including one young man whom she married but lost just 1 month later. In 1918, she married J. W. Garrett, another wounded soldier, but they were divorced a few years later.

It was shortly after the war that Eileen Garrett's powers of medi-umship began to blossom. She had joined a group of women who wanted to use table tipping to contact those whom they had lost during the war, and one day she slipped into a trance during their séance. She reported being able to see dead people standing around the table where they were sitting. Garrett was so unsettled by the phenomenon that she consulted a hypnotist, who put her back into a trance. While Mrs. Garrett was entranced, the hypnotist reported, he communicated with an entity named Uvani, who had contacted him through his hypnotized subject. The spirit had told him that he was to be Garrett's spirit guide for communication with the spirits. Garrett resisted this, but it was no use. She had been selected as the messenger between the spirits and the living world.

Although she became a highly respected medium and accepted that she had a precious gift, she remained skeptical about her ability to act as a conduit between the world of the living and that of the dead. Two years before her death in 1970, she wrote: "I prefer to think of the controls as principals of the subconscious. I have never been able to wholly accept them as spiritual dwellers on the threshold, which they seem to believe they are" (Time-Life Books 1989c, 85).

A curious and intelligent woman, Garrett wished to understand more about her powers and about the task the entity told her she had been assigned. She presented herself to the British College of Psychic Science in London, where, between 1924 and 1929, she worked with a rising star in the ASPR by the name of Hereward Carrington.

Hereward Carrington

Hereward Carrington (1881–1959) was a handsome, distinguished British-born investigator and author of reports of paranormal phenomena who became a member of the ASPR in 1900 at the tender age of 19. After Professor James Hyslop took over as president of the society, Carrington became his assistant and held that position until 1908. Until he had occasion to witness some of the phenomena produced by Eusapia Palladino, Carrington was a skeptic's skeptic who appeared resistant to most evidential displays of spirit communication.

Among the initial accounts in Dr. A.'s journals is a letter to the editor of *The Progressive Thinker* in Chicago. In it, he reflects on a

recent article in the journal on the investigation of mediums at Lily
Dale by one Hereward Carrington. Dr. A. writes:

> Mr. Carrington's "exposure" of mediums at Lily Dale came as a
> great surprise, no doubt, to many who had thought that the phe-
> nomena there were worth serious consideration. However, if
> nothing better occurs than what appears on the face of Mr. Car-
> rington's report, then the mediums at Lily Dale, or those he inves-
> tigated, are at most arrant humbugs, and the visitors at this famous
> camp, patrons of those mediums, the silliest of dupes. Nonetheless,
> Mr. Carrington's testimony, as a member of the American Society
> of Psychical Research, will have great weight, especially with those
> who have never investigated phenomena at Lily Dale, but to one
> who has, it is not overwhelming (Dr. A., summer 1908).

Fully aware of the risks he took by publicly challenging a notable
figure such as Hereward Carrington, Dr. A. nevertheless confirmed
his avowed position as a seeker of truth and knowledge. Frauds there
were, by the dozen. But there were also debunkers who had neither
the intellect nor the strength of purpose to effectively challenge those
things they were aiming to discredit. Dr. A. was seeking truth on all
fronts. He was characteristically both fair and incisive in his lack of
appreciation for Carrington's conclusions. His letter continues:

> I was there on the 16th day of August last [1907], the day Mr.
> Carrington says he left the place. I went over the same ground,
> visited the same mediums immediately after him, so I know
> whereof I speak. . . . It is quite evident that Mr. Carrington did not
> visit Lily Dale in a sympathetic spirit. Anyone who has been there
> cannot help but note the contrast between the delightful place and
> his prosaic description of it. His primary object seemed to be to
> expose mediums, rather than to investigate psychic phenomena.

It is possible that Carrington was encouraged by Dr. A.'s challenge
to be more open-minded in his investigations, for he went on to write
17 books on various topics dealing with the paranormal. He became

a devoted student of psychic phenomena and in 1921 founded the American Psychical Institute and Laboratory. Carrington's work with Eileen Garrett so moved him that he followed up the research with the publication of *The Case for Psychic Survival* (1957), a study of mediumistic phenomena. The book includes a full account of the testing done with Garrett to establish once and for all whether Uvani, her spirit guide, was the spirit of the long-dead Arab or merely an active dramatization of the medium's subconscious mind.

Carrington was much impressed by Mrs. Garrett's skills as a medium, but equally impressed by her desire to assist in the examinations. In the preface to the book, he acknowledges her help with consummate grace.

> We were indeed fortunate in securing the services of an outstanding psychic "sensitive"—Mrs. Eileen Garrett, well known through her own writings. . . . Her wholehearted cooperation in these tests is hereby acknowledged—and deeply appreciated. Mrs. Garrett is unique in that she herself is scientifically interested in the nature of her own phenomena. When giving a séance, she passes into deep trance and, after a short wait, her usual "control" makes his appearance—that is, "he" speaks through her mouth, addressing the sitter and inviting questions (Carrington 1957, 13).

Mrs. Garrett, who at the time of the testing in London was editor of the magazine *Tomorrow* and president of the Parapsychology Foundation, was known worldwide for her work as a medium. But it is equally important to point out that those who knew her well would never have called her a spiritualist. In Carrington's words:

> It is an interesting and curious fact that the normal Mrs. Garrett is not spiritualistically inclined; she seems to be more or less "on the fence" regarding the interpretation of her own phenomena; she frankly states that she does not know the source of her own information, or anything much about her own Control (Carrington 1957, 60).

Testing Sessions with Mrs. Garrett

The tests given to Mrs. Garrett in both normal state and in trance state as Uvani were scored and interpreted.

The Bernreuter Personality Inventory measures four aspects of personality: neurotic tendency, self-sufficiency, introversion-extroversion, and dominance-submission. Mrs. Garrett and Uvani's results showed internal consistency (i.e., Mrs. Garrett's answers remained fairly homogeneous from one question to the next, as did Uvani's). However, the results showed that Mrs. Garrett and Uvani had directly opposing behavioral tendencies.

On this measure, Uvani's scores indicated a high degree of emotional stability; Mrs. Garrett, on the other hand, scored quite low on the same scale. Whereas Uvani was somewhat submissive, fairly introverted, and average in dependence on others, Mrs. Garrett was rated as having a high tendency to dominate and being fairly extroverted and not at all dependent on others.

Page's Behavior Analysis gave an indication of the number of what Carrington refers to as "schizoid traits"[20] that were present. Mrs. Garrett's results showed her to possess 15 schizoid traits, a score within the average range of responses for normal individuals. Uvani's results showed 36 schizoid traits, a score decidedly beyond both

---

Put to the Tests

The following battery of tests was given to both Mrs. Garrett and to Uvani:

- Bernreuter Personality Inventory

- Page's Behavior Analysis

- Thurstone scale (to measure attitudes toward the Church)

- Woodworth Neurotic Inventory (administered to Mrs. Garrett only due to lack of time)

---

normal and psychotic individuals. Carrington is quick to point out that Uvani's score is so far beyond the range that it is indeed impossible to interpret since no norms are available for comparison.

On the Woodworth Neurotic Inventory, which was not administered to Uvani, Mrs. Garrett scored a fairly high tendency toward neuroticism, which was consistent with her low emotional stability rating on the Bernreuter.

Carrington and his colleagues also administered various other tests to Mrs. Garrett and Uvani, some of them to see if the transfer of training could take place between the woman and her spirit guide. Uvani and Mrs. Garrett were each asked to memorize two different lists of words. Whereas Uvani succeeded in memorizing all of the words on his list as well as many of the words on her list, Mrs. Garrett had great difficulty memorizing even her own words. She explained that she had had trouble with learning in school and that memorization had never been a strong skill.

When dealing with Mrs. Garrett's ability to tell sitters items that only they and their loved ones could possibly know, the investigators were interested in knowing whether the medium was using telepathy to "read" the minds of the sitters. Several measures were put into place to examine this, all with the same result: No telepathy was detected. Additional instruments measuring everything from galvanic skin response to blood pressure were used at various stages throughout the testing cycle.

Over the course of 24 experimental sittings, a secondary control calling himself Abulatif made his presence known, along with two well-known figures in the history of the ASPR, Dr. Richard Hodgson, a one-time secretary of the society, and Dr. James Hyslop, founder of the ASPR, who had passed away in 1920.

Among the results achieved through Carrington's exhaustive set of measures, little or no evidence of supernatural contact was ever established. Some results were conclusive, however. It was agreed that, based on these results, Mrs. Garrett was truly in a trance state when Uvani and the other entities communicated. Uvani himself seemed to be consistent in his attitudes from one sitting to the next. Interestingly, however, his accent was not so consistent. He spoke with a strong Middle Eastern accent at the beginning of the séances, then

... more or less lapses into modern English as the sitting progresses—only occasionally catching himself up, as it were, and speaking with his characteristic accent for a few words before again lapsing into the language of the medium (Carrington 1957, 118).

Carrington's conclusions indicate the great weight of trial, which he acknowledged went with them, of interpreting the first results ever received from quantitative methods to answer a question investigators had been asking for decades. Carrington stated categorically that Uvani and his second, Abulatif, were shown to be nothing more than secondary personalities of Mrs. Garrett, "which have attained unique independence, but which are, nevertheless, not the truly independent spiritual entities which they claim to be" (Carrington 1957, 127). When it came to the other entities who communicated through Mrs. Garrett, and who often supplied supernormal information, the investigators were less sure.

Although Carrington was never prepared to give a final verdict regarding the existence of contact with the spiritual world, over time his stance changed quite considerably from ardent cynicism to scientific curiosity to, ultimately, baffled acceptance of the unknown. In

A Rose by Any Other Name

A striking characteristic of the majority of spirit communicators is their penchant for using Hollywood-style stage names. Throughout the history of spiritualism, the names of disembodied spirits were not those one would typically associate with someone down the street, but rather unusual names one might make up for a particular purpose (e.g., to indicate nationality or uniqueness). Specific examples are Abulatif and Uvani (Eileen Garrett's controls), Nada and Afid (medium Florence Cook's controls), Nepenthis (a female spirit materialized by Madame d'Espérance), and, of Dr. A.'s acquaintance, Lee Long and Blue Light.

The Story of Psychic Science he wrote: "I may say that I have never, in all that time, witnessed any phenomena which have appeared to me undoubtedly spiritistic in character—though I have, of course, seen many unquestionably supernormal phenomena" (Carrington 1930, 68). Among the "unquestionably supernormal phenomena" might surely have been the materialized hands that an astounded Carrington reportedly held and saw disappear from his grasp during a séance.

In 1932, shortly after the scandal erupted involving the medium Margery Crandon, Carrington may have been reluctant to accept some of the phenomena that had previously astounded him, but his reluctance didn't last long. In later years he was to confirm his willingness to remain open to all possibilities. Some time after completing the exhaustive work with Eileen Garrett, he wrote:

> I can now say that our experiments seem to have shown the existence of mental entities independent of the control of the medium, and separate and apart from the conscious or subconscious mind of the medium (Fodor 1966, 42).

Controversy continued to rage over whether mediums were communicating with aspects of their own personalities or with discarnate entities from beyond the grave. Carrington avoided making such a decision, fearing, perhaps, that taking one side or the other on such a controversial question might constitute for him a professional point of no return.

Short of saying precisely what he thought the "entities" were, he appears to have finally come to the conclusion to which many great philosophers have come: that there is an unavoidable presence of uncertainty when dealing with life and death.

> For my own part—while still holding my final judgement in suspense—I must say that our experimental tests seem to have furnished material which is at least **indicative** of survival—which in itself is a conclusion of no little significance (Carrington 1957, 128) [emphasis in the original]

THE END OF AN ERA

But time was marching on. The heartbreaking memories of robust young men whose lives were cut short by the war were fading into the past, and by the mid-1930s, spiritualism had lost much of its popularity. That is not to say, however, that it had disappeared completely. As with all controversial pursuits, those who are really serious about their subject will continue to pursue it, although perhaps not as publicly as before. So it was with spiritualism. The great stage mediums had gone, and the great investigators had shuffled off this mortal coil.[21] But perhaps when times are tough, it is only the toughest who survive. Leslie Flint is a case in point.

Leslie Flint

Of all the mediums we have seen in this text, perhaps Leslie Flint (1911–1994) will be the most memorable, if only because he is of our time. After all the other mediums, particularly those known as physical mediums, had faded into obscurity, Flint continued to hone his craft.

Born in a Salvation Army home in the London district of Hackney, Leslie was abandoned by his mother when still very young and taken to live with his poverty-stricken but hardworking grandmother. Soon after, he began to experience visions. When he was 17, he attended a few séances at a home circle and was startled when he himself fell into a trance and began relaying messages of relevance to sitters. Having no recollection of what occurred during the trance state and receiving nothing but grief from his grandmother over the séances, he decided he was not interested in pursuing what the other sitters tried to convince him was a great gift.

He took up his second most consuming interest, ballroom dancing, developing it into a career in performing as well as in teaching. In 1932, Flint had the good fortune to become reacquainted with Mrs. Edith Mundin, one of the sitters of his original home circle. She persuaded him to return to the circle. He eventually agreed to become its medium, and his skills began developing.

An eager fan of silent films, Flint often stopped at the cinema on his way home from dance class or a séance. But it wasn't long before this young sensitive became persona non grata in movie theaters. One evening while sitting and enjoying a film, he became aware of strange whispering going on around him.

> I could catch only an odd word here and there. But the voices were those of both men and women and it was made very clear to me that other members of the audience could also hear them because I was constantly being told to shut up or thumped angrily on the back by those sitting behind me (Flint 1971, 73).

Astounding as it was, Leslie had begun receiving direct-voice communication from the spirit world. He eventually had to give up going to the cinema altogether when he realized what was happening. At about the same time, the situation at home with his grandmother became untenable and he moved out. He became a grateful paying guest in the widowed Mrs. Mundin's house, from where he was happily able to pursue his passions for both dancing and mediumship without criticism or interference.

It wasn't long before the circle began to hear spirit voices at its séances. At first they were simply confused whisperings, but later they became clearer and more discrete as spirits began identifying themselves by the names they had used on earth. Flint noticed that he was now able to be a part of the conversations because he no longer needed to be in a trance state in order for the spirit voices to manifest.

Excited about his developing psychic skills, Flint was in the throes of deciding whether to drop his career in dancing so he could pursue full-time mediumship. Strolling down a side street one bright day in 1934, he met his dance partner and paramour Gladys, who promptly struck him in the face in full view of dozens of people. She accused him of living with a woman old enough to be his mother, then turned and walked out of his life. At that moment Flint's decision was made. He would give up his career in dancing and devote his life to mediumship and the pursuit of evidence of "the glorious, comforting truth of man's survival of his bodily death" (Flint 1971, 75).

His gifts developed rapidly, as did his relationship with Mrs.

Mundin. The two were married later that same year. Then, one night in 1935, his life took an abrupt turn toward the limelight. During one of the weekly séances in the Mundin/Flint house, the sitters were clutching one another's hands when suddenly a voice with a distinct Italian accent began, as clear and crisp as if the speaker were sitting in the room.

I have come tonight to say how happy I am that this young man has at last accepted the life path he must tread and I want to tell him that one day when he is a famous medium he will hold a séance in the room which was my bedroom in Hollywood and I will come and speak to him there when he does so (Flint 1971, 76).

The voice, pleasant and cultured, informed the group that he was Valentino—Rudolph Valentino—the Italian-born American actor, romantic hero of such silent films as *The Sheik*. Flint was filled with overwhelming joy, and then and there determined that he would pursue this nebulous career in all its glittering possibilities.

With his wife's tactful help, he set out to polish his speech and manners to make him more socially "acceptable" for public appearances before all levels of society. A few months after the Valentino appearance, the first chance occurred for him to appear in public. It happened that the medium at the local spiritualist church where Edith was a member had just eloped with a member of the congregation. The post was vacant, and the church committee, having heard of Flint's successes, invited him to take the place of the former medium.

The congregation soon knew it had made the right choice. At his very first sermon in the fall of 1935, Flint went into a trance and gave a most interesting discourse and followed it with a brilliant demonstration of clairvoyance while under the control of a spirit who introduced himself as 'White Wing' (Flint 1971, 78). While his séances were still in their early stages, Flint was joined by a spirit entity who identified himself as Mickey, a cheerful 11-year-old Cockney newspaper boy who had been killed when he was run over by a truck.

Mickey became Flint's main control and doorkeeper to the spirit world and remained with him throughout the years of his mediumship.

Over the next several years, even while World War II raged and air-raid sirens interrupted every other séance, conscientious objector Leslie Flint gave hundreds of private and public séances, suffering badgering from audience members who felt it was their duty to challenge his placement in a noncombatant corps in lieu of fighting in the war.

Some of the sittings, however, provided what Flint called much needed "light relief." At one private séance in 1940 with a woman named Alice Bowering who wanted to talk to her departed husband, Flint was surprised when two jovial male voices joined them from the spirit world. It seems the woman had been married twice, and the cremated remains of both of her late husbands now sat side by side on the mantelpiece. Their disembodied spirits had gotten to know and like each other on the other side, and together they were watching over their widow!

Leslie Flint's name was on the tips of thousands of British tongues, but the talk wasn't always flattering. In 1948, Reverend Charles Drayton Thomas, a member of the committee of the Temple of Light Church where Flint was resident medium, a member of Flint's home circle, and a member of the SPR, heard a rumor that a number of fellow SPR members were suggesting that Flint was using ventriloquism to produce the voices they had heard at a recent séance. Thomas challenged his SPR fellows and set up a sitting during which he personally took care of fraud precautions. He recorded the measures he took:

> On February 5, I placed over his tightly closed lips a strip of Elastoplast. It was 5½ inches long and 2½ inches wide and very strongly adhesive. This I pressed firmly over and into the crevices of the closed lips. A scarf was then tied tightly over this and the medium's hands tied firmly to the arms of his chair: another cord was so tied that he would be unable to bend down his head. Thus, supposing he endeavoured during trance to loosen the bandage, it would be quite impossible for him to reach it (Flint 1971, 159).

Dr. Samuel Augustus Aykroyd, DDS, at age 79

Walter Ashurst, full trance medium

Walter Ashurst was a smoker; one of the boxes that he emptied.

The Shadow: Walter's favorite reading

Detective Fiction Weekly: Walter's other favorite reading

Dr. Aykroyd's journals
filled 83 scribblers
like this.

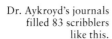

Dr. Aykroyd's journals were
discovered in this trunk where
they had been hidden for
50 years.

The author at age 8 with his mother,
when he first started attending the
séances of Dr. Aykroyd's circle

The masthead of *The Progressive Thinker* to which
Dr. Aykroyd had a lifetime subscription

Hereward Carrington (1881–1959), British
psychical investigator and author

Mina "Margery" Crandon (1881–1941),
leading spiritualist medium

Sir William Crookes (1832–1919), pioneer
in the field of subatomic phenomena

Sir Arthur Conan Doyle (1859–1930),
Sherlock Holmes author, closely
involved with spiritualism

Harry Houdini (Ehrich Weiss) (1874–1926), legendary escape artist

William James (1842–1910), founder of the American Society for Psychical Research (ASPR)

A glass lantern slide of a portrait of Baron Albert von Schrenck-Notzing (1862–1929) of Germany; an outstanding original pioneer in scientific psychic exploration, leading to the first photographs of materialized forms and materialized thoughts

Emmanuel Swedenborg (1688–1772).

Precipitated spirit painting of Azur, the helper, attributed to the Campbell Brothers, hangs in the main parlor of the Maplewood Hotel in Lily Dale, New York.

Precipitated painting of Clara, attributed to the Bangs Sisters, hangs in the Lily Dale Museum.

Precipitated painting of Nora, attributed to the Campbell Brothers around the turn of the century, hangs in the main parlor of the Maplewood Hotel in Lily Dale, New York. By request of the deceased girl's mother, the portrait appeared in full light at an evening Campbell Brothers auditorium séance.

A wide-angle photograph of a frontal view of the medium, Mary Marshall, with a teleplasmic mass that resembles a hand emerging from her mouth at a séance held at the home of Dr. Thomas Glendenning Hamilton on April 27, 1932

This spirit photo was taken in Lily Dale, New York, about 1921, and shows Dr. Aykroyd in a meditative mode with the heads of four individuals, presumed to be deceased, appearing (hovering) around him.

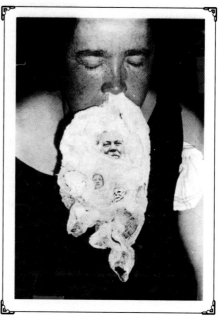

Photograph of the medium, Mary Marshall, with a teleplasmic mass attached to her nose featuring the second materialization of the face of Sir Arthur Conan Doyle during a séance at the home of Dr. Thomas Glendenning Hamilton on June 27, 1932

Replica of typical séance trumpet which was reported to float around the séance room and from which emanated the voices of spirits. The replicas are sold at Lily Dale as curiosities.

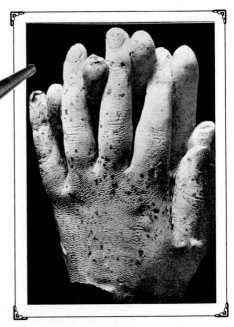

Wax hand cast, produced by Franek Kluski (1874–1944), a physical medium reputedly capable of producing detailed ectoplasmic materializations of animal or human forms

Slates with "spirit writing." After 75 years, the original red chalk appears to be fused with the surface and cannot be smudged. The written message on the slate reads, "My Dear Nephew, I am not far off. I can be of help. Command me at any time. Uncle Andrew Aykroyd."

The séance produced precisely the same voices, in their usual clarity and volume, as on any other occasion. The experiment was repeated on May 7, 1948, in the presence of four guests at Flint's home. Among those present was the research officer of the SPR, Dr. D. J. West, who had examined the medium's cabinet before and after the sitting and had personally attached tape to Flint's mouth and tied his arms to the chair.

A few days after the séance, Flint received a letter from West saying that he was not satisfied with the test results. He stated that when he examined the plasters covering Flint's mouth after the séance, one of them was no longer in line with the indelible pencil marking he had made. It suggested, he said, that the tape had been removed and reapplied. He accepted partial responsibility, suggesting that perhaps his methods had not been stringent enough. On the face of the observation, however, he had come to the conclusion that the results were without value. He asked Flint to submit to further testing, this time on the premises of the SPR. Flint refused.

The lack of SPR sanction did not tarnish for a moment Leslie Flint's reputation among believers. Over the next 28 years he continued to practice his craft, holding séances for thousands of people, among them dozens of members of British high society, including Her Royal Highness Princess Louise, daughter of Queen Victoria and wife of John Campbell, Marquis of Lorne, the former governor general of Canada. He also had several sittings with Mae West, some of them held in her Hollywood home on one trip to California and New York that Flint made in the '60s. But the trip ended on a sad note. When he returned to London, he found Edith in very poor health. She had suffered a stroke while he was in the United States and was now confined to a wheelchair. She died a few months later.

Although Flint gave up public appearances in 1976, he continued to hold private séances. Over the next several years, he communicated with the spirits of such people as Charles Richet; Lord Birkenhead, the former lord chancellor of England; famed British actress Ellen Terry; former British prime minister Sir Winston Churchill; and author Emily Brontë.

Flint submitted to scores of sittings for retesting, and voices spoke during many of these sittings. On more than one occasion, while viewing a sitting through an infrared telescope, one researcher claimed he had seen the ectoplasmic larynx appear to the medium's left side. In one experimental séance in 1972, a mass that looked like a ball of mist was photographed hovering just above Flint's left shoulder.

Although he never again submitted to testing with the SPR, Flint refers to himself in his autobiography as "the most tested medium this country has ever produced" (Flint 1971, Foreword). The record shows that no one ever found him guilty of fraud because, Flint says, no fraud was ever committed. In his own words:

> I have used my rare and strange gifts as honestly, as selflessly, and as devotedly as I have been able for thirty-five years now and my sixtieth birthday is almost here. I do not know how much longer I have left to serve and I am deeply concerned that I know of no one who can follow me (Flint 1971, 220).

My personal dream of one day attending a séance with Leslie Flint sadly never came true. I was able, however, to acquire recordings of séances that had been conducted with this great medium between 1962 and 1984. The tapes I procured included some rather startling communications with Maurice Chevalier beginning on October 12, 1975. Whereas the other disembodied spirits related that they were somewhat perplexed at being able to communicate with the sitters, Chevalier seemed to be more analytical than the others about what was happening.

In the earliest taped sequences, Chevalier seems extremely disoriented. He constantly asks sitters to repeat their questions, as if he cannot hear them very well or cannot understand what they are trying to say. One gets the sense that he does not quite understand what is happening, or indeed that he may not even realize he has died. In later sessions (1982 and 1984), his voice is much more relaxed, and at one point he suggests that the other side is *"magnifique."* He is asked by what possible means he is able to speak and be heard by people in the living world. He seems mystified yet accepting of it all. He offers no theories on how it is done and sounds quite satisfied not to know.

The tapes are fascinating, but there are conundrums. Although some of these discarnate entities identify themselves by first names, none identifies him- or herself absolutely.[22] It is our knowledge of these historical characters, and perhaps in some cases our experiences with their stage personas, that permits us to connect their disembodied voices to the names we know so well. Curiously, Charlotte Brontë is heard, during a séance taped on April 5, 1973, referring to Jane Austen[23] by her full name.

There are also further curiosities pertaining to these tapes. In some sessions, the male voices sound uncannily alike. The voice of Charlotte Brontë sometimes sounds very much like the voice of a 5-year-old boy named Bobby Tracy and the young newsboy, Mickey. This, of course, could simply be because they are produced through the same larynx—that of the medium, Leslie Flint. Perhaps one day someone might decide to subject such tapes to forensic audio analysis to discover whether the speech was produced by one voice or by a variety of different voices. What determination could be made one way or the other is unclear, but it would at the very least add to the body of knowledge of the paranormal.

Leslie Flint passed to the spirit world in April 1994, and, as we shall see, the essence of Leslie Flint's concern, "Where have all the great mediums gone?" has yet to be answered.

Chapter 3

Ghosts Today

> At one point I had to explain how I differed on a certain point from both Catholics and Fundamentalists: I hope I shall not for this forfeit the goodwill or prayers of either.
>
> —C. S. Lewis (Wilson 1990, 274)

Any discussion of a quasi-religious topic such as spiritualism is sure to be contentious. It would take a stronger soul than I to walk into such an arena without some fear or trepidation. Nevertheless, our subject could not be approached without first looking at the present state of the world and its spiritual makeup.

Although not a religion per se, the New Age movement appears to have developed a significant following over the last decades, with substantial increases since the turn of the millennium. Researchers estimate that New Agers number as many as 10 million to 12 million worldwide and constitute 12 to 15 percent of the US population. According to Naisbitt and Aburdene:

> At the dawn of the third millennium there are unmistakable signs of a worldwide multidenominational religious revival.

American baby boomers who rejected organized religion in the 1970s are returning to church with their children in tow or joining the New Age movement (1990, 270).

THE NEW AGE BELIEF SYSTEM

The term "New Age" was popularized by the American media in the late 1980s to describe a spiritual subculture interested in such things as meditation, channeling, reincarnation, crystals, psychic experience, holistic health, and environmentalism. The term also includes other fields associated with pseudoscience, anomalous phenomena, and various other mysteries such as UFOs and crop circles. Although there is an established belief system in the movement, New Agers typically construct their own personal journeys based on ideas taken from various principles.

New Age is a broad, diverse movement of the 20th century and contemporary Western culture whose adherents represent the most affluent, well-educated, and successful segment of the baby-boom generation, and its practices and beliefs may be seen as a form of alternative spirituality. Characterized by an individual and eclectic approach to spirituality, many of the ideas of the New Age movement are elements of older traditions from both Eastern and Western philosophies. Virtually all the world's major religions have influenced New Age thinking: spiritualism, Buddhism, Sufism, shamanism, Hinduism, occultism, and neo-paganism. The New Age movement has in turn influenced literature, art, crafts, and musical styles that are seen around the world.

With roots in transcendentalism, mesmerism, Swedenborgianism, and the Hermetic arts of astrology, magic, alchemy, and cabbala (or Kabbalah), the constituent elements of New Age are embedded in some of the practices of spiritualism, Theosophy, and some forms of the metaphysical movement. Although New Agers generally believe in the theory of monism,[1] they tend to emphasize a relativist approach to truth, often using the Vedic statement "one truth, many paths," which is similar in intent to the Zen Buddhist dictum "many paths, one mountain," to describe their personal journeys. This relativism is not only a spiritual relativism, it also extends to physical theories, with physical phenomena being considered largely from an experiential rather than a scientific viewpoint.

Among the influential promoters of the New Age movement are the actor Shirley MacLaine, whose television mini-series *Out on a Limb* created a wave of interest in New Age ideas, and James Redfield, who in 1992 self-published *The Celestine Prophesy* to great response. Both works were instant successes that managed to shake the perceptions of millions of people and reawakened a worldwide interest in spirituality.

One of the most interesting aspects of New Age illustrates how closely tied it is to spiritualist concepts: the use of channelers. Although there are some distinct differences between channelers and mediums, the two are quite similar. A medium is an intermediary between the world of the living and those who have passed on. In the majority of cases, mediums go into a trance. Using one of the "clear senses" or direct voice, the medium brings through messages from spirits who have lived before and who are usually, although not always, connected in some way to the people being contacted.

According to Buckland (2006, 68), channelers go into a trancelike state while remaining fully conscious of all that is around them. While in this state, they bring information from sources who may or may not have lived at any time on earth, and who are often not at all connected to the people being contacted. Among the sources communicating through channelers are entities who claim to have lived in Atlantis; others have claimed to be from other planets and universes. Mediums usually work with small groups or individuals. Channelers typically deliver their information in a public forum.

Although channeling appears to be a newer practice, related as it is to the New Age movement, it is really as old as recorded time. Artifacts from Egypt indicate that masks were worn by priests when channeling messages from the Egyptian gods, and archaeological evidence suggests that Mayan priests played the parts of gods while allegedly relaying information and instructions from them. As it is with mediums, there may be frauds and charlatans among channelers, but there are many who have a genuine gift.

SPIRITUALITY VERSUS RELIGION

New religious practice has come with a whole set of difficulties, not the least of which is confusion in terminology. What precisely constitutes a religion? Dictionaries tell us that religion is adherence to a particular set of beliefs, and that has been the standard understanding among most people. Religion would seem to refer specifically to groups composed of those actively involved in following a strict code of behavior and doctrine, yet many of the belief systems popular today appear to permit various degrees of latitude in interpretation.

A contradiction is apparent here. While a lack of a clear doctrine has been put forward as a reason that many people sever daily ties with some church groups, flexibility and concession to individual needs have been the very qualities that have attracted others to what might be considered unconventional forms of ideology.

Statistics seem to tell us that interest in religion is down, and yet, if one considers the burgeoning New Age movement, the rise of interest in holistic healing, and the increased belief in the power of such things as crystals and magnets, it appears that the metaphysical realm is heading toward a popularity similar to what it enjoyed in the Victorian era.

Popular media reflect these trends. Consider the premises of the handful of television series that are not focused on crime solving. *Medium, Ghost Whisperer,* even *Smallville,* to name but a few, all indicate that people are interested in the paranormal. Since an interest in paranormal occurrences suggests an openness to believe in their existence, it is not a great stretch to assume that the popularity of such story lines indicates a willingness to consider a supernatural source for these events. It would seem, certainly on the face of it, that something spiritual is at work here, and people who are open to the existence of supernatural forces could be called spiritual. But are they spiritualists?

The term "spiritualist" may be used to describe a person who manifests concern for things that are divine (i.e., proceeding from God), but it may also refer to those who care about things that have to do with the higher qualities of the mind and the meaning of life and may, in practice, have nothing whatever to do with an "ism" (for example, capitalism, communism, socialism, spiritualism).

Interestingly, there is little in the literature to absolutely define the term "spirit." Even the spiritualists themselves have failed to give more than fleeting attention to the lack of definition for what, other than indestructible life, is actually implied. Many religions view the spirit and the soul as one and the same. To many in the distant past, the soul's intangible nature only served to prove its importance to man's full existence. Somewhat of a tautology, the argument nevertheless had huge masses of people convinced.

Nándor Fodor, a spiritualist and author of the *Encyclopaedia of Psychic Science* (originally published in 1933), is somewhat more, dare we say . . . down-to-earth when he writes that the spirit resides *in* the soul and is "the innermost principle, the divine particle, the vital essence, the inherent actuating element of life" (Fodor 1966, 356).

Spiritualists draw inspiration from other religions, in some instances the established religions in which they were raised. Many of today's enlightened spiritualists are those whose backgrounds include Christianity, Hinduism, Islam, and Buddhism, as well as those who

The Seven Principles of Spiritualism

- The divine eternal parenthood (sometimes called "the fatherhood of God")

- The family of humankind (sometimes called "the brotherhood of man")

- The interconnectedness of all creation

- The communion of spirits and the ministry of angels

- The continuous existence of the human soul

- Personal and social responsibility (including compensation and/or retribution in the hereafter for the good and evil deeds done "on earth")

- Eternal progress open to every human soul

were formerly adherents of newer belief systems such as Eckankar.[2] Considered a "personal" religion, the spiritualist church belief system includes seven accepted principles, and all members are permitted full individual liberty of interpretation of these principles.

Today, most spiritualist churches in America are affiliated with the National Spiritualist Association of Churches (NSAC) or with the Universal Spiritualist Association (USA). The NSAC, established in 1893, is the largest and oldest organization for the science, philosophy, and religion of modern spiritualism in the United States, and it has its general office in Lily Dale, New York. The USA, founded in the United States in 1956, describes itself as "a nondenominational association teaching, preaching and practicing the great religions" (Buckland 2006, 421).

Churches within the NSAC are autonomous, although they must be chartered by the organization (see Table 1). In the United Kingdom, most spiritualist churches are affiliated with the Spiritualists' National Union, which came into existence in 1902 when the National Federation of Spiritualists, established in 1891, changed its name. Many of the groups around the world belong to the International Spiritualist Federation, founded in Belgium in 1923. Seen as an umbrella group for the entire movement, the federation holds a conference every 2 years in a different part of the world.

TABLE 1: SPIRITUALIST CHURCHES IN THE UNITED STATES AND CANADA

US STATE[3]	NUMBER OF CHURCHES
California	34
Florida	16
Connecticut	7
Arizona	5
District of Columbia	2
Georgia	2
Arkansas	1
Colorado	1

CANADIAN PROVINCE	NUMBER OF CHURCHES
Ontario	30
British Columbia	15
Quebec	4
Alberta	3
Manitoba	3
Nova Scotia	2

In my research, I discovered several sources that fail to list spiritualism as a religion and others that label as "spiritism" any system of beliefs that is not mainstream. Still others use those two terms interchangeably. But there are clear differences between spiritualism and spiritism, and they should never be considered synonymous.

Robert Henry Thouless, a reader in educational psychology at Cambridge University and a fellow of Corpus Christi College Cambridge, agreed that there was a lack of agreement on the definition of spiritualism and suggested that the term "spiritism" would be more appropriate for the beliefs and practices associated with communication after death.[4] He contended that the suggested term would alleviate confusion with the general metaphysical meaning of spiritualism, which asserts the reality of the nonmaterial world.

Spiritualists, however, never adopted the suggested label. Unbeknownst to Thouless, the term "spiritism" had already been preempted. A well-respected and influential set of doctrines and practices known as Spiritism is still widely practiced in Brazil and the Philippines. Spiritism is correctly used to define only the religion that exists today almost exclusively in those countries.

KARDECISM, THE SPIRITISM OF BRAZIL

French physician and writer Hippolyte Léon Denizard Rivail (1804–1869), who became known as Allan Kardec, proposed and supported a belief system, a modern religion if you will, based on the central tenet of reincarnation. It is not surprising that Brazil, exposed for centuries as it has been to African spirits and superstition, would be home to Christian Spiritism. *Kardecismo,* as it is called in its birthplace, remains a powerful religious force in contemporary Brazilian society. Kardecist centers have been established all over the country, and current statistics suggest that 1.3 percent of the population of Brazil classify themselves as Spiritists.

Steaming and lush, Brazil has 125 million people who profess to be Catholic, yet only 30 percent of them attend mass regularly. The Charismatic Renewal branch of the Catholic Church is growing fast, while its conservative branch is in decline. More than 2 million[5] people in Brazil today, some who formerly called themselves Catholic, appear to be turning to less traditional methods of worship, including Kardecism, Afro-Brazilian syncretism, Umbanda, and Candomblé.[6]

Interestingly, Kardecism had a somewhat unusual start. In 1857, Allan Kardec codified Spiritism in his book *Le Livre des Esprits* (*The Book of Spirits*), which outlines clearly a belief not only that the soul of man survives bodily death, but also that surviving spirits can and do communicate with the living. Brazilian Spiritists (they call themselves *espíritos*) believe that they have "restored Christianity to what it was at the time of its founding: a faith based firmly on the immortality of the soul, regarding Jesus as the medium of God" (Playfair 1975, 15).

Kardecismo's early days witnessed the same type of fervor for the performance of curious manifestations that the rest of the world was experiencing. Brazil was not immune to the trends. But it had its own homegrown kind of mediums.

Chico Xavier

Francisco Cândido Xavier (1910–), known as Chico, was born in Pedro Leopoldo, Brazil. He left school at the age of 13 after completing primary level, then went on to become a household name and the country's most prolific author. He began writing in 1932 and, although virtually blind in one eye, has written nonstop since then, producing an average of three books per year. But there is something very unusual about how Chico writes. His writing is all achieved through a process referred to in Brazil as *psicografia:* what we call in English "automatic writing."[7]

According to Guy Playfair in *The Flying Cow* (1975), Chico does not claim ownership of any of the material he writes. He lives on a government pension and all proceeds from his books go to charities. He does this because, in fact, it is not his material.[8] His hand is controlled by spirits, unseen by all but Chico, who dictate to him under the control of his spirit guide, Emmanuel. Among the many spirits who have dictated works through Emmanuel are novelist André Luiz; pioneer of tropical medicine Dr. Oswaldo Cruz; and poets Castro Alves, Augusto de Anjos, and Casimiro de Abreu.

The works of poetry were published in 1932 in a volume entitled *Parnasso de Além-Túmulo* (*Parnassus from Beyond the Tomb*). Poet and academician Humberto de Campos, who was a leading figure in Brazilian literary circles, declared that the poetry showed precisely the same characteristics as the poems of these men when they were alive and declared them to be authentic. De Campos died shortly after publication of *Parnasso* and began dictating work through Chico that very same year.

Between 1937 and 1942, Chico published five books signed by de Campos—works that were received with the same amount of awe and reverence Chico's other works had prompted. Sadly, not everyone was impressed. De Campos's widow took Chico to court in 1944, claiming author's rights since the books were written by her late husband. The judge declared that it was not possible to establish whether or not de Campos's spirit had actually written the books. In any case, he said, de Campos was officially dead and had no more rights. The case was dismissed.

The furor over the trial gradually subsided. Chico Xavier, perpetually modest and lacking any need for publicity, judiciously signed any subsequent books written by de Campos as Brother X. He has continued his writing and has proved to be an inspiration for hundreds of thousands of Brazilian *espíritos.*

Carlos Mirabelli

No discussion of Spiritism could exclude Carlos (formerly Carmine) Mirabelli (1889–1951), a Brazilian of Italian descent who remains a most controversial and legendary figure. Particularly skilled at trance speaking, physical mediumship including levitation and apport, and automatic writing and painting, Mirabelli's abilities first came to the attention of others when he was working in a shoe store in São Paulo. One day, shoes began tumbling off the shelves in typical poltergeist fashion. This event was followed by several others until Mirabelli was taken to a psychiatric hospital for several days of observation, after which he was declared healthy but abnormal. The diagnosis: an extraordinary excess of radiant nervous forces within him.

Born and raised within 200 miles of São Paulo, Carlos Mirabelli, the son of a comfortably well-off Lutheran minister, showed early financial acumen. Although his business and real estate interests earned him a good living quite separate from his mediumship, he was not among the large group of psychics who gave their services without charge.[9]

In the early 1920s, Mirabelli presented himself at the newly established Academia de Estudos Psychicos Cesare Lombroso in São Paulo, where he submitted to several weeks of intensive and controlled experiments. According to Fodor, a paper on the findings was published in 1926. It reported on more than 300 sittings during which "astounding" phenomena were witnessed by a total of 555 people. Among the phenomena were trance speaking, during which the medium allegedly spoke 26 languages, including 7 dialects, and automatic writing, during which Mirabelli wrote in 28 languages and produced numerous pages: 14 pages in French in 19 minutes, inspired by Flammarion,[10] on the existence of inhabited planets in the universe; 9 pages on the independence of Czechoslovakia in 20 minutes; 5 pages in Japanese on the Russo-Japanese war in 12 minutes; 15 pages in Syrian inspired by Harun el Raschid; and 3 pages of untranslatable hieroglyphics in 32 minutes. Of the 63 materialization experiments carried out on Mirabelli, 40 were made in daylight and 23 in bright artificial light. Results indicated that 47 of the 63 tests of a physical nature showed negative results (i.e., there was insufficient manifestation).

The report showed that the testing produced some astounding results, yet the phenomena were greeted with some reticence by mainstream investigators, none of whom had been present at the experiments. Eric J. Dingwall of the SPR reviewed the report some time after its translation into English and declared:

I must confess that, on lengthy examination of the documents concerning Mirabelli, I find myself totally at a loss to come to any decision whatever on the case. It would be easy to condemn the man as a monstrous fraud and the sitters as equally monstrous fools. But I do not think that such a supposition will help even him who makes it (Fodor 1966, 244).

Dingwall was not alone in his caution. Professor Hans Driesch[11] traveled to São Paulo in 1928 to investigate Mirabelli for himself. He was impressed by the telekinetic phenomena he witnessed, among them the movement of a small vase and the closing of folding doors in daylight. Both events occurred without any apparent cause. But for the remainder of the medium's reported abilities, Driesch was less convinced. Witnessing no evidence of materialization or apportation, and hearing only Italian and Estonian spoken by Mirabelli, Driesch was unable to confirm the declaration of mediumship.

Meanwhile, Mirabelli had aligned himself with a number of Kardecism centers in São Paulo and Rio de Janeiro, providing them with both financial and spiritual support. Flamboyant and vain yet benevolent and altruistic, Mirabelli did not enjoy the favor of all *espíritos*. Many felt that his theatrics were not quite in keeping with the seriousness with which they wished to be taken. Yet many other members of the Brazilian public reacted quite differently: They embraced Spiritism as a direct result of the fascination with psychic phenomena that Mirabelli's performances created.

In the 1930s, the medium began to use his skills for faith healing, and his methods were anything but ordinary. On one occasion he claimed to have received the spirit of someone who had died of tuberculosis. To prove the point, he began spitting up real blood, a pint of it in less than a half hour, after which he recovered completely. Despite the theatrics, it seems that there were people who benefited from his abilities. Many doctors of the time claimed that Mirabelli gave them accurate diagnoses of patients in their care, diagnoses that helped them to treat their patients much more effectively.

But as Playfair observed (1975, 84), many of the phenomena that Mirabelli produced seemed utterly pointless: large pictures were smashed over sitters' heads, watches disappeared and reappeared somewhere else, ladies' mislaid eyeglasses showed up on their night tables at home, levitations occurred for no apparent reason, and unusual formerly lost articles, including the body of a woman whose decomposed remains her son had exhumed and stored in his house, reappeared.

Even today among modern devotees of Spiritism, many consider Mirabelli's feats to have been little more than fascinating theatrical displays.[12] His antics, in fact, must have annoyed a number of people during his lifetime. At the time of his death at age 62, Mirabelli had survived 15 lawsuits for the illegal practice of witchcraft. Other than the few healings he had managed to perform, Mirabelli's mediumship, even if genuine, seemed to have been largely performance for performance's sake.

Mirabelli's story is one tragic event in the saga of mediumship, and perhaps of spiritualism in general. It has already been stated that authentic mediums are bound by a code that they will use their gifts for the good of humankind without seeking financial or other gain. There is no doubt that, human nature being what it is, most mediums were tempted by the fame and fortune that awaited them for taking their skills to the stage. The consumers as well were subject to human weaknesses that caused them to demand more frequent and more sophisticated manifestations. As Playfair suggests about Mirabelli: "At times, the power left him, and he would indulge in some harmless conjuring tricks in order not to disappoint his audience" (1975, 108).

But the conjuring tricks resorted to by Mirabelli and some other mediums were anything but harmless. They fueled skeptics and nonbelievers in their relentless and visionless pursuit of fakery, which, over time, resulted in a climate of hostility for all mediums. Perhaps, if Mirabelli had not been so consumed by the magnet of fame and so easily flattered by those who turned him into a celebrity, his powers would have been fully investigated. As it is, the world will never know precisely the true nature or extent of his gifts.

MEDIUMSHIP NOW

In many ways, mediumship today in Brazil is taken much more seriously than it used to be. There is far less emphasis on stagey physical phenomena and more on the healing of mind and body. Indeed, around the world, mediumship is considered to be a viable occupation, although it is still viewed by many as an occult practice or as being among the cluster of carnival amusements that include fortune-telling and teacup reading. If you had the opportunity to speak to a real medium today, you would find not an individual somewhat reluctant to share details of an age-old practice, but one whose kind has been ridiculed and persecuted for centuries. Spiritualism has suffered a similar fate, but not all mediums are spiritualists.

According to the tenets of spiritualism, human beings are made up of three distinct parts: the body, the soul, and, at the highest level, the spirit. All three are vitalized by infinite intelligence and constitute the "triune being" central to this belief. It seems, indeed, that mediums today are concentrating their skills on healing that triune being. Yet not all mediums maintain a connection to spiritualism per se, nor do spiritualist churches support resident mediums as most did in the past. Statistics compiled by the Lighthouse Spiritual Centre in Toronto[13] show a total of 70 practicing (and licensed) mediums worldwide at the present time, yet there are more than 1,100 spiritualist churches (see Table 2).

The ratios of mediums to churches are barely adequate if a medium is considered to be an essential part of spiritualist practice. The statistics seem to underscore the suggestion that the connection between mediumship and the spiritualist religion is not necessarily a very strong one.

TABLE 2: SPIRITUALIST CHURCHES AND MEDIUMS WORLDWIDE

COUNTRY	NUMBER OF SPIRITUALIST CHURCHES	NUMBER OF PRACTICING MEDIUMS
England	810	29
Australia	75	4
United States	68	21
Canada	57	8
Scotland	42	4
South Africa	35	N/A
Wales	25	2
New Zealand	16	N/A

Northern Ireland	2	N/A
Pakistan	1	N/A
Sweden	1	N/A
Switzerland	1	N/A
Israel	N/A	1
Netherlands	N/A	1

A Worldwide Mediums Survey Internet poll[14] conducted in 2000 by Worldwide Mediums and Psychics may shed some light on modern-day mediums and their beliefs. Of 1,209 mediums surveyed regarding their faith and beliefs, 17.2 percent said that they did not believe in spiritualism as a faith. Unfortunately, those who responded positively to this question were not asked if they generally believed in spiritualist teachings; if they were, the response may have given us a slightly different picture. Many of today's mediums are not connected to any church or belief system, preferring to be seen as separate from anything organized.

But there may be other reasons for the low numbers of mediums listed in statistical reports. Richard MacKenzie, first minister of the Spiritualist Fellowship Church in Winnipeg and a medium himself, claims that the numbers reflected in online or mail-in surveys may in fact be only a fragment of the real picture and that there are probably 10 times that many. To illustrate his point, there are seven mediums of his acquaintance in his city alone, yet Lighthouse Spiritualist Centre statistics show only eight for *all* of Canada.

Why are these people not represented in polls? One reason, MacKenzie suggests, goes back to the spiritualist belief in free-thinking and individual journeys. The mediums are happy to simply do what they do and perhaps don't feel a great need to be recognized or identified by an outside agency.

To further underscore MacKenzie's contention that mediumship is not a dying art, he reminds us that there are currently several full-time teaching institutions around the world that specialize in mediumship. Among them are Arthur Findlay College, "the world's foremost college for the advancement of spiritualism and psychic sciences," in Stansted,

Essex, England; Camp Chesterfield, "a Spiritual Center of Light," in Chesterfield, Indiana; and the Morris Pratt Institute in Milwaukee, one of the Bureaus of Education for the NSAC, which offers full-time courses in the history, science, and religion of spiritualism, in healing, and in comparative religions.

With such comprehensive courses being offered, perhaps now we can answer Leslie Flint's question: "Where have all the great mediums gone?" It appears that they are alive and well and busy doing their work. But what exactly is their work?

And What Do You Do for a Living?

In researching this book, it has become quite clear to me why a medium might dodge such a question at a cocktail party. The answer would probably be followed by snickers or a reaction like a Monty Python "wink, wink, nudge, nudge."

What exactly are modern mediums doing today, you might ask. Table tipping? Materializations? Some, perhaps, but it appears that mediums have become more helpful than they seemed to be in the past, and many are practicing now what was largely the preserve of the shaman: psychic healing—of both the spirit and the body.

Dr. Stanley Krippner, in an article based on his lecture presented at the Dynamics of Healing: Altered States, Ritual and Medicine[15] conference held in Beverly Hills, California, on April 28, 1991, writes about several modern shamans who, working quietly and effectively for generations, have healed by restoring the balance of the body. The imbalance may be a misalliance within the body such as heat/cold or light/dark, or it may be between the individual and some outside source, such as the community or the spirit world. In any case, the healing succeeds when the balance is restored.

The second principle of shamanic healing is holism. The shaman works not only with the body and the mind, but also with the emotions and spiritual aspects of the human psyche. In many ways this reflects the monistic beliefs of some New Age practitioners. The third principle of shamanistic healing is imagination—the idea that if we believe it can happen, it can happen. If we believe that the laying on of hands will bring our inner energies to restore health to an ill part of the body or that a ritual performed near a dying person will ease his or her transition into the next world, it will.

Krippner reports that studies involving psychological testing have been conducted on shamans in various primitive villages. The healers scored significantly higher than their fellow villagers, most notably in the areas of creativity, imagination, and consensual reality. Although there have been no reports of mediums being tested in this way, it is safe to assume that their sensitivities and abilities are not much different from those of shamans. It may not be a stretch to suppose that mediums heal using the same three principles: balance, holism, and imagination. Whether or not they are spiritualists matters not at all to the outcome of their ministrations, which often produce astounding results—such as those produced by the Brazilian Spiritist Edivaldo Silva.

SOME MODERN HEALERS
Edivaldo Oliveira Silva

In his relatively brief life, and even briefer career, Brazilian psychic healer Edivaldo Silva (1930–1974) successfully treated more than 60,000 people. Edivaldo was 32 when he discovered his healing gift, and he performed his early surgeries without making an incision or drawing blood. He later went to more invasive kinds of surgery, which were, although not bloodless, quite painless, according to patients.

His surgery was usually done while in a trance state, with the skilled hands and mind of Edivaldo's spirit guide Dr. Calazans, a Spaniard, controlling his incisions. A true multiculturalist, Edivaldo was also aided at various other times, according to Buckland (2006, 373), by medical spirit guides from England, France, Japan, Germany, Italy, and Brazil.

His apparently brusque manner did not deter the thousands who flocked to his clinics in the hope of finding relief for their ailments. Nor did it affect the volunteer witnesses he solicited from the crowds of onlookers.

One such brave soul who not only witnessed Edivaldo's psychic surgery but also experienced it firsthand was Guy Playfair. In 1971, in the interest of research,[16] the brave young British writer underwent psychic surgery with Edivaldo Silva for a digestive condition that had been relentlessly plaguing him for the better part of his adult life. Excerpts of his account follow:

Edivaldo's hands seemed to find what they were looking for, the thumbs pressing down hard, and I felt a very distinct plop as they penetrated the skin and went inside. My stomach immediately felt wet all over, as if I were bleeding to death. I could feel a sort of tickling inside, but no pain at all.

[Later,] I peeled off the bandage on my stomach . . . there was a bright red mark on the place where Edivaldo had pressed with his thumbs and nearby there were two bright red dots. The red line was not a scar, just a jagged line only about three inches long, above and to the left of the navel. By the following morning the line had faded and within two days it had disappeared. . . . The following day I felt just about normal (Playfair 1975, 173).

Looking at all the evidence, one would wonder if Playfair had been under the influence of some drug or hypnotized by a clever hoaxer. But he maintains he was sober and was in full control of his faculties. (Well, perhaps he wasn't completely sober. He had "sipped at a very excellent Scotch at lunch" [1975, 171].) After one more "operation" and two more checkups, Playfair was declared cured, and for more than a year he was absolutely pain free. At the time he wrote his book, he was still astonished by (and grateful for) what had occurred.

Such healings occur daily in Brazil. Sadly, they are no longer done by Edivaldo Silva. He was killed in a traffic accident in 1974 at the age of 44, his death a great loss to Spiritism and to the people of Brazil. But healings are happening elsewhere. In the Philippines, where psychic medicine has been practiced for centuries, mystical healings are just part of everyday events. Today, the best-known psychic surgeon, spiritualist, and healer in the Philippines is Alex Orbito.

Alex L. Orbito

Born in the small town of Cuyapo on the outskirts of Manila, Alex Orbito (1940–) was the youngest of 14 children of farming parents. He was unaware of his great gifts until the age of 14, when a local woman who had been paralyzed for 10 years had a dream in which she saw young Alex healing her. She sent her son the next morning to fetch Alex. Coincidentally, Alex had also had a dream the previous night. In his dream, he was healing a crippled woman. He lost no time getting to the woman's house, where he prayed, then urged her to stand and walk. Which she did.

In no time at all the news of Alex's ability as a healer spread from one barrio of the Philippines to another. According to the *Psychic Reader Newspaper* (July 2004), Alex is not alone in his abilities. His brothers Marcos and Roger are practicing healers, his sister Felicitas is a medium, and his mother is considered one of the founders of the spiritualist movement in the Philippines.

A humble, pious man, Alex continues to practice psychic medicine and magnetic healing[17] and is considered by some to be the world's greatest psychic surgeon. His reputation has spread worldwide, and it is estimated that he has treated more than a million people, among them Shirley MacLaine and members of the Saudi royal family.

But as skilled and famous as Alex and a host of other psychics have become, few can outdo the prominence of an Indian mystic who goes by the name of Sai Baba.

Ratnakara Venkata Satyanarayana Raju, aka Sai Baba

According to the International Sai Organization, there are an estimated 1,200 Sai Baba centers in 130 countries worldwide. Various estimates place the current number of Sai Baba followers at anywhere between 6 million and 100 million people. This man is not just a guru, he is a phenomenon.

The followers of Bhagavan Sri Sathya Sai Baba[18] (1926[19]–), the controversial South Indian guru, claim that he has divine powers and is able to work miracles such as healings and materializations, and possibly to perform bilocation (being in two different places at the same time).

As described in an article in the *Journal of the American Society for Psychical Research,* Erlendur Haraldsson[20] and Karlis Osis took three field trips to India between 1973 and 1975 to study Sai Baba. They came away baffled.

> The investigators were able to observe at close range some unexplained occurrences which took place in the presence of Sri Sathya Sai Baba. Although no conclusions can be reached on the phenomena observed and described in this account because they occurred under informal conditions,[21] it seemed worthwhile to report the events because of the challenge they offer to carry out further studies of the well-known Indian religious leader under well-controlled experimental conditions.[22]

The informal observations were of paranormal appearances of items such as *vibuti,* the holy ash that in Hinduism is a symbolic representation somewhat akin to the bread and wine of Christianity, and a single and then a double *rudrashka,* a rare acornlike botanical stone or pit. On one occasion, he made an enameled image disappear and then reappear on a ring he had given to one of those present. The investigators filmed Sai Baba during some of these performances and had the films viewed by other scientists and several magicians. One magician, Douglas Henning, claimed he could duplicate everything he saw on the film except for the ring incident, which he said was beyond his skill as a magician. The others were unable to explain anything they saw.

LILY DALE, NEW YORK

Like any religion, ours requires a leap of faith.

—*Gretchen Clark, Lily Dale medium*

My memories of those séances in Ontario are getting a bit fuzzy around the edges. I am, after all, an octogenarian, and some leeway must be granted to those of us who have memories that go back that far. But somehow, those images of Walter and my grandfather and his friends as they gathered around the square table niggled at me. My journey, clearly, was not over. It was essential that I visit Lily Dale to retrace Dr. A.'s footsteps of almost 100 years before.

On August 25, 2005, I checked into the Athenaeum Hotel in Chautauqua, New York. I had misjudged the popularity of Lily Dale and found, to my disappointment, that all the rooms in the town were taken. A brief cab ride, however, got me from my comfortable lodgings to the village that I realize, in retrospect, I'd waited all my life to see.

The cab let me off near the Lily Dale Assembly offices on Melrose Drive. The building that houses the offices looked pretty much the same as it had in photos from the time of Lily Dale's founding. The gingerbread houses were still there, like they had been on the day of Grandpa's visit. And there were quaint, freshly painted Victorian-style houses that had been made over into shops and cafés.

I walked 2 blocks northeast toward the lake and found myself surrounded by cheerful, pleasant people and clean streets lined with masses of pink and orange daylilies. I passed gift shops offering crystals and bookstores whose windows were stacked with volumes on spiritual healing. I avoided them all. The shopping could wait.

Due to a brief stopover in New York City, I had missed the opportunity to meet with James van Praagh, the subject of the CBS miniseries *Living with the Dead*. Considered to be one of the best-known mediums in North America, he had been in residence at Lily Dale only 2 weeks before my arrival.

James van Praagh

Born in Bayside, New York, van Praagh (1958–) is purported to be a survival-evidence medium, able to bridge the gap between the living world and the world of the dead. He claims to be clairsentient and clairvoyant.

Raised as a Catholic, James was an altar boy in his early years. At the age of 8, while praying in his room, he asked God to reveal himself, and "an open hand appeared through the ceiling of James' room emitting radiant beams of light."[23] James entered the seminary at age 14, but his interest in his religion gradually waned and was replaced by spirituality. He abandoned his pursuit of the priesthood and entered university.

After graduation from San Francisco State University with a degree in broadcasting and communications, he moved to Los Angeles, where he soon developed an interest in metaphysics and psychic phenomena. His interest led him to investigate some of the area's mediums, and within 2 years he had begun receiving messages from beyond and giving readings to friends. It did not take long for news of James van Praagh's abilities to spread. He now travels the world, teaching classes in mediumship, hosting cruises to spiritual destinations, and conducting seminars that are typically sold out.

As with almost every other medium we have discussed, James van Praagh has his share of detractors. Among the most zealous and distinguished of his challengers is Dr. Michael Shermer, and if these two ever have a chance to do battle, it will be like witnessing a clash of the Titans.

Shermer is founding publisher of *Skeptic* magazine and the executive director of the Skeptics Society. A former marathon cyclist, Shermer is the author of numerous successful books, several of which deal with the topic of why people cling to irrational or insubstantial beliefs.

While working on a piece for *20/20*, Shermer had the opportunity to spend a great deal of time with van Praagh, both at home and on the road. Although fascinated by how van Praagh manages to develop such a following, he is convinced the man is a fraud.

> Van Praagh is an actor playing the part of a medium. Like all acting, it requires practice—a LOT of practice it turns out. Although I know all of his lines by now, I had not memorized them, nor did I have the deep reserve of backup lines for contingencies he frequently encounters in readings.[24]

Shermer is convinced that van Praagh practices "cold reading," a technique used to convince a person that one knows more about him or her than one actually does. Typically used by fraud artists and con men, the technique allows a person to easily obtain a great deal of information from another by carefully (and quickly) assessing such things as body language, grooming, sexual orientation, education level, manner of speech, and so on. Although practitioners sometimes make erroneous assumptions, they can usually get back on track by asking leading, innocuous-sounding questions.

Although it is true that some people are naturally gifted with heightened sensitivity and may use it to help others, there are some who study and perfect their technique to purposely swindle. Shermer allows that van Praagh may be more self-deceived than deceiving. Nevertheless, he cautions that van Praagh's behavior probably fits into the latter category. By the looks of the entries on Shermer's Web site (www.michaelshermer.com) devoted to his theory, it would appear that he intends to eventually prove it.

Van Praagh, for his part, missed a perfect opportunity to turn the entire accusation of his use of cold reading on its heels. In the early 1990s, University of Arizona psychologist Dr. Gary E. Schwartz[25] and his colleague Dr. Linda Russek conducted an exhaustive series of experiments with a group of mediums in order to discover whether the personality survives bodily death. Experimental controls that were put into place virtually eliminated the possibility of cold reading: There were blind readings, during which the medium could not see the sitter, and blind-mute readings, during which the medium was unable to either see or hear the sitter, but instead received monosyllabic answers through an intermediary.

Among the results reported in Schwartz's 2002 book *The Afterlife Experiments* was an overwhelming suggestion that the correct answers (i.e., answers verified by the sitter) were statistically beyond what would have been attainable by chance or with even the most skillful cold reading. Schwartz reports that James van Praagh declined to respond to repeated requests to be part of the experiments, but later, apparently, he was supportive.

Since I had missed my chance to meet with van Praagh, I set out for my reading with one medium who *was* involved in the Schwartz experiments and who was reported to be the most powerful medium in Lily Dale.

Anne Gehman

Those who must see to believe don't believe enough to see. And those who believe enough to see won't stop believing, no matter what they see (Wicker 2003, 163).

Anne Gehman's principal residence is in the Washington, DC, area, where her husband is a professor of English at Georgetown University. She spends her summers in Lily Dale. Anne's background is somewhat typical of other mediums we have met. She came to her gifts very early in life, as the youngest of eight children born into an Amish-Mennonite Florida farm family. The first manifestation she produced was causing dishes and cutlery on the table to move without touching them. She progressed to healing her mother, who was suffering from an unidentified illness. But nothing she did allayed the fears of her zealously religious father, who treated her skills as an affliction that needed to be prayed away.

Anne left home at 14 to pursue an education, but after being on her own for a few years, her loneliness and depression drove her to attempt suicide. As Anne was struggling between life and death, a woman appeared to her in a vision. That apparition gave her a new lease on life. When Anne regained her strength, she felt a strong compulsion to attend a spiritualist camp at Cassadaga Lake (aka Lily Dale). She presented herself to a medium by the name of Wilbur Hull, who declared her a natural medium. He had had a vision similar to Anne's, in which the woman had told him she was sending him "the greatest natural medium she had ever known" (Wicker 2003, 175). The rest is history.

So there I was, about to meet a legend in the world of spiritualism. I had come prepared, or so I thought. I had put fresh batteries into my tape recorder while in my hotel room, yet when the meeting began the thing failed to start. Frustrated at not being able to record my time with her, I sat and wrote my recollections the moment I got back to my room, because, you see, the visit had a specific purpose.

After I arranged my things and settled on the chair Anne had provided, we proceeded to chat about a number of things. She went in and out of a trance, giving me what I considered to be some general evidentiary material pertaining to my life. Then she suddenly asked, "Who is Anna?" That certainly got my attention! Anna was a long-ago love of Dr. A's.

I acknowledged this.

Then she asked, "James. Who is James?"

I had no idea. I shook my head.

"William James!" she whispered, and then slipped into her trance voice. "He is helping you with your work. He comes and goes. Not here all the time."

I nodded and smiled. I figured I couldn't get much better assistance in my writing than from William James!

"You have two books ahead of you," she said. "Not one. Two."

I had not mentioned *anything* to her about writing a book. Things were looking up.

"Jane? Who is Jane? Very sweet disposition. Lovely smile. Stout. Plump. Especially around the middle."

My grandmother Ellen Jane, perhaps? It certainly sounded like a description of her. Not perfect, but close. I held my tongue and feigned ignorance, wary of a cold reading.

"There's a man here. Handsome, always in a suit and tie. A mustache. Keeps his thoughts to himself. Finds it difficult to speak up. To speak out."

It sounded very much like a description of my father Maurice James, and I told her so. It went on like this for several more minutes, while I sat wondering when and how (or even if) I would broach the subject of what I held in my hand.

Not long before I made my trip to Lily Dale, my daughter-in-law, the actor Donna Dixon, experienced the passing of a very dear friend. I had brought with me a small box containing a piece of jewelry that the friend had given to Donna before her death. I wondered whether Anne would be able to make any contact, and if she would be able to divine what was in the box.

But time was running out, and I'd spent most of it hearing about things pertaining to me. I had to remind myself that I was there for Donna. I took a chance and slipped Anne the little box.

I quickly told her about "a woman I will call Donna" and her friend's passing. I purposely didn't tell her what was in the box, nor did I tell her what my relationship is to Donna. Anne took the box from me, still unopened. She hesitated for a moment before closing her eyes, appearing to go in and out of a trance.

"I see a cross . . . ," she said softly, her eyes closed, her fingers wrapped gently around the little blue box. She went silent for about 30 seconds, then said, "This friend of Donna's . . . I feel a sudden blow to the head, and then blackness." She fell silent again, then opened her eyes. "That's all. I'm getting nothing more . . . but this Donna, is she a spiritualist?"

"No," I answered. "But I would certainly say she is a spiritual person."

Without really appearing to be interested in my answer, Anne continued.

"She's going to do a lot of traveling soon, to the west." A pause before she resumed. "She is on her own quest, and there is a person near her that doesn't share this, but this will change, this person will become much more supportive."

With that, my reading was over. I had gotten at least some of what I had come for. The little box, if you are wondering, contained a ring emblazoned with a small cross that was given to Donna by her friend, the photographer Berry Berenson, the late wife of actor Tony Perkins, not long before she died on September 11, 2001. She was on the ill-fated American flight from Boston that was hijacked by terrorists and subsequently crashed into the World Trade Center, killing all aboard. We will never know Berry's final moments, but what consolation for those who loved her to know that she experienced only "a sudden blow to the head, and then blackness."

Even though some of the details may have been weak, Anne had apparently somehow picked up that my daughter-in-law was a traveling person. Soon after my visit to Lily Dale, Donna visited Chile. Some time later she traveled to Israel, Africa, and the South Pole. We never discovered who the less-than-supportive person was, and Donna is unsure of any particular quest she may be on. Perhaps those things will come to pass. Perhaps they won't. But now I was on my own quest, and my next stop was to find the channeler John White.

John White

The consensus of the natives I consulted on the porch of the Maple-wood Hotel was that John White was considered by everybody to be "very good." On a table on his front porch a schedule of his appointments showed an opening at 11:30 a.m., so I put my name down. Returning at the appointed hour, I knocked on his door and he looked me up and down and said, "Your mother is with you." Schooled as I had been in the cold-reading techniques of channelers, I didn't pay much attention to this on the basis that somebody of my age would hardly have a mother who was living, so it would be a good guess that my mother was in the spirit world. In retrospect, it might have been a mistake for me to be so skeptical because over the years, I've come to believe that my mother *is* my muse. I did not respond to his introduction, not revealing by any gesture or other indication that what he had said interested me.

I am happy to report that my tape recorder came back to life, and I was able to record, in full sound, both sides of the conversation with John White. The first part was mostly what I might call "stabs in the dark." After inquiring as to the name of my wife, he proceeded to tell me she has difficulties with her breathing, which is true; about Dan he related that he is a good son, which he is; my granddaughter Danielle, he suggested, is artistic, which is true; and regarding my other granddaughter Belle (whose name he thought was spelled Bell, like the Liberty one), he suggested that she thought she knew it all and would soon find out that wasn't true, which may sometimes be true of Belle and about 99 percent of other teenagers I have ever known.

He asked if I wanted to know anything specific. I did. I wanted to know more about the Aykroyd family patriarch, Samuel Aykroyd—in particular, what he had done for a living. I didn't give John the name, but I did say what his relationship was to me, and I handed him an envelope containing the spirit photograph taken at Lily Dale in 1922. What I wanted was information to flesh out our family's rather sketchy profile of the man who had started the Aykroyd New World line, emigrating from England circa 1780 and settling in Hudson, New York.

I must say, John gave it the old college try. He closed his eyes and seemed to be weighing the envelope, lifting it up and down in slow motion. He talked about my ancestor holding a Bible, a King James version to be precise, while questioning its validity. He told me that the man he was seeing ("I'm just following the pictures," John said) had a great quality of observation and a questioning mind about the nature of the heavens. He told me the man he was seeing was not that literate, having about a grade-six education, and that he was fond of scribbling notes. John told me the man was interested in medicine— primitive medicine. During his description, John said he saw people in barns and people taking care of horses—a coach business, with many irons in the fire. A man who was not physically rugged, had a love of music, and an interest in politics. He suggested that the man arrived in America alone, his wife having died en route.

The frustrating thing was, I had no idea if any of this was true. I was also disappointed. I had come looking for answers without having any way to prove or disprove them. Furthermore, the descriptions were so vague as to be true for the vast majority of Europeans who settled in America in the 18th century. A history book would have given me as many clues about the family patriarch as I got from John. So I changed the subject. Donna was still on my mind. With a few minutes still left in our reading, I decided to pull out the small box once again and try for a proxy reading.

I started differently this time, giving John Donna's name, as well as her relationship to me. But I didn't tell him what was in the closed box, only that it had once belonged to a deceased friend. I explained that I was hoping for some message to bring back to Donna about her friend, and that I thought the object in the box might help. He held the box and closed his eyes.

"Okay. Let me see what I get. [Sigh] No, I'm not getting the person who's passed on. Let me just do this . . . let me tune in to Donna first."

John said he sensed a boy child around Donna. No, I said. No boys. Then he asked if Donna's friend had died from a cancerous condition. No, I answered, not cancer. Sugar diabetes? No, wrong again. Feeling we'd come to the end of a silly guessing game, I reached for my box and prepared to leave.

As John was passing the little box over to me, still firmly shut, he quietly said, "All of a sudden I saw the symbol of a cross."

"You did what?"

"I saw a symbol of a cross."

It stopped me in my tracks. I sat back down and let John tell me his interpretations of the person related to the object that he had correctly identified. He said that although he couldn't "get it directly," that this person was "living in their own divine mind, and aware of their own divine mind and where they are right now."

I had another message of some comfort to bring back to Donna. It wasn't much, but it at least suggested that her friend was not a troubled, lost soul. It would be enough for me to feel I had somewhat succeeded in my self-appointed task. As I turned to leave John's office, I had reason to be confident about his words.

But my own quest was not over. I made my way to the Fourth Street address of medium Pauline Kay. Now that I had information for Donna, I hoped to get from Pauline not so much contact with the dead as information and perceptions on the life of a medium. And perhaps, if there was time, to find out a bit about my future. Again, my technical equipment failed to do its proper job, for this time it didn't pick up my voice at all, only Pauline's. And that was scratchy and full of static. But I have her comments, which were, after all, what I was after.

Pauline Kay

As Pauline tells it, she came reluctantly to her gifts. In the United Kingdom, where she was born and raised, there was much talk of Winston Churchill for several weeks when Pauline was young. He was ill and people around Pauline were discussing how long he would live, "and right out of my mouth without any control at all came 'Oh, he'll die before 12 o'clock on Sunday.'"[26]

Pauline said she was shocked by the occurrence and so humiliated by her outburst that, as she relates it, "if the earth could have swallowed me up, I would have loved it." To her satisfaction, nothing else of a psychic nature occurred to her for many decades. At the age of

40, while waiting to go into a job interview after just having returned from volunteering overseas in East Africa, it happened again. As she sat bemoaning her age, her lack of education, and the reality of competing against 120 other applicants, she felt a child's small hand slip into hers. I asked Pauline if this was just a sensation of a child holding her hand.

"No," said Pauline. "The child was real. Her name was Saffron."

When the child took her hand, she suddenly had the awareness that she would get the job. It was not just a feeling. It was an absolute conviction. And she did.

She went on to tell me about her open views on everything from psychic readings—"I've no idea what I'm saying to you, just so long as it has meaning to you, that's what counts"—to reincarnation— "We've got annuals and we've got perennials, and we've got evergreens in the plant world. So why can't those apply to human beings in some shape or form."

I thought it was time to move into my future. Pauline didn't mince words. "I feel you are well organized in your thoughts and your ideas, so I feel here that the outcome is good for whatever it is you are looking to seek to achieve. . . . One way is to start with what you know, then with what you've learned, and then with your perception of the outcome. . . . You've got to be careful with the outcome. And what I mean by this is, if you make any statements in the book, or make any observations in the book, make sure you've got materials to back it up. Otherwise, you're in trouble."

I was glad I'd taped the remainder of our meeting. The last few minutes were spent with Pauline talking in somewhat vague generalities about relationships and spirituality, but I wasn't really listening any longer. The phrase "otherwise, you're in trouble" haunted me for the rest of the reading and all the way back to my hotel room, where, like a mad researcher, I double- and triple-checked every single source I'd listed, working long into that night.

As I made my way by cab to the airport the next morning, I looked over my shoulder at Lily Dale. I saw the soft pastel hues of the gingerbread houses, homes to the 24 mediums working there, trying to communicate with the invisible world. I couldn't help but wonder how different things would have been had my engineer father, M. J., been successful in his desire to invent a machine that would replace them.

ELECTRONIC VOICE PHENOMENON:
The Aykroyd Circle's Unfinished Business

I am inclined to believe that our personality hereafter will be able to affect matter. If this reasoning be correct, then, if we can evolve an instrument so delicate as to be affected by our personality as it survives in the next life, such an instrument, when made available, ought to record something.

—*Thomas Edison*

Thomas Alva Edison believed that an electronic device could be built to communicate with the dead. The famous inventor was also fascinated by spirit photography and believed that spirits could be captured on film. He and many others believed this could be accomplished through a controversial anomaly that became known as electronic voice phenomenon (EVP), the recording on audiotape of a voice for which there is no known source. In the October 1920 issue of *Scientific American* magazine, Edison announced that he was working on such a device, though it was not completed before he died in 1931 and he left behind no plans.

My father, an engineer with Bell Canada, was present at most of Dr. A.'s séances. I can imagine that he quietly went back to his study in the evenings thinking of ways, in his keen technical mind, to do what Edison had failed to accomplish. It seemed that vibrations were the key, and the closest the Aykroyd circle got was a series of conversations on the subject with Blue Light on March 20, 1933:

At a séance held on the above date at Hogarth Avenue, [Toronto], Blue Light gave us a talk on vibrations. We asked him how much more rapidly the vibrations the spirits use are than those of the medium, or our vibrations when we are talking. He said about 100 times more rapid. He also said that the vibrations are so fine they form a continuous line of magnetic force. We asked him about an electric instrument to communicate with us by the use of their vibrations. He said such an instrument can and will be invented and that we will also be able to communicate with the inhabitants of the planets in not so very distant time. He said he would bring a man (from the spirit world) who would be able to instruct us in the building of such an instrument.

In another few moments the expression on the face of Walter the medium changed so drastically that the sitters knew another spirit was about to speak. In an unusual move,[28] this spirit began by introducing himself.

"My name is Gruestock," he said. "Austrian with German mixture. I will come again, when I will give you a drawing to go by in constructing an instrument by which you will be able to communicate with us. It will be simple in construction and will make communication of a very wide range, so that many more people will be able to come in touch with the spirits without the use of the human body as medium."

Alas, neither Blue Light's spirit man nor Gruestock's drawings ever manifested. Dr. A. passed to the spirit world in December of that year, 1933, never having been able to see the materialization he had so hoped for. But my father's plans for an EVP machine did not die with his father, and the Aykroyd circle séances continued to be held for another 10 years. At one of those séances, one that I vividly recall, the sitters were visited by an illustrious personage who made them believe for another brief period that perhaps the machine was not just so much imagination run wild.

By now, I was a frequent member of the group, although my place as a 10- and then 11-year-old confined me to sitting and observing without comment. The strictures were not in the least punishment, for I viewed the happenings at these sittings with the same childlike acceptance that I viewed the chubby man in the red suit at Christmastime or the beautiful, white-clad fairy who purchased teeth from me. I wasn't awed or mesmerized. I was simply seeing something happen that was not that unusual, and something that I was a part of.

The event that I will now relate was, apparently, anything but usual. Regretfully, I wasn't there. But my mother was. Very much sought after in her social circles for her teacup readings, my mother was not only a skilled fortune-teller, but also a brilliant *raconteuse*. Her retelling of this particular incident made it a vivid piece of family history.

It began as a typical séance and, as they were nearing the end of it, my grandmother had retreated to the kitchen to put the teakettle on and place on the large tray the carrot cake she had baked in the afternoon. Walter suddenly rose from his chair and turned his back to the table. Still in the trance state, his actions smooth yet deliberate, he slowly raised one leg and then the other and knelt on the chair seat facing backward. When he spoke, his voice was shaky and just loud enough for the sitters to hear, and it sounded completely different from anything they had heard before.

"Steinmetz here. You will not succeed," the spirit said through Walter, who remained kneeling on the chair, still facing away from the table around which the group was seated.

"The instrument you contemplate is not possible. Vibrations are too fine, too many. Ideal convergence of vibrations can never be created by those who remain on this plane."

It was not until later that my father discovered who Steinmetz was: Carl Proteus Steinmetz (1865–1923), a Prussian American mathematician and physicist who enlightened the world of engineering with his brilliant description of the alternating current, enabling engineers to design electrical motors using applied mathematical calculations rather than by trial-and-error. Steinmetz had a mind like a steel trap, but his body was encumbered by a debilitating deformity that prevented him from sitting upright. He did most of his work while kneeling on his chair!

Plug-In Psychics and Electronic Voice Phenomenon

Although the visit from the Steinmetz spirit effectively halted the Aykroyd circle's pursuit, others continued research into what is now known as EVP.

On June 12, 1959, Friedrich Jürgenson, a Swedish painter and film director, made an astonishing discovery while taping birdsong in the woods. While reviewing the tapes, he heard voices in the background that were unclear but unmistakably human, even though he had begun with a blank tape and was taping in an isolated area.

Wondering if he had somehow tapped into stray radio signals, he decided to research the effect in an attempt to duplicate it. As his research progressed, he received longer, more distinct phrases. The voices soon began to address him by name and to comment on his work. At first, Jürgenson believed the voices emanated from an extra-terrestrial source, but he later came to the conclusion that the transmissions were from deceased persons.

His findings were published in two volumes: *Voices from the Universe* (1964) and *Radio Contact with the Dead* (1967). Considered today to contain rather flimsy research, his work was the inspiration behind further research during the '50s and '60s by others, including Dr. Konstantin Raudive, a Latvian professor of psychology who used Jürgenson's methods to catalogue a vast collection of more than 70,000 unexplained recorded voices.

In the midst of the excitement over EVP, the SPR commissioned an electronics expert by the name of D. J. Ellis to investigate some of the EVP findings. Ellis concluded that the voices heard were likely due to natural phenomena (dust on the tape, ambient sound, atmospheric electrical interference) and cautioned that the interpretation of such sounds was highly subjective, susceptible as it was to imagination.

On the other hand, perhaps Jürgenson was correct in his first assumption that he had tapped into stray radio signals. In *Spook* (2005, 189), author Mary Roach points to other possible sources of unusual sounds. Roach tells of a German woman who was apparently spoken to in English by her oven every time she opened its door, and a man from the same neighborhood claimed his heating system was talking to him. When engineers investigated the reports, they concluded that the voices were none other than episodes of a program on the radio being broadcast internationally by an American station. Apparently a gap, either between two pieces of metal or between a piece of metal and the ground, caused what is known as a "semiconductivity event," which resulted in the metal appliances picking up stray radio signals.

Some investigators believe the "voices" on the tapes are the products of experimenters who inadvertently imprint the tapes by psychokinesis in their zealousness to capture spirit voices. Still others believe they are nothing but fraud.

Despite the cautions, the interest in EVP and its relative instrumental transcommunication (ITC)[29] continued, with thousands of researchers around the world purportedly recording messages from the dead. The Association for Voice Taping Research was founded in Germany in the 1970s. The next decade ushered in the American Association of Electronic Voice Phenomena, founded by Sarah Estep, who provided a system for classifying the quality of sound from various EVP messages. In 1992, Mark Macy started the International Network for Instrumental Transcommunication, but the organization folded several years later,[30] partly as a result of a lack of support from the scientific community. Until a suitable paradigm has been established to enable science to grapple with this phenomenon, EVP and ITC will likely continue to attract the attention of curious and intelligent people (see Comments, Chapter 3, ii, for some modern cinematic treatments of these topics).

The Aykroyd circles gradually wound to a close without the so-hoped-for materializations or the so-cleverly-contemplated machine ever becoming a reality, though the notes and the legacy lived on, as did my yearning for understanding. If the Aykroyd circle and its league of cooperative spirits could not achieve materialization, why were others able to? Are spirits attempting to communicate, and if so, what purpose do they have and why do some appear to reach us while others do not? Are there specific abilities that spirits or mediums possess that permit these manifestations to occur, and if so, what are these special spirit skills?

I was not content to accept cursory judgments or sketchy research, and until I would be able to delve further, I had to console myself with the words of Steinmetz: "No man really becomes a fool until he stops asking questions." For me, the questions about materialization, spirit painting, speaking in tongues—manifestations of the type observed during séances—were still largely unresolved.

Chapter 4

Extraordinary Skills

Exceptional human experience is an umbrella term for many types of experiences generally considered to be psychic, mystical, encounter-type experiences, death-related experiences, and experiences at the upper end of the normal range, such as creative inspiration and exceptional human performance.

—*Rhea A. White, MA*[1]

Some people believe displays of extraordinary skill to be attempts by disembodied spirits to contact us in the physical plane. Others believe that the phenomena are the result of superhuman powers exhibited by very real people. There are still others who attribute these phenomena to various causes (other than fraud): blips in the machinery, extraterrestrial communications, or sunspots and other cosmic disturbances. These distinctions have been the bugbears of investigators such as Sir William Crookes and Charles Richet, et al., who consistently reminded their critics that they were not questioning religious or spiritual beliefs, but rather looking for some natural or scientific proof to explain what *appeared to be happening.*

Regardless of the roots of the phenomena, there is no doubt that it takes a very special person to act as a conduit between the seen and the unseen, manifestations that can be photographed but not observed, voices that can be recorded yet have no apparent source. People calling themselves "mediums" today are rare. Taking their place these days are channelers, the New Age, distinctly 20th-century version of mediums who are in abundance in Lily Dale and elsewhere across North America and in Europe. In California alone, more than a thousand channelers are listed on Web sites, in phonebooks, and in special New Age directories. But what about the name change? Is there any evidence that the channelers of today are different from their counterparts of yesteryear?

A channeler will put the paying client in contact with a discarnate spirit who dispenses advice and perhaps even a glimpse into the future. Ectoplasm is nowhere to be seen, and materializations are of the "mental" type (i.e., the entity is not observable to anyone but the channeler). The spirit imparts its message to the channeler through extrasensory pathways, and the channeler conveys the message to the client. Sometimes the voice of the spirit comes through the channeler and can be heard by the sitter, but more often, the channeler relays the spirit's message in his or her own voice.

It seems clear that not just anyone can perform the function of channeler, yet the numbers would suggest that many people believe they can be conduits to the spirits. Or do they? In a 1989 article in the *Skeptical Inquirer,* James E. Alcock, a York University psychology professor and author of *Parapsychology: Science or Magic?* (1981), points to the sometimes overwhelming vice of greed as one of the driving forces behind the channeling fad.[2] The rise of numerous do-it-yourself workshops and conventions is evidence of that. To be sure, many of those people who are taking training as channelers appear to be seeking self-improvement and enlightenment on a strictly personal level. But there is no doubt that skilled channelers today can develop a loyal and generous following just as the famous mediums of the 1920s and '30s did, and for some people, the lure of fame and fortune is just too great to ignore.

There are pitfalls in all of this, not so much for the channelers themselves as for their clients. Alcock suggests that there is a danger in following advice from channelers, particularly if one has real problems. He suggests that "the pastiche of pop psychology and metaphysics offered up by channelers may prove as deleterious for the psyche as the fake treatments proffered by medical quacks can be for the body."

Individuals who wish to become professional mediums or channelers today can be certified by one of the many professional organizations set up for such a purpose. The examinations administered by these organizations ensure that mediums and channelers display certain characteristics, which include, as the British medium Maurice Barbanell suggests, "sensitiveness, the ability to register vibrations, radiations or frequencies which cannot be captured by any of the five senses" (Buckland 2006, 249).

ALL IN A DAY'S WORK

With such diverse training available, one may wonder if mediums actually avail themselves of these opportunities. And furthermore, whether anyone is doing any quality assurance monitoring. In the 2001 Worldwide Mediums Survey Internet poll conducted by Worldwide Mediums and Psychics, a sample of questions related to medium training and development showed that, like other professionals, most mediums take their work seriously. It also appears that interest in investigating mediums is nowhere near as popular as it used to be. Just as well, for it would seem that many mediums are not really open to being scrutinized.

Not one of the 1,196 mediums who responded to the section on investigation had ever taken part in the investigation of another medium, and only two had themselves been investigated, one by the media and one by other mediums and teachers in a classroom setting. Of this group, only 15 percent stated that they felt mediums should be investigated by scientists; 24 percent responded negatively to the idea. The remainder did not respond. But what, other than personal development, are modern mediums spending their time doing?

Only 54 mediums responded to the question on physical manifestations (production of ectoplasm, table tilting, automatic writing, etc.), suggesting that perhaps this is a dying art form. Of those who responded, only 15 mediums had experienced materialization, and they reported it as a mental manifestation, meaning that it was unseen by others. In this group, 89.11 percent were aware of their spirit guides, most of whom were viewed both in the medium's mind and physically by the medium. Thirty-five percent of this group became aware of their spirit guides in childhood; 56 percent became aware of their spirit guides within 1 year of their development as mediums.

The section on superclarity of the senses was answered by 2,093 mediums. The results indicate that this little-understood aggregation

Superclarity of the Senses

All of the words below are derived from the French for "clear."

- Clairalience/clairessence (clear smelling): the strong and particular odor produced at some séances that is associated with the spirit being contacted. Occasionally the smell can be experienced by all present; at other times only the medium experiences it.

- Clairaudience (clear hearing): the hearing of sounds, music, or voices not audible to normal hearing

- Clairhambiance/clairgustance (clear tasting): the ability of the medium to experience a very specific taste associated with the spirit being contacted

- Clairsentience (clear sensing): the psychic sense perception of taste, smell, touch, emotions, and physical sensations that contribute to overall psychic and intuitive impressions

- Clairvoyance (clear seeing): the perception of current objects, events, or people that may not be discerned through normal senses (Buckland 2006, 75; Guiley 1991, 111)

of abilities is experienced by a great number of practitioners: clairvoyance by 93.8 percent, clairsentience by 92.6 percent, clairaudience by 87.0 percent, clairessence[3] by 87.0 percent, and clairgustance by 38.5 percent.

The overall results indicate that the role of the medium has changed significantly since the early days of spiritualism-based mediumship. Perhaps the whole nature of communication between the planes of existence has changed, or perhaps we are simply more able to accept as part of the natural order some skills that we previously thought were paranormal.

The skills required by modern communicators with the other side seem to be more of the type we typically associate with the supersensory, as opposed to the supernatural. We likely all know people with hearing so hypersensitive that it forces them to remove clocks from a room before they can sleep, or people whose sense of smell is so keen they can detect when a car's antifreeze is low. We may marvel at their ability, but we don't look upon it as anything supernatural. Must the acceptance of such observable phenomena require *fides spirituosa* (spiritual faith)? Perhaps it is sufficient to apply *fides humana* (human faith) to help one accept what appears to be unexplainable.

Lawrence LeShan in *The Medium, The Mystic, and the Physicist* (originally published in 1974) suggests that if we could accept that multiple realities may be equally valid under terms from different concepts of the cosmos and that different things are possible in different metaphysical systems, then no paradox would exist. But right now, let us simply take a tour, a traveler's journey of a sort, through the various manifestations we have been discussing. We will find out what the scientists say might be going on when mediums actually do produce extraordinary phenomena, and then perhaps we will be better able to decide, or at least feel comfortable about not deciding. But we will first have to consider the issue of fraud.

THE SPECTER OF FRAUD
One White Crow

To upset the conclusion that all crows are black, there is no
need to seek demonstration that no crows are black; it is sufficient to produce one white crow; a single one is sufficient.

—William James, 1890

Wherever reports of psychic manifestations occurred, close behind
were the debunkers, the investigators and the naysayers. And just as
close behind were the frauds and tricksters who knew a good thing
when they saw it: a gullible segment of the population willing to suspend disbelief long enough to be bamboozled by sleight of hand.

The task for legitimate practitioners was ticklish. In an environment
rife with staged performances of legerdemain and magic, the typically
trivial demonstrations given in parlors were paltry compared to the
sensational feats being viewed elsewhere. For the mediums, there was a
clear and present danger of losing one's audience and, as a result, one's
means of support. To counteract such effects, some legitimate psychics
admittedly resorted to trickery, and that perhaps was the greatest pity
of all, for it made investigators wary of them as a group. Many investigators, as we have seen, were men of science, out to prove only the scientific basis of what they saw and having no vested interest one way or
another in what they found. Such a man was William James.

William James (1842–1910) was a professor of psychology at Harvard University and one of the founders in 1885 of the American
Society for Psychical Research (ASPR). Born in New York City and
educated at Harvard Medical School, he also received honorary
degrees from the universities at Princeton, Edinburgh, Harvard, and
Padua. Brother of author Henry James, William made contributions
to both psychology and philosophy and was considered one of the
most influential thinkers of his time.

Strongly influenced in his early life by the writings of Emmanuel
Swedenborg, James remained intrigued by paranormal phenomena
for the rest of his life. A cautious investigator, he was determined to

take a pragmatic approach to the investigation of psychical activity, and he attended the Lawrence Scientific School at Harvard University to pursue it. More interested in mental mediumship than its physical counterpart, James considered that survival after bodily death to be a possibility. But although his psychical research convinced him of the validity of telepathy, it did not go so far as to prove the existence of life beyond the grave.

After 18 months of investigation of the medium Leonora E. Piper (see Comments Chapter 4, i), James delivered his famous white crow lecture suggesting that Mrs. Piper was analogues to "one white crow," or proof that not all mediums were fakes.

Once the popularity of mediums, particularly physical mediums and their confreres, reached epidemic proportions, the field of psychic investigation experienced a parallel surge. Everyone, it seems, had an opinion. And although people like Sir Arthur Conan Doyle, William James, Sir William Crookes, and Gustave Géley relished their time in the spotlight as investigators, some were later to be found lecturing in defense of the very mediums they had set out to expose. Sadly, many of these men had been tricked into believing what they were told, simply because they could not explain what their eyes and minds told them was impossible. Maintaining high scientific standards in the face of this was difficult at best, although some investigators of the time attempted to control the folly.

A review written by James H. Hyslop and published in a 1917 issue of the *Journal of the American Society for Psychical Research* suggests that several occurrences of levitation at séances could, in fact, have been staged. In his review of W. J. Crawford's[4] three titles covering his experiments with the Goligher circle (which you will read more about later), Hyslop suggests that tampering and embellishment are all too possible in a séance situation, particularly where physical phenomena are involved.

> The physical phenomena of spiritualism have always been more difficult to investigate and more exposed to skepticism than the mental, and this is because the conjurer could so easily imitate them.[5]

But not all the investigators were naïve. While the crowned heads of Europe were vying for invitations to private séances with the new stars of the supernatural stage and psychic investigators were becoming stars in their own right, an uppity little rabbi's son from Appleton, Wisconsin, began making a few lives miserable.

Harry Houdini

Ehrich (nicknamed Harry) Weiss (1874–1926), a young magician who billed himself by the exotic-sounding name of Houdini,[6] began incorporating the fashionable events called séances into his stage act. It amazed him when people he thought reasonable would pull him aside after a performance and ask him to verify that he was actually being helped by the spirits, and that his skills were preternatural.

One day while shopping for props for his act, he stumbled upon evidence that local mediums were ordering their supplies from the same magic shop he frequented. Houdini was an honest young man, and he realized that he had been misleading his paying public. He abruptly stopped calling his sessions séances, billing himself instead as a magician and escape artist. Although throughout his brilliant career he maintained that he did not have psychic powers, he never divulged any of his magician's secrets. All that he would say when anyone asked was that "he had one secret that explained everything he did" (Kalush and Sloman 2006, 222).

However, as he became more famous, people suggested that he did have such powers. Sir Arthur Conan Doyle himself believed this until 1922, when Houdini began showing Doyle evidence that what he was seeing in séances was nothing more than sleight of hand. Though he had been nicely dodging Doyle's insistence of a supernatural connection, he could no longer tolerate Doyle's apparent lack of judgment.

Houdini had a strong sense of showmanship; however, he felt that the people who were calling themselves mediums should own up to what they were really doing. They weren't communicating with the dead. They were illusionists, just like him. Maybe not as good, but illusionists all the same. Houdini spent the next few years trying to uncover the fakes, and we will meet him again on our journey through extraordinary skills.

An Influential Book from the Beyond

Around the turn of the century, many people were convinced of the reality of séances, and a large number of mediums were serious practitioners who used the spirits to improve the lives of those around them. Harriet Beecher Stowe, a spiritualist, never denied the prevailing idea that she wrote under the guidance of spirits. Her novel *Uncle Tom's Cabin,* published in 1852, was arguably one of the major influences that led to the American Civil War. Subsequently translated into more than 60 languages, it has become an iconic representation of the horrors of slavery.

AUTOMATIC WRITING

Automatic writing is probably one of the less spectacular feats of a medium, and in truth, it can be very prone to fakery. Numerous mediums from Mrs. Leonora Piper to the Davenport brothers exhibited automatic writing, typically putting down on paper information that they could not have received through normal means about people who had passed to the spirit world.

Numerous literary and religious compositions have been produced through automatic writing. Among such works are the writings of an intellectually brilliant 7th-century Arab merchant who, on the 17th night of Ramadan in the year 610,[7] was enveloped in the overpowering embrace of an angel who recited passages that purportedly came from God. The word of God, spoken for the first time in Arabic, was heard by Muhammad ibn 'Abd Allah over a period of 23 years. Muhammad, who could neither read nor write, recorded for posterity the verses that became known as the Recitation, or the Qur'an, the most important writings of the Islamic faith.

> Muhammad used to enter a tranced state and sometimes seemed to lose consciousness; he used to sweat profusely, and often felt an interior heaviness like grief that impelled him to

lower his head between his knees, a position adopted by some contemporary Jewish mystics when they entered an alternative state of consciousness. . . . It is not surprising that Muhammad found the revelations such an immense strain: not only was he working through an entirely new political solution for his people, but he was composing one of the great spiritual and literary classics of all time. He believed that he was putting the ineffable Word of God into Arabic (Armstrong 1993, 140).

Twentieth-Century Communications

Automatic writing is not solely a peculiarity of the past. On September 9, 1963, Jane Roberts, a resident of Elmira, New York, went into a spontaneous trance and began writing. The ideas culminated in the full-length nonfiction book *How to Develop Your ESP Power* (1966). Inspired to delve further into the paranormal, a field in which neither she nor her husband had any background or experience, Jane borrowed a Ouija board and began to contact various personalities from the spirit world. In December of that same year, they communicated with an entity who called himself Seth. It was a contact that would change their lives.

Over the next several months, Seth communicated through the Ouija board and later clairaudiently, and, still later, directly through Roberts. While her husband took dictation in multiple notebooks, Seth talked about the human condition and specifically about reincarnation. His teachings, communicated to Roberts over the next 20 years, were published in two full-length books: *The Seth Material* (1970) and *Seth Speaks* (1972).

Jane Roberts died in 1984 at the age of 55. Until shortly before her death, she and her husband continued to share Seth's wisdom in workshops and private classes.

Perhaps one of the most famous automatic writers of all time was an American woman named Pearl Curran, a poorly educated St. Louis, Missouri, housewife who began writing in 1913 after a brief session at a Ouija board, during which she was contacted by the spirit of a 17th-century Englishwoman who identified herself as Patience Worth. Over the next several years, Patience Worth dictated by spelling out words on the Ouija, and Pearl Curran wrote an astonishing 4 million words, filling 29 bound volumes. The works, which were eventually published, include plays, short stories, and 2,500 poems, as well as six full-length novels set in diverse historical frameworks. One of them, *The Sorry Tale,* a 300,000-word epic about the life of Christ, took more than 2 years to dictate through the Ouija board.

Although the Patience Worth writing is astonishing, its source is controversial. Scholars who analyzed the works declared them to be authentic in their historical details. Others, focusing on the language, maintained that it appeared to be too archaic (by several centuries) for the time period in which Patience Worth ostensibly lived. Some hypothesized that the unschooled Curran was tapping in to the Jungian collective unconscious to access the Old English language that was used for much of the writing. As dismissive as this may sound, the skill that Pearl Curran would have had to draw on in order to create these works is nothing short of astounding.

Such is the dichotomy among those who accept the existence of automatic writing and other psychic phenomena but adhere to different schools of thought on how it is produced. The disunion has resulted in what could be characterized as an internecine battle: On one side of the discussion are those who maintain that automatic writings and other psychic manifestations are created by discarnate beings, and on the other, those who maintain that the phenomena are created through the use of supernormal abilities. At the very least, serious debaters on both sides have been together on one level: their abhorrence of fakery.

Over the years and for countless mediums, apparently strenuous experimental controls have been put in place to expose fakery. Sometimes it was proven, sometimes not. I have absolute confidence that neither my grandfather nor his medium Walter Ashurst, nor any of the regular sitters, was anything but honest in their reporting of the phenomena they experienced. There was someone else associated with my grandfather's séances, however, who was not above chicanery.

The Aykroyd circle had a brief but entertaining experience with a close relative of automatic writing known as spirit writing. Unlike automatic writing, in which the spirit requires a living scribe, with spirit writing, the spirits themselves are said to write messages, sometimes by way of a materialized hand. On this occasion, however, I can assure you that the hand involved in the writing was anything but spiritual.

A Bit of Mischief

It was the summer of 1931. I was 9, and as usual, I was at the Lake Loughborough country home of my grandparents. Séances were being held weekly in the old farmhouse, as all concerned thought a materialization was imminent. And I, as usual, was given permission to attend as a silent witness. One evening, Lee Long, Walter's control, suggested toward the end of the séance that the sitters should leave out on the table India ink and a fine-point brush. He told them that he would visit during the night and leave them a very special message. The séance closed with various predictions about what the message might say and with the sitters eager to come back the next evening to see for themselves.

I lay in my bed pretending to be asleep until darkness finally fell and my grandparents went off to bed. Slipping down the stairs, avoiding the creaky step whose location I was very familiar with, I snatched up the ink bottle, brush, and paper from the dining room table and snuck into the cellarway, closing the door before snapping on the chain of the overhead light.

My eyes swept the shelves of kitchen condiments, past the vinegar bottle, the crock of molasses, a tin of sugar, until they fell on the exotic shape of the soy sauce bottle. In less time than it takes to tell about it, I scratched out a series of Chinese characters from the label onto the paper, then scrambled back toward my room, replacing Lee Long's writing materials in more or less the same location where I'd found them.

In the morning and then again in the evening when the Aykroyd circle sitters arrived, there was great excitement. The excitement seemed to die down considerably when someone (my grandmother I'm guessing—perhaps with a nose for mischief) suggested that the message was of little use to them since none of them read Chinese. By the next day the message had disappeared, along with all talk of it. It was just as well. I'm sure if anyone had thought of taking it to the owners of the local Chinese restaurant to decipher, they would have found it offered no more cryptic a message than "Bottled in Hong Kong"!

I know how I did it. But what do the experts say is happening when mediums manifest automatic writing? Some psychologists believe that automatic writing can be the result of a self-induced mild trance, allowing the writer to move out of metacognitive awareness. In such an alpha state, the brain is able to reach into its more intuitive, creative right side and use it, along with the orderly left side, to access information it may not be aware that it knows.

Believers, of course, maintain that automatic writing is the product of communication from beyond, and that the insights received by the mind and the writing produced by the hand do not stem from the writer at all, but from a spirit entity using the writer as an instrument.

Earthbound writers sometimes talk about experiences of writing for hours with the words just tumbling out of them as fast as they can write them, while they are virtually unaware of the passage of time. As mysterious and elusive as this phenomenon is, writers don't typically feel compelled to give book-jacket credit to the spirits.

DIRECT-VOICE MEDIUMSHIP

Direct voice mediumship is the manifestation of a voice produced in space without a visible source. Many instances of the direct-voice phenomenon were experienced through the medium's trumpet (see photo insert for a reproduction of a trumpet of the type used in Lily Dale). Among the mediums who produced this phenomenon were Margery Crandon, Eileen Garrett, Leslie Flint, and Etta Wriedt, the latter of whom Dr. A. had the pleasure of meeting in 1921 when he and his wife witnessed the amazing phenomenon.

Sir Arthur Conan Doyle, in particular, seemed quite overwhelmed by a series of séances he attended in 1911 with Mrs. Wriedt, during which he "heard her talking to, even arguing with, some spirit person with whose opinion she did not agree" (Doyle 1926, 1:159). Doyle turned to the ancients to look for examples of oral communication from the spirits and felt he had found a thread in Socrates and Joan of Arc, although he admitted that there was no evidence the voices could be heard by anyone else. Frederic Myers countered the idea of spirit summonings with a suggestion that the Socratic voices were "a profounder stratum of the sage himself" (Doyle 1926, 2:152), which Doyle found rather unhelpful. Doyle parried with an argument about the "*vox divina*"[8] and about voices that were said to emanate from structures such as the famed statue of Apollo at Delphi, to which Myers (according to Doyle) had no comeback.

Talking statues aside, the question of how voices could be produced in a séance that would yield the results encountered with mediums such as Walter, D. D. Home, Mrs. Wriedt, or indeed with any medium in whose presence voices manifest is clearly one with which scientists have wrestled. One answer considered was vibrations.

Fodor has many interesting things to say about vibrations as they occur in the séance room, and one of the most poetic quotes he uses comes from the spirit world itself: "We can walk on the vibrations made by your laughing," Margery Crandon's control Walter once said. Fodor suggests that vibrations, strong enough to require soldiers to break step across a bridge and to shatter crystal exposed to certain wavelengths, could be responsible for the production of many mysterious psychic phenomena. Could vibrations create a pathway for voices to cross the borderline between the spirit world and this one?

Indeed, vibrations were at the basis of Edison's contention, as we saw in the previous chapter, that an instrument could be designed to allow the living to communicate with the dead. The major question, of course, remains. If spirits use vibrations to communicate with the living, how is it done? Are sound waves from beyond stimulated in such a way that they change in rapidity or frequency, thus allowing them to penetrate into the areas of a living brain dedicated to hearing? Do the spirits who wish to communicate with people on this plane convey through extrasensory perception (ESP) thoughts that are then transformed into audible messages? Or is there another way the spirits create voices?

One theory of the production of the phenomenon comes to us from J. Arthur Findlay,[9] who received the following message circa 1920 from an unidentified spirit source:

From the medium and those present, a chemist from the spirit world withdraws certain ingredients which for want of a better name is called ectoplasm. To this the chemist adds ingredients of his own making. He then, with his materialized hands, constructs a mask resembling the mouth and tongue. The spirit wishing to speak places his face into this mask. . . . The etheric organs have once again become clothed in matter resembling physical matter, and by the passage of air through them your atmosphere can be vibrated and you hear his voice (Fodor 1966, 92).

In truth, the accounts from the investigators themselves of such manifestations often produce more questions than answers. One consistently repeated observation was that while the spirit voice was being heard most mediums were unable to speak. Margery Crandon is an example. Records indicate that when Margery Crandon's spirit control spoke, there was usually a mass on her shoulder that was connected to her left ear and nostril with ectoplasmic tubes. Fodor observed: "this psychic microphone seems to be very closely associated with the medium's organism" (Fodor 1966, 92). Fodor cites even more examples of unusual observations: Medium Mrs. Everitt[10] could never speak simultaneously with her spirits. Her control claimed he needed her breath in order to speak; the Reverend Monck[11] and his spirits always had an "impasse" when they tried to speak together; Medium Harry Bastian's[12] spirits could speak when his mouth was full of water, but not if his nose was also "stopped up." Some real-world explanations may need to be considered.

Ventriloquism

In direct-voice mediumship, where the voices are heard somewhere distant from the medium, there is the possibility of ventriloquism, an ancient art of which trace evidence can be found in Hebrew and Egyptian archaeology. The North American idea of ventriloquism has probably been largely shaped by Edgar Bergen's verbose dummy Charlie McCarthy, but practitioners of old did not use dummies. The art was in throwing the voice, making it sound as though it were coming from a source distant from the speaker.

Once thought to be the result of a particular use of the stomach during inhalation (hence the name: *venter* + *loqui* means "belly speaking"), it is now understood that in ventriloquism words are formed in the usual way, but the breath is allowed to escape slowly. Such breath control muffles the tones and allows the speaker to keep the mouth open as little as possible. At the same time the tongue is retracted so that only its tip moves, causing pressure on the vocal cords and diffusing the sound. The greater the pressure on the vocal cords, the greater the illusion of distance.

I do not have any firsthand experiences of this phenomenon because Walter Ashurst was not a direct-voice medium. Lee Long, Mike Whalen, Blue Light, and all the other manifestations of spirits who were permitted access to the Aykroyd circle spoke openly through Walter's vocal mechanisms. My recollection of Walter's voices is vivid, but my sister Judy Harvie's is even more so. Many years older than I was when she attended the sittings, she was perhaps more attuned to details, she recently provided substantial fleshing out of my own experiences:

"In the séances, my most vivid memory is of Walter. He went back like this [tilts her head back] and he was totally transformed—clearly in a trance. When the various characters came through and talked, such as Blue Light and the Chinaman, Walter's total physiognomy changed. He couldn't have acted like that. The voice changed, but also the stance. For some people he would sit up straight; you could tell he was older or younger than the one before. Just the whole persona seemed to change."

Judy's account is not unusual. Others who have been present at séances where spirits have manifested through the voice boxes of mediums have been percipients of similar transformations. So have psychiatrists dealing with patients under mental stress. Does this description sound like it might characterize Walter? "Different modes of being and feeling and acting . . . exist independently of each other, coming forth and being in control at different times." It is a definition of dissociative identity disorder, or multiple personality disorder.[13]

I am not saying that Walter had a mental disorder. I find the idea ludicrous. If there had been the slightest concern of mental instability, my grandparents would never have had him live with them, as they did for nearly 12 years, and would certainly never have permitted their grandchildren the freedom we had to be with him. But might some of the same mechanisms, some of the same extraordinary skills at work in the dissociative identity disorder mind also have been working for Walter?

In my research for this book, I had the good fortune to be put in contact with Dr. Joe Nickell, senior research fellow at the Center for Inquiry, an affiliate of the Committee for Skeptical Inquiry in Amherst, New York. Although I had made it clear to him that I felt Walter Ashurst incapable of deceit, Nickell, a self-confessed skeptic, explained that some voice production is quite frankly fraud. In one case in which he was involved several years ago, he and psychologist Robert A. Baker obtained a tape recording of a woman who purportedly had channeled a dead Scotsman. A professional linguist declared the dialect to be fake.

In other cases, Nickell said, some people "are able to go into a dissociative or self-induced 'hypnotic' state, speak in a voice of an imagined discarnate spirit, and apparently not remember what occurred." He explained that such a person might be sincere and sane, but might exhibit other traits suggestive of a fantasy-prone personality.

Perhaps Walter Ashurst was creating all the voices he spoke. Not fraudulently, mind you, but sincerely. And yet . . . being fantasy-prone was one thing when speaking English. But could Walter have dissociated well enough to speak Chinese?

Glossolalia (and Its Close Cousins)

A specialized skill sometimes exhibited by direct-voice mediums is glossolalia, which, according to Guiley (1991), has three categories: glossolalia, speaking in a language unknown to the speaker or hearer; xenoglossolalia or xenoglossy, speaking in a language unknown to the speaker but known by the hearer; and heteroglossolalia, speaking in a language known by the speaker but understood by hearers in their native tongues. Although Richet used the term "xenoglossis" to refer to both the written and spoken forms of this phenomenon, Fodor (1966) uses "xenoglossis" to describe the written word and "glossolalia" for speaking in tongues unknown to the speaker. Since Fodor's definition seems to suit our purposes best, we will make use of it here.

Using that definition then, it would seem that the Aykroyd circle séances never experienced xenoglossis since Lee Long never actually produced a message in Chinese through Ellen Jane, who was the circle's practitioner of automatic writing. The group did, however, have its own repeated demonstrations of glossolalia.

From the very early days of Walter's séances with the group, Lee Long, Walter's Chinese control, spoke in what the group assumed was Chinese. In Dr. A.'s words:

> All the English he knows he has learned from the sitters. . . .
> He is very anxious to learn English and will ask us to repeat a word over and over again for him so he can say it, and it is amusing to hear him try to get our pronunciation. He will talk Chinese very rapidly, especially to a new sitter whom he seems to like to surprise.

It must be remembered that Walter knew no language other than English; however, whether or not the language that Walter spoke while in trance was in fact Chinese is open to conjecture, for no one in the group could speak or understand it. But Walter Ashurst would not have been the first medium to exhibit the skill of glossolalia.

The first to do so, at least in the history of spiritualism, was Miss Laura Edmonds of New York. According to her father, Judge John Worth Edmonds, a staunch spiritualist, Laura began to exhibit the skill in 1851. He maintained that an entranced Laura regularly enabled foreign sitters to converse in their own languages with the spirits, and although she spoke the words and answered sitters, she did not understand what she was saying. Among the nine languages in which she could apparently converse fluently were Greek, French, Spanish, Latin, and Polish, yet in a waking state she knew only English and the smattering of French she had learned at school.

Other than Judge Edmonds's accounts, most of which contain no specific dates or mentions of who was present, there is little evidence that the trance conversations were exactly as he portrayed them.

Interestingly, however, written accounts[14] of glossolalia were recorded long before Laura Edmonds or her father were born: some 2,000 years ago to be precise, in the words of the Apostle Paul in Acts 2:1–6.

> And when the day of Pentecost was fully come, they were all with one accord in one place. And suddenly there came a sound from heaven as of a rushing mighty wind, and it filled all the house where they were sitting. And there appeared unto them cloven tongues like as of fire, and it sat upon each of them. And they were all filled with the Holy Ghost, and began to speak with other tongues, as the Spirit gave them utterance. And there were dwelling at Jerusalem Jews, devout men, out of every nation under heaven. Now when this was noised abroad, the multitude came together, and were confounded, because that every man heard them speak in his own language.

The account of the Holy Spirit's appearance to the apostles after the death of Jesus is the foundation for Pentecostal churches and Pentecostal movements among Latter-Day Saints, Mormons, Quakers, and others who advocate glossolalia as one sign of the Holy Spirit's presence in a worshipper.

Most glossolalia, however, is little more than gibberish, made up of sounds and utterances that bear no resemblance to any language. Christie-Murray (1978) points to several differences that occur between glossas (the utterances produced in glossolalia) and normal languages. They are more repetitious and have a lower "inventory of sounds" than normal languages, and they are typically reproduced making frequent use of features of the mother tongue and diminishing features not found in the mother tongue. He cites the example of a language in which the mother tongue commonly uses *ee* and not the *eo* sound, observing that the same relative use will be made of those sounds in glossas. Regularity of cadence is also heard as a type of echoism, which Christie-Murray describes as the "exaltation of feeling" of words expressing judgment, love, or other strong emotions.

In most modern churches other than the charismatics, speaking in tongues is considered an aberration, and some view it as a sign of demonic possession or, more frequently, the result of mental or emotional upset.[15] And yet it must be admitted that the ability to speak or even to appear to speak convincingly in an unknown tongue is an amazing skill.

Clever Acting or Speech Center Stimulation?

Performers must use some form of this skill when they feign accents or utter phrases in foreign languages. We have heard comedians blurt out snippets of conversation in a foreign language they may not know. One of my favorite examples is from an old British television comedy set in France during World War II. The owner of the café (a British actor) would regularly burst into French to give his opinion of the German occupiers. It was brilliant—but it wasn't French!

Consider American Meryl Streep playing the Danish heiress Karen Blixen;[16] or Sam Neill, who is from New Zealand, performing as the American archeologist Dr. Alan Grant;[17] or Tom Hanks perfecting the Deep South accent for the role of Professor Goldthwait Higginson Dorr III.[18] These are only a few of the talented actors who have slipped eloquently into a role requiring a dialect. A great deal has been made of Emma Hardinge Britten's accounts of medium Jenny Keyes and the fact that she sang in Italian and Spanish, languages with which she was unfamiliar.[19] Yet opera singers regularly sing fluently in German, Italian, and French even though they may not be able to speak these languages. And it may not be such a rare skill. Ask a member of any church choir how they manage to sing in Latin even when they can't understand a single word of it. Think about auctioneers or evangelist preachers. Although not using a foreign language, they possess a unique ability to orate with an amazing speed and fluidity that takes years to perfect.

Yet spiritualists argue otherwise. They dismiss ventriloquism and mimicry as explanations for the voices heard during séances and offer several possibilities to account for the medium's utterances, in either familiar or unknown languages. One suggestion is that the thoughts of the spirit entity influence the speech center of the entranced medium's brain, thus stimulating it to produce language. If the entity uses a language foreign to the medium, one of two things may occur: i) the medium, either consciously or unconsciously, interprets the message in his or her own language, or ii) the medium unconsciously transmits the utterance in the language in which the message originated.

For cases of direct-voice mediumship where the voices of entities are heard coming from the air or a voice trumpet rather than via the voice mechanism of the medium, spiritualists have a different explanation. They explain that in such cases, the medium becomes an energy focal point, enabling the spirit voice to speak from the ambient air. This would be particularly effective, they suggest, in cases in which the spirit must use a language foreign to the medium. Since the medium's vocal apparatus is not involved, the spirit entity is free to speak in the language of choice.

Are the "spirit voices" heard during séances a function of ventriloquism, thought transference, energy focus, or playacting? The debate will continue. We can conclude, however, that not all incidents of voices heard during séances are evidential of spirit communication, and that if spirits are in fact communicating through spoken language, how they do it remains unclear.

SPIRIT PHOTOGRAPHY

A temporary sensation in the Aykroyd circles was caused by two photographs known within the family as "The Faces in the Windows." The photos were two black-and-white snapshots taken with a small Kodak camera one weekend in 1921. The subject was my brother Maurice, posing with his fishing rod in front of the farmhouse.

Some weeks after the photographs were developed, friends and family members noticed that behind the living subject, tiny faces were visible inside the farmhouse window: an old gentleman, a child with bobbed hair, a woman with a sweet-faced child at her knee. All these could be detected in the photo background, yet no one else was about the property at the time the snap was taken. In his notes, Dr. A. wrote the following quasi-scientific explanation:

We had been holding séances in those rooms for some time. . . .
The mediums, and perhaps others at the sittings as well, gave off

what the scientific investigators are now calling "ectoplasm" or "psychoplasm." The rooms, acting as cabinets, were impregnated with this substance and the spirits absorbed it to the extent of being solid enough to reflect the rays of light onto the sensitive plate of the camera. The thought occurs to me that they materialized in miniature to make the "medical substance" go round, so that as many could appear as possible. Minute faces may also be accounted for by supposing focal distances to be immaterial on the other side, as distance is "annihilated" under the conditions of the four dimensions of space.

Despite the attempt to rationalize the effect as objective proof of the presence of spirits that the medium had been "seeing," Dr. A. and the others likely soon realized that they had been gullible. Their strong will to believe in the presence of spirits had permitted them to see something that wasn't there. It was eventually accepted that the "faces" were likely due to the play of light on the window or perhaps just the pattern of leaves from nearby trees reflecting on the pane of glass, creating for the human mind the appearance of faces.[20] No more was ever made of it.

But there was one Aykroyd photograph that has remained an enigma. Published for the first time in *A Sense of Place* (Aykroyd 2002, 138) and reproduced in the photo insert, it has been the subject of countless hours of discussion and the cause of inspiration for many within our family, right down to the present generation.

At some point during a visit that Dr. A. made to Lily Dale, he had a photographic portrait of himself taken by an on-site spirit photographer. Taken outdoors on a verandah in full sunlight, the photograph shows the subject squinting slightly as he looks into the sun. By the time Dr. A. received the print, it showed several additional images (known as "extras" in spirit photography). His reaction to the photo is recorded in a letter he wrote to Azoth, the pseudonym of a writer whose column appeared regularly in *The Progressive Thinker,* in 1921:

Some years ago, I sat for a spirit photograph at Lily Dale, New York and received one which was not completely satisfactory, the faces being not as clearly or readily identified as we

EXTRAORDINARY SKILLS

139

would like. But after some time when we looked up some old photographs, we thought we could see resemblances between these photos and two of the faces on the picture.

The partially visible face of the young woman who appears almost directly above the subject's left ear was identified as Anna, the long-ago love of Dr. A.'s. The second recognizable face in the photograph was described as "an attempt to represent a photograph of my father-in-law, not so much in expression as in general make-up." So excited was Dr. A. by the discoveries that he immediately had a copy made of the photograph. He bundled it, along with the letter and an old tintype photo of the same Anna, and sent it off to Azoth as an example of a true spirit photograph, an unsolicited appearance on film of spirits from the other side.

Is the Medium the Messenger?

Although some view the phenomenon of spirit photography as nothing more than deliberate attempts to defraud the naïve, the initial appearance of "spirits" or "ghosts" in photographic portraiture is thought

---

Forever Young

I have often wondered why spirit photographs typically show the subjects in fine form, fully clothed, and at an apparent age that would put them roughly at the apogee of their physical beauty and strength. Jeffrey Burton Russell gives us a possible explanation in *A History of Heaven*. In his discussion of the leaders of the monastic school of Saint Victor, Russell suggests that their views on heaven led them to conclude that "the resurrected body will be identical with our earthly body, but transfigured; it will be immune from death and sorrow; it will be at the height of its powers, free from disease and deformity and around thirty years old, the age at which Christ began his ministry" (Russell 1997, 119).

---

gory, and whether their mediumistic abilities came to the fore prior to their work in photography or vice versa is immaterial. The fact was that their psychical skills enabled them to reproduce spectral images, whether originating from materialization or thought, in visible form. The question of how the process was enabled in the spirit world, however, proved to be a greater mystery.

Thought Forms and Spirit "Extras"

William T. Stead, the British journalist who had been communicating regularly through automatic writing with his spirit guide Julia, was fascinated by spirit photography, and he, too, wondered how it was accomplished in the spirit world. In 1895, Stead sat for London photographer and medium Richard Boursnell. While being photographed, Stead kept thoughts of Julia in his mind, hoping that Julia's image would thus be captured by the camera's lens. When the film was exposed, he was pleased to see the image of a beautiful young woman sharing the frame with him.

When he later communicated with Julia via automatic writing, he was surprised by what he read. Julia told him that it was not her image in the photo at all but her "thought form" poured into the mold of another woman. She told him that whenever spirits wanted to manifest themselves, either by materialization or by photography, they simply reused an existing mold, much as an artist would use a woodblock or a photographer would use a negative to make multiple prints: "You get the block and you go on printing. We get the mold, and go on producing copies when they are wanted" (Jolly 2006, 47).

It is interesting to read about the various lengths people have gone to in order to explain the appearance of spirits in photos or, in some cases, to produce the phenomenon. One of the best-known spirit photographers was an American named William Hope (1863–1933), who became a devout spiritualist after he photographed a friend only to find the man's dead sister standing beside the subject in the developed prints.

Hope, a carpenter, turned his hobby into a profession and became one of the most sought-after spirit photographers of the time. Investigated by some of the best, including Sir William Crookes, he was caught in a fraud more than once. In 1920, skeptic pamphleteer Edward Bush fooled Hope into producing a "spirit photograph" of a man who was still very much alive. That embarrassing exposure was followed by another in 1922, in which investigator Harry Price[23] and his colleague, SPR research officer Eric J. Dingwall, inconspicuously marked a photographic plate before giving it to Hope to process. When the plates were exposed with a spirit "extra" in full view, Price and Dingwall found that the plate was not the marked one they had given him. They accused Hope of substituting their plate with one that had been doctored beforehand. Hope maintained that it was a setup during which someone switched his photographic plates.

The spiritualist community came to the man's rescue with what Jolly describes as "the spiritualist escape clause that even genuine mediums were sometimes weak enough to resort to trickery" (2006, 100). Nothing was proven either way and Hope continued to work and make himself available for testing until his death.

Ghost Photographs (www.ghostresearch.org/ghostpics), a Web site operated by Illinois photographer Dale Kaczmarek, posts dozens of photos from various people who purport to have captured spirits on film. Kaczmarek acknowledges that there are "no experts in the field of spirit photography analysis" and that his interpretations are based on his own expertise in photography and his knowledge of film defects and natural phenomena. Avowed expert or not, Kaczmarek is no amateur. Not only does he give critical analysis of every photo posted, he has also published in the field an article, "Evidence for Spirit Photography," which appeared in *Pursuit Journal,* volume 19, number 1, in 1986, and a book, *A Field Guide to Spirit Photography* (2002).

Apart from the fact that the Web site's copyright is registered in the name of the Ghost Research Society, suggesting that Kaczmarek may be open to the existence of supernatural forces, this man, in his own way, seems to be like the objective scientific researchers of old, using his knowledge without the complication of a hidden agenda. The Web site's home page divides submissions into two lists: photos in which no technical weakness was detected (i.e., apparently authentic) and photos showing effects that appear to be the result of operator error or technical malfunction. For both lists, details are given of the conditions under which the photograph was taken, the camera and film types, exposure levels, and so on.

In accepting photos from the public, Kaczmarek is obviously operating from the standpoint of believing in people's honesty. Even though some of the photos he has listed as apparently authentic seem, to my critical eye, a little staged, he has responded negatively only to those in which he can detect and identify some specific technically based fault: overlong exposure time, lens flare, dirty lens, reflection in the distance, and the first or last print on a roll, which apparently often show red or orange glows resulting from faulty handling of the film.

In addition to pointing out the potential for failures of technique or equipment, Kaczmarek warns any modern would-be spirit photographers that photos of apparent "orbs" taken with digital cameras are rarely anything more than digital flaws that arise in low-light conditions due to a lack of pixilation.

A catalogue of so-called spirit photographs was published in 2004 as a companion piece to an exhibit called The Perfect Medium: Photography and the Occult, held at the Metropolitan Museum of Art in New York on September 27, 2005. The book is a compendium of spirit photos taken over the last 100 years. Among the many reproduced photos are the lurid ones taken by Schrenck-Notzing of bifolded magazine pictures or cheeseclothlike material oozing out of Eva C.'s nose, and the more aesthetic ones taken by Ada Emma Deane, a British photographer who worked during the 1920s and whose beautiful "spirit" subjects frequently appear artistically posed with gossamer veils floating around their faces. Other Deane photos show clouds of veil-like mist appearing like cartoonists' thought bubbles above the subjects' heads. In one case at least, a fine string can clearly be seen attached to the bubble, anchoring it to something off-camera.

So many of Deane's "spirits" so closely resembled photos published at the time in magazines and newspapers that one would wonder at her ability to stay in business. Yet Deane continued to work even after she was accused of fraud, producing more than 2,000 "spirit photos" over the course of her career.

In spite of what some saw as obvious fraud, spiritualists and believers continued to defend spirit photography, making use of a number of rationales for the existence of apparent anomalies in the images taken by spirit photographers. The repeated appearance of the same image in photos of different sitters they countered with the spirit Julia's explanation of the recycled mold made from an etheric substance. About veiled or conspicuously "posed" shots (e. g., Ada Deane's images), they explained that spirits, unlike living subjects, were not using photographs as a way to display their egos, but were captured in modesty of both character and body. Likenesses that appeared flat or one-dimensional, they said, were the result of spirits' prudent use of the available energy and materials. And as a defense for the most frequent criticism of all, double exposure, they explained that the earth's atmosphere, being of a density different from their psychic auras, caused an effect of "double refraction."

One of the most comprehensive and rational books ever to deal with the subject of spirit photography was published in 2006. Martyn Jolly's *Faces of the Living Dead* reproduces plate after plate of some never-before-seen photographs gleaned from various archives of spirit "extras" and materializations. The narrative is crisp and eminently pragmatic, giving us a sense of both the flaws in logic of the early psychic investigators and the human frailties that could account for them.

Whether carried out under the reign of biological or mechanical metaphors, the quasi-scientific investigations of Crawford, Geley, Schrenck-Notzing or Richet shared two characteristics. They myopically concentrated on accumulating and analyzing mountains of evidence, which they had to break down into smaller and smaller details in order to fit them incrementally into their predetermined psychic theories. And they cultivated glaring blindspots—to the possibility for instance, that their apparently simple and guileless mediums might actually be colluding with that medium's supposedly genuine and solicitous protectors. But the investigators were driven men following a long trail of tantalizing evidence. They were led on as the intensity of the phenomena seemed to swell in direct response to the urgency of their search (Jolly 2006, 5).

Truth in Photographs

Perhaps like no other, the case of Margery Crandon illustrates the point Jolly makes regarding investigator myopia. Mina "Margery" Crandon (1888–1941), née Stinson, was born on a farm in Ontario and, while still a teenager, moved to Boston to pursue her talents in music and acting. Her second husband, Dr. LeRoi Goddard Crandon, was a prominent and wealthy Boston physician and a professor of surgery at Harvard. Dr. Crandon's interest in spiritualism led him to experiment with table tipping using his wife as the conduit to the spirits. To their surprise and pleasure, Mina was a natural. Able to produce table rappings and tippings with ease, she went into a trance during some of the earliest sittings and was soon producing automatic writing, psychic music, and, eventually, direct voice. Her control and spirit guide during these times was her deceased elder brother Walter.[24] Mina's manifestations became so frequent and so impressive that she was soon a local celebrity, adopting the name "Margery" for public performances.

By the end of 1923, the year in which her first séance took place, she came to the attention of a Harvard group that was conducting scientific investigations. The phenomena produced in Margery's presence were remarkable, and she was soon invited to Europe, where she was investigated under what were billed as strict controls. In 1924, a committee formed by *Scientific American* magazine began its own investigation of her on the urging of Sir Arthur Conan Doyle.

Margery's popularity likely stemmed from the fact that she was a member of Boston high society by virtue of her marriage—a rarity in the rough-and-tumble world of the public medium. Therefore, it was simply assumed that she was what she claimed to be, and even obvious fraud would have been washed away along with whispers of impropriety. Nice women like her surely wouldn't wad damp cheesecloth into their armpits or swallow crumpled-up bits of *Le Miroir* or stuff pieces of raw animal innards into their vaginas, all for later retrieval to present to astonished onlookers . . . or would they? Victorian ladies and gentlemen might not have had the boldness to consider such things, but there were other facts to this case that might have made modern observers a little more skeptical than their ancestors.

Dr. Crandon's profession gave him credibility, but it also gave him ample opportunity to collect specimens of human tissue. Yet even the most glaring possibilities for the placing of foreign substances into Margery Crandon's body didn't compel people like Doyle and investigator J. Malcolm Bird to challenge her. Even Hereward Carrington fell for the charms of the beautiful medium.

As you will remember, Carrington's inexhaustible pursuit of truth as it applied to psychic phenomena was responsible for hundreds of pages of illuminating and debunking text. Time after time his experiments uncovered dubious practices. Although his evidence failed to allow him to declare that all mediums were frauds, he nevertheless continued in his relentless attempts to expose fraudulent practitioners. Until he met Margery Crandon. It was then that his defenses and his determination seemed to evaporate. Following the lead of those who had investigated her before him, he made public statements about the genuineness of this medium.

But even Margery's charms didn't seem able to penetrate the determination of that exasperating magician from Wisconsin. Throughout 1924, Harry Houdini attended every séance of Margery's he was invited to, and it seemed that the more he examined and questioned, the cockier Margery got. Then, in 1925, it looked as though Margery's star might plummet to earth. In January of that year, Margery, in a deep trance and wearing nothing but a dressing gown and long silk stockings, held a private sitting for Eric J. Dingwall (of the London SPR), who wished to photograph the ectoplasmic extrusions that Margery had begun producing. Having received permission from Margery's control Walter to take the photograph by magnesium flash in the dark, Dingwall captured the photograph of an ectoplasmic hand that seemed to have emerged from somewhere near Margery's navel, quite visible at the front of the wide-open dressing gown. Jolly gives us an account of what transpired next:

> Dingwall brought the photographs to William McDougall, chair of the *Scientific American* committee and professor of psychology at Harvard. Under his magnifying glass, they looked to him more like an animal's trachea and lung cut crudely into

the shape of a wrist, palm and fingers, than "genuine" ecto-plasm. Dingwall next showed the photographs to a gynecologist who confirmed that the substance, whatever it was, could be packed into a vagina and expelled (2006, 75).

In what was perhaps an example of nature complaining quietly, Margery suffered a uterine hemorrhage very shortly after this event. Were the ectoplasmic extrusions some sort of uterine growth that had gone undetected? Or was it fraud?

Dingwall was at first completely convinced that Margery was a genuine medium capable of producing some unique phenomena: blob-like extrusions unlike anything he had seen before, and long, flexible rods of ectoplasm protruding from various body cavities. But after several observations of the "production" of this ectoplasm in dim, flashing red light, Dingwall had to admit that he had never actually seen the ectoplasm being extruded from Margery's body, but was only able to view it after it was partly or fully formed.

Having been examined by some of the best in the field, the legiti-macy of Margery's mediumship soon divided investigators into two opposing factions. Although Dingwall fell short of issuing an outright disclaimer of Margery's genuineness, he ceased to be a supporter, and others followed suit on the negative side: William McDougall of Har-vard, Henry Clay McCommas of Princeton, and Harry Houdini, among others. On the positive side were Doyle and Carrington, and Margery's husband LeRoi Crandon, who had garnered unequivocal support from the American Society for Psychical Research, which by 1925 was largely controlled by spiritualists.

The Witch of Lime Street

With the ASPR in her corner, Margery somehow managed to pass off the threat of public scandal and within no time at all was back per-forming even more new feats. The woman known as the Witch of Lime Street, so named for the Crandons' Boston residence at 10 Lime Street, was back in action. She heralded her return to public life in 1926 with yet another addition to her already amazing repertoire.

Her new skill was producing wax impressions of spirit fingerprints.

With the aid of wax obtained from her dentist, Dr. Caldwell, who was an occasional sitter in her circle, Margery "psychically" created mold after mold of finger- and thumbprints right in front of her sitters. A blob of wax would be placed in a bowl on a table out of Margery's reach, and the spirit would be summoned as usual. After the lights were turned back on, prints would be found to have been embedded into the wax. Usually the prints were alleged to belong to her spirit guide, Walter; at other times, to other spirit entities. A fingerprint expert whom the Crandons themselves had hired took fingerprints of everyone in the room on several occasions, including Margery and her husband. The expert declared that the molds were different from any of them. He further attested that the prints were identical to prints he had managed to get from one of the deceased Walter's old razors. Then the roof fell in.

In 1932, in what turned out to be a lethal show of bravado against Houdini and his fellow doubters, Dr. Crandon hired E. E. Dudley, one of their circle's regulars, to catalogue prints of everyone who had ever attended a Crandon circle séance. Unfortunately for the Crandons, Dudley was an honest man. The prints that allegedly belonged to Walter the spirit were a perfect match for those of Dr. Caldwell, Margery's dentist. Try as it might, the ASPR was unable to keep the news from the media, and within days the shocking headlines hit the *New York Times*. With such damaging publicity, even Margery's most ardent supporters either backed away from her or added their own public condemnation.

Hereward Carrington, until then a staunch supporter, retreated from Margery and from the scandal that erupted, and it was soon ascertained that reports of her genuineness had been anything but objective. Both Carrington and Margery admitted that during his investigations they had been having an affair. J. Malcolm Bird, who had previously claimed to be a loyal Margery ally, admitted that he had sometimes slanted reports in her favor. The Crandons were socially and professionally disgraced.

To be fair, over the brief period of Margery Crandon's active mediumship, she produced some startling phenomena, particularly those that accompanied materializations. Unlike the gauzy, netlike ectoplasms that were a preliminary to materializations by other mediums, Margery's emanations were reportedly made from a warm, rubbery organic substance that was materialized into crude fingers and hands: "It could be touched and examined, it felt like skin, it contained bones, its temperature was around forty degrees" (Chéroux et al. 2005, 217). None of the investigators was ever able to discover how she produced them.

Margery fell into chronic alcoholism and died in 1941 at the age of 54. Nándor Fodor, psychic investigator and paranormal chronicler, was at her deathbed, expecting her to confess that it had all been a fraud. Defiant to the end, Margery laughed and told him that he and other psychic investigators would be guessing for the rest of their lives.

Kirlian Photography and Crystallization of Thought

The hunt for explanations for the appearance of spirits in photographs continued. In the early 1940s, a Russian couple, Semyon Kirlian, an electrical engineer, and his wife Valentina, a biologist, experimented with the photography of objects that had been electrically charged. They found that there was more to be seen than the naked eye could detect and called the aura they observed "bioplasma." One famous photo using this technique shows a leaf. Just before the camera was activated, one of the experimenters snipped a corner off the leaf, yet in the photograph the luminous outline of the original leaf is clearly seen, even the part that had been cut away!

Although controversial, these techniques have been thought by some to be useful in healing, since the fingers and hands of psychic healers are seen in Kirlian photographs to radiate flares of light during the time of healing. Areas of intense color and light have also been observed at the precise points where acupuncturists have chosen to insert their needles. Some scientists say Kirlian photography reproduces a physical form of psychic energy, revealing the etheric body. Others believe it reveals nothing more than a discharge of electricity. Although it is a fascinating subject, there is no evidence to conclude that Kirlian photography is a paranormal phenomenon.

Yet another explanation for the appearance of "extras" on film was

initially put forward by J. Traill Taylor (1827–1895), a British spiritualist who began investigating spirit photography in the mid-1800s.
Taylor suggested that the "spirits" appearing on film might be "crystal-
lizations of thought," a novel idea at the time and one that caught on
like wildfire among those who tried to avoid the *fides spirituosa* trap.
By 1885, a year after the SPR published its second volume of *Proceedings,* which included a detailed set of experimental observations on
hypnosis and telepathy undertaken by Edmund Gurney, both Frederic
Myers and Gurney had begun stating publicly that the idea of thought
transference could, in fact, be the basis for all psychic phenomena.

Not surprisingly, the telepathy bandwagon gradually rolled to a point
in the road where only the most ardent supporters stayed on, though
many today continue to believe that some people can project thoughts
powerful enough to be picked up by sensitive photographic equipment.
When one considers a number of the spirit photos taken by Schrenck-
Notzing and Dr. Glen Hamilton, it is easy to understand why.

AUTOMATIC PAINTING

While automatic writing is the most common automatism, automatic
painting is the second most common. There have been numerous documented cases of people with neither artistic training nor ability who produced works of art, some showing astounding similarities in technique to
the works of famous, long-dead artists. Some automatic art is the product
of an unknown spirit or results when a spirit acts as an artist's model.

William Blake, who is probably best known as a British romantic
poet (*The Tyger, Songs of Innocence, Songs of Experience*), was also
an artist who often painted psychically, sketching his spirit visitors as
if they were posing. He drew them with enthusiasm and composure,
looking up from time to time as though he had a real sitter before him.
If the vision disappeared, he stopped painting until it reappeared.

Artist Robert Swain Gifford (1840–1905) was an American oil
painter, etcher, and watercolorist whose favorite subjects were misty
landscapes and coastal views of his native Massachusetts. Six months
after Gifford's sudden death, a New York City engraver by the name
of Frederic Thompson suddenly felt the urge to paint. His chosen sub-

ject: gnarled trees and coastal landscapes. Whenever he felt urged to paint in the style that Gifford had been known for, Thompson would announce, "Gifford wants to sketch."

In the first 2 years of these psychic interludes, Thompson produced more than 2,000 very small drawings that he painted with a zeal that amounted to obsession. Although initially fearing he might be going mad, Thompson and those who knew him eventually became convinced that the paintings were done by Thompson's hand being guided by Gifford's spirit.

Psychic artist Luís Antônio Gasparetto (1949–) is a Brazilian who is said to have had no artistic training and to be unable to paint a stroke. Yet he has been known to turn out paintings at a staggering rate and in a variety of styles reminiscent of famous artists such as Picasso, van Gogh, Renoir, Manet, and Goya, among others. In a televised demonstration in England in 1978, Gasparetto produced 21 sketches, one after the other in rapid succession. Some were done with both hands simultaneously, with one hand drawing one picture and the other drawing a second picture upside down. In a public demonstration in California in 1988, he turned out another amazing handful of paintings in the styles of the masters, all within a few minutes.

Gasparetto considers himself to be a channeler, able to produce the images on canvas only after receiving psychic skill from long-dead artists. Art experts are not so sure. Although his skill and dexterity are arguably well beyond average, and although his art does resemble the styles of the masters, art critics say the work is not up to the standards of those he purports to be channeling. Be that as it may, he has achieved a significant following and is able, through the sale of his paintings, to make a living.

Numerous other channelers and mediums have painted canvases over the years and claimed their hands were guided by spirits. Some people swear that the paintings are absolutely true to the styles of long-dead artists. Others wonder if perhaps the talent is coming through a shared memory, a Jung-like collective artistic ability. Still others are willing to accept only that automatic paintings are produced by people who are exceptionally talented at mimicking styles. But Dr. A. wrote in his notes of another kind of automatic painting, one that truly seems to defy explanation: precipitated painting.

Precipitated Painting

Unlike standard automatic paintings, precipitated paintings are created by artists who never touch the canvas. The image appears without the aid of brush, or paint, or even hands. Sometimes the paintings are produced inside the medium's cabinet while the medium remains outside. At other times, the paintings are said to appear in broad daylight and in full view of an audience. In those cases, the medium simply sits near or waves a hand in front of the canvas and the painting gradually becomes visible.

In a letter to the *Kingston Whig-Standard* dated 1913, Dr. A. talks about a "self-luminous" portrait that had been exhibited in Kingston the previous week. Although it has been impossible to discover who exhibited the painting or indeed anything about its provenance, Dr. A.'s notes indicate that it was "postulated as being a painting of Christ" and that it was painted by Elizabeth S. Bangs (1859–1922) and May Eunice Bangs (b. 1864), the late 19th-century American mediums who produced many of the paintings that now hang in Lily Dale.

The Bangs Sisters

Known as Lizzie and May, the young Chicago-born ladies who slipped into the pages of history as the Bangs Sisters began their mediumship while still children. Much of the phenomena they produced were unremarkable: slate writing, apports, and table turning, much the same as effects produced by a host of other mediums of the time. But it is their paintings, which they began producing as early as 1894, that continue to baffle.

Relatives or friends would be asked to bring along a photograph of the deceased person whose portrait they wished to have painted. They were never asked to show the photograph to the sisters, nor were they asked for any description of the spirit who was about to become the artists' model. Behind the cover of a curtained-off area or cabinet, Lizzie and May would produce a painting of the deceased person, the completion of which required several sittings by the living relative. Later on, the paintings were produced in full color and in a fraction of the time. Nándor Fodor describes one such event:

Two identical paper-mounted canvases in wooden frames were held up, face to face, against the window, the lower edges resting on a table and the sides gripped by each medium with one hand. A short curtain was hung on either side and an opaque blind was drawn over the canvases. With the light streaming from behind, the canvases were translucent. After a quarter of an hour the outlines of shadows began to appear and disappear as if the invisible artist made a preliminary sketch, then the picture began to grow at a feverish rate and when the frames were separated the portrait was found on the paper surface next to the sitter. Though the paint was greasy and stuck to the finger on being touched, it left no stain on the paper surface of the other canvas which closely touched it (Fodor 1966, 27).

Fodor's description of the artists' material is consistent with other accounts. An additional letter sent by Dr. A. to the editor of the *Whig-Standard* in 1913 tells of an account written by Vice-Admiral W. Usborne Moore of the British Navy. The account, which appeared in Moore's book *Glimpses of the Next State* (1911), described a visit the vice-admiral had with the Bangs Sisters on January 18, 1909, during which Moore asked for a picture to be precipitated of his deceased wife, Lola. Dr. A. says that Moore wrote:

After a few minutes, the canvas assumed various hues, rosy, blue and brown; it would become dark and light independently of the sun being clouded or not. Dim outlines of faces occasionally appeared in different parts of the canvas. From the time the face and bust appeared to the time the canvasses were separated and the finished picture was put on a sofa in the next room, twenty-five minutes elapsed. Neither of the psychics had ever seen the carte-de-visite[25] in my pocket. . . . When the portrait was finished, it bore a very close resemblance to the photograph. . . . At the same time the picture is by no means a slavish copy of the photograph. It's [*sic*] pose is more upright, the face spirituelle [*sic*], and the dress not exactly the same. There is a firmness, a decision, and an appearance of calm and contented happiness.

The pose and the material were not the only aspects of the Bangs Sisters' art that were remarkable. It seems that even as the paintings were being produced, changes, often requested mentally by the sitters, were accomplished. In one case, a sitter by the name of Howe mentally asked for his late wife's name to appear at the bottom of her portrait and for a yellow rose to be placed in her hair. The finished portrait contained both, even though the photograph he had brought with him to the sitting contained neither.

I had read Dr. A.'s description of the portrait exhibited in Kingston and wondered what it was that could have so moved him. It wasn't until I actually saw ones like it when I was in Lily Dale in 2005 that I realized what he was trying to convey: the luminosity, the softness, the eyes! There are at least a half-dozen fine examples of precipitated paintings hanging in Lily Dale, some at the museum, some at the Maplewood Hotel. Several of the paintings have been reproduced here in full color in the insert, some for the first time, so that readers can see for themselves.

My conversations with Ron Nagy, Lily Dale historian and, according to Buckland, "one of the country's leading experts on the phenomena" (2006, 30), further captured my interest. According to Nagy, author of *Precipitated Spirit Paintings* (2006), art experts have examined the portraits and cannot explain what art medium was used. It is neither oil- nor water-based paint; it is not pastel and it is not crayon. In truth, it is impossible to see even the minutest brushstroke, and the entire effect is soft and ethereal. "It looks as though it has been applied with a modern airbrush and has the consistency of the powder on a butterfly's wings" (Nagy 2006, 11).

Few investigators have made serious examinations of the material used in these beautiful and mysterious paintings, although some are still attempting to postulate how they may have been created. One of these is Dr. Joe Nickell, whom we have already met. In addition to holding the position of senior research fellow at the Center for Inquiry of the Committee for Skeptical Inquiry (CSI) in Amherst, New York, Nickell is a frequent talk-show guest who has appeared on *Larry King Live, 20/20,* and *Oprah,* among others. He writes a regular column for the *Skeptical Inquirer* and is considered to be one of America's most accomplished investigators of the paranormal.

In investigating the paintings hanging in Lily Dale that were allegedly precipitated by the Bangs Sisters, Joe Nickell brought into play more than just his doctorate in literary investigation and his many years of experience in the forensic analysis of historical documents. Like Houdini, his predecessor in the art of debunking frauds, Nickell made use of his knowledge as a former magician.

Nickell discovered Floyd Thayer's 1928 *Quality Magic Catalog,* an index of materials and instruments for the enhancement of performances of stage magic, and it led him to some interesting speculation. One description explains that two canvases, when placed face-to-face in a frame and powerfully lit from the rear, could be used with a particular device to achieve much the same effects as those produced by the Bangs Sisters, who also, curiously, required two canvases.

Recognizing the similarity in procedure and outcome between the Bangs Sisters' phenomena and those of magicians of the time, Nickell was sufficiently inspired to attempt to recreate a precipitated painting of his own. Although Nickell had no access to the Thayer device, he succeeded in producing "what seems a very similar effect." The account of Nickell's hypothetical reconstruction of the Bangs Sisters' method was published in the June 2000 issue of *Skeptical Briefs,* a quarterly newsletter for CSI members.

Nickell explains that before being asked to take a seat, the sitter would be given an opportunity to examine the room. A previously prepared picture, rolled up and placed out of reach in advance, would remain undetected. As in the scenario described earlier, two blank panels were placed face-to-face, stood up on a table, and held by one sister on either side. An opaque blind was pulled down. Then:

> The spirits are invoked, while under cover of the drawn blind, one sister uses her free hand to extract the (previously prepared) picture from its hiding place and attach it to the face of the rearmost panel which is laid on the table behind the other panel. All is now ready for the blind to be raised.
>
> Light is seen streaming through the blank panel, which will function as a sort of screen on which the seemingly materializing image will be projected from the rear. At a suitable time, one of

the sisters, using her free hand behind the curtain, stands the picture panel upright a few inches from the other, an action which creates a shadowy, clouded effect upon the "screen." Slowly the picture panel is moved forward, and, as it approaches the screen, colors appear, followed by a blurry face which eventually comes into focus and is recognized. Finally, the completed picture is revealed in full light at the end of the séance.[26]

Nickell believes that the use of two canvases had a dual purpose: One, it served as a screen to permit rear projection of the image, and two, it was used as an effective shield to hide the previously prepared portrait from view.

Were the Bangs Sisters frauds? Perhaps no one will ever know for certain. But as Nickell observes, they were "obviously effective, given the many testimonials they elicited." Yet although their name is perhaps synonymous with spirit painting, the Bangs Sisters were by no means the only, or even the earliest, mediums to produce this phenomenon.

In *Skeptical Briefs'* March 2000 issue,[27] Nickell gives a comprehensive overview of spirit painting beginning with the appearance in the mid-1860s, when the Bangs Sisters were still toddlers, of the Glasgow medium David Duguid and his small, trance-painted landscapes. Henry Slade also produced spirit pictures around this time, some with a slate and chalk, some with paints. And then there were the notorious Campbell "Brothers."

The Campbell Brothers

Another painting pair, the so-called Campbell Brothers, were not siblings at all. Allen B. Campbell (1833–1919) and Charles Shourds (d. 1926) were close friends who ran an import/export business out of New Jersey. After brief careers as solo spiritualist performers, Campbell as a medium artist and Shourds as a materialization medium, they appeared together on stage for the first time in 1897.

Their duo performances included the production of spirit typewriter messages, slate writing, and spirit painting of miniatures on porcelain. Among their most spectacular productions were precipitated paintings done in much the same style as those of the Bangs Sisters. Buckland relates a typical scenario that was described in Ron Nagy's book *Precipitated Spirit Paintings* (2006):

> The examined blank canvases were placed on a table with oil paints in a receptacle underneath the table, and all was then covered with a black cloth. The mediums and sitters would join hands or place their hands down on the table. When the cover was lifted there would be a finished painting, the like of which would take a professional artist many days to produce (Buckland 2006, 60).

One of the most astounding of the paintings precipitated by the Campbell Brothers was produced in a single 90-minute sitting on June 15, 1898, in the Campbell Brothers' Egyptian séance room. It was a life-size portrait in oil of Allen Campbell's spirit guide Azur (see photo insert) that hangs in the Maplewood Hotel at Lily Dale. The six-pointed star appearing behind Azur's head was not originally in the portrait. It is said to have later materialized, and it remains visible today.

Nickell's explanation for how the Campbell Brothers produced *Azur* builds on a scenario that was offered by Hereward Carrington at the time of the painting's creation. Carrington believed that the spirit oil paintings were produced with the aid of a previously completed fresh but dry oil painting. By adhering a blank canvas over the completed oil and then removing it behind the curtain or cabinet, the medium would appear to have "painted" the portrait in minutes. A light application of poppyseed oil on the paint's surface would aid in the illusion.

On close examination of the Azur painting in Lily Dale, Nickell found that all four corners were slightly marred. It was a finding consistent with Carrington's suggestion of a blank canvas having been fitted over the top of the previously completed one. Nickell has more to say about the later appearance of Azur's star-shaped halo:

> I suggest that the star, which is not particularly bold, was not at first noticed. When the sitters' attention was called to it, and they then focused on it, they were deceived by the power of suggestion into thinking it had spontaneously materialized.[28]

Plausible? Nickell certainly thinks so. But those who staunchly believe in the reality of the spirit connection to these portraits dismiss his explanations, and Carrington's, as ludicrous.

Joe Nickell does not seem at all uncomfortable with the idea of dissonance, and rightly enough. Without open discussion and varying points of view, no new theories would ever be developed. And even though Nickell's ideas about these enigmatic portraits may not sit well with those who ascribe their creation to a transcendental realm, his research has gone a long way in compiling a history of this amazing yet controversial phenomenon.

SLATE WRITING

Skeptics and believers are equally puzzled over a particular phenomenon that has had them profoundly divided. The ability to write on slates bound face-to-face without removing the bindings seems, on the face of it, to be a rather astounding skill. Yet Henry Slade (d. 1905) managed to perform this phenomenon time after time in front of onlookers with an ease that would suggest it was an everyday occurrence. Skeptics said it was a trick. Believers said it was a spiritual manifestation. In 1876, the debate became overheated.

Little is known about American Henry Slade's early life, but by the time the controversy over his spirit skills had divided the forces on either side of psychic phenomena, he had already spent 15 years as a professional medium whose levitations and slate writing were astounding onlookers.

Then, in 1876, Madame Helena Blavatsky (see Comments, Chapter 4, iii), a gifted Russian materialization medium whose travels in pursuit of the study of her art took her to India, Tibet, and Egypt, invited Henry Slade to demonstrate his slate-writing skills to investigators at the Imperial University in St. Petersburg. On his way to St. Petersburg to accept Blavatsky's invitation, Slade stopped in London for a number of weeks to make several public appearances. The visit would prove his undoing.

At one of the séances attended by a sizeable crowd, a Professor Edwin Ray Lankester (1847–1929), a member of the British Association for the

Advancement of Science, had paid his £1 fee and, after seeing one demonstration, returned for a second séance, determined to discover what he felt sure was a trick. Before Slade had a chance to "write" anything, Lankester snatched the slate from the medium's hands and untied the twine holding them together. The onlookers stared as the bindings were taken off the slates to reveal a message already written on them.

Within days, Lankester had disclosed the sordid story in the *London Times* and sued Slade for taking money under false pretenses. Slade was convicted in October and sentenced to 3 months hard labor, but he never served his time. During an appeal, the conviction was overturned on technical grounds. Lankester registered to have the case reopened, but before another summons could be issued, the medium skipped the country and returned to New York.

Henry Slade continued to practice his art and to separate the believers from the skeptics, yet throughout his career there was evidence that he was more fraud artist than wonder-worker. To wit: Two sealed slates prepared by Camille Flammarion were in Slade's possession for more than 10 days in 1877, yet no writing was produced, and Slade was caught with prewritten messages in 1883 in New York and again in 1885 on a visit to Australia. During the latter visit, a sitter also saw his foot move a table he was presumably levitating. Then, caught cheating in West Virginia in 1886, Slade and his business partner were arrested.

In the midst of all this bad publicity for Slade (and ultimately for slate writing in general), Richet publicly made two important points: Slade's honesty was open to question, but more significantly for psychic investigation, slate writing was susceptible to trickery.

There were other mediums who performed slate writing, but Slade's name (and his dishonesty) will perhaps forever be what people think of in connection with it. In using the tricks he did, or in not being good enough to perform them well, Slade opened a floodgate of suspicion against all mediums who produced slate writing.

In truth, there are many odd features of slate writing that could point to trickery. Investigators of various slate writers noticed quite early on that there were inconsistencies in penmanship on slates, even when the writing was purported to come from the same spirit. They also noted the mediums' usual request for a small stub of chalk.

When the messages were general, the writing was usually of normal size, with clear, well-formed letters. When the messages were in response to a specific question asked by a sitter, the writing was usually cramped, uneven, and sometimes almost illegible. Investigators came to the conclusion that they were dealing with fraud. General messages could of course be written beforehand. But since questions could not be anticipated, specific messages in answer to a sitter's query could not be prewritten on the slates. In such a case, the medium would write on the slate, which was usually held under the table, by activating with his foot a rod or rigid device attached to the chalk stub. The chalk needed to be small in order to fit into the gap between the slates. This technique explains why specific response messages were not only produced in minute writing, but were typically confined to the border around the slate's periphery rather than centered.

Trickery or not, the skill needed to produce slate writing is considerable, and it was one of the exciting phenomena the Aykroyd circle sitters experienced but which I was not fortunate enough to witness. Luckily, we have my sister Judy's recollections of one of the more memorable séances:

"At this one séance they had the slates, and they were tied together. They brought them up quite early and set them on the table. Not on the table where we were sitting, but on the table in the corner. I can recollect that during the séance I heard scratching . . . that's all I heard. And then they were opened at the end [of the séance] and there was writing there."

Judy recalled that no one went near the slates during the séance. She didn't remember what was written on them, and the slates from that particular séance do not seem to have been preserved. But the results from another such séance many years before have been saved.

A set of old-fashioned school slates sits in my writer's hideout at the lake. On one of them a message is written in red chalk. After the 90-odd years that the slate has lain in storage, the writing now appears to be fused with the surface and cannot be smudged. The message is brief but still legible. It reads:

My dear nephew
I am not far off. I can be of help.
Command me at any time.
Uncle Andrew Aykroyd[29]

TABLE TIPPING

Séance sitters sat in a circle facing one another, usually around a table. Why a table? The séance table and phenomena related to it are often an integral part of a séance and have been the subject of much speculation. Is the table there for some simple, practical purpose (e.g., to rest one's hands on or to make sitters feel less exposed)? Or is there a more sinister reason: to conceal some device or trick being used by the medium?

Table-related phenomena, regardless of the controversy, are usually referred to as table tipping or table turning, but in fact during manifestation the table can make quite a variety of fascinating moves. Table tipping appears to have originated in America, then gradually spread to Britain and Europe. But tables have been used for divination since ancient times and have been occasionally somewhat troublesome to those who would use them as oracles. Ammianus Marcellinus (ca. 330–395) recounts in *The Late Roman Empire* a story of two Byzantine wannabe psychics who had been sentenced to torture for creating an oracle to divine who would be the next emperor. The table they employed was engraved with the alphabet. A ring suspended above it, when set in motion, moved back and forth across the tabletop, spelling out words in answer to questions.

Although tables continued to be used in more modern forms of divination, they were usually ordinary, unengraved tables, often folding card tables. Although I would like to say there were instances when heavy oaken dining tables were made to tilt and tip, I must admit I have not read of any.[30] Reports of table tipping tended to involve light, easily transported ones, and it was, perhaps, facts such as this that led a few to wonder about fraud. But that possibility did not seem to hamper the eagerness with which Victorian séance-goers greeted the phenomenon. That, however, was soon to change.

Michael Faraday (1791–1867), English physicist, chemist, and curious observer of unusual phenomena, wondered what was happening in the popular table-tipping episodes of his day. He theorized that the force moving the tables was the result of involuntary contractions of the muscles of sitters who wanted to see the table move, and he set out to demonstrate it.

He constructed a table with two tops, one on top of the other, held together by heavy rubber bands. The uppermost one was divided from the lower one by a layer of ball bearings. When they began their séance, the sitters were amazed when only the top table—the one in contact with their fingers—moved. The other remained immobile, indicating that it was their fingers, and not the spirits, moving the table. The same action can be suggested as being responsible for the movement of the planchette on a Ouija board.

A modern series of events that perhaps brought the phenomenon of table tipping to incredible new heights and to public attention was one known as the Philip Experiment.

The Philip Experiment

In 1972, members of the Toronto Society for Psychical Research participated in a series of experiments in Toronto to see if they could produce an entity able to manifest the phenomena of table tilting and rappings of the type that had, by many in the past, been credited to spirits. They hoped to eventually get such an entity to materialize. The team was led by Dr. A. R. G. Owen, a mathematician in the Department of Preventive Medicine and Biostatistics at the University of Toronto.

The first part of their plan seemed simple: create an identity for this entity, which included a description of physical characteristics and a name, and then agree on a background—where he was from, what kind of events he experienced, what things in his life caused him to be the person he was. It was precisely the kind of personality creation done by fiction writers when they work to bring into being a well-rounded, "alive" character.

Table Tipping

In order to encourage manifestation of the phenomenon of table tipping, sitters need to be evenly situated around the table with their fingertips resting lightly on its top surface. This action is ostensibly to keep a constant, unbroken circle of "energy" from the sitters. Feet are to be planted flat on the floor. Legs are to be uncrossed. Sitters are often asked to close their eyes. The medium (or group leader if no medium is present) asks for a spirit to make contact. If contact is successfully made, the table may begin to shudder slightly. Soon it will tip on two legs, or even tilt over on one leg and start to spin. At this point, questions can be asked and the spirit will answer by moving the table in a specific direction or by tapping out answers according to a code as directed by the leader (e.g., one tap for yes, two for no). Contrary to what one might initially think, table tipping is *not* a phenomenon of levitation, but rather one known as telekinesis or psychokinesis, in which the medium can make the table move without touching it. The ability of some mediums to move tables (and other objects) with physical contact that is apparently insufficient to explain the movement (e.g., touching with the fingertips) is referred to as parakinesis (Buckland 2006, 295).

Exhaustive research was conducted, along with the travel it entailed, and the character was created. They named him Philip Aylesworth, and they gave his life a setting. He had lived in England in the 17th century in a manor house in Warwickshire. The researchers created a backstory for him that included a love affair with a gypsy named Margo who, after being accused of casting a spell on him, was burned at the stake as a witch. Philip's tragic story ended with his death by suicide over the guilt he felt at his failure to come to Margo's defense.

The second part of the team's plan was more complicated: to enable the fictitious entity to manifest. Their first attempts to do so were failures. Then, in 1973, they had a breakthrough. By mimicking the atmosphere of the séances of old—near-darkness, a casual atmosphere, singing—they had their first manifestations: table knocking, with the sound apparently coming from nowhere!

At first astounded, the team continued to meet and to receive information from the "entity" via coded knocks. The information he gave of his life contained nothing more about him than the team knew collectively, but he added historical information about his time period that was later found to be accurate. The team theorized that it was, in fact, their collective consciousness being manifested. But they were in for a surprise. Philip, the fictitious entity, began to develop a distinct personality, with a notable mischievous bent.

Within months, the manifestations in the session room escalated to the point where, on more than one occasion, the table chased visitors who had attended to witness the phenomena. At those times, the sitters' hands were not in contact with the table. At other times, lights turned on and off without anyone in the room touching the switches. The experiments were repeated with different group members, and each group was successful in producing its own version of Philip, only with different names and identities.

What were the Philip experiments tapping in to? It could be suggested that the phenomena produced were evidence of past-life recall of one or more sitters. Or perhaps it was the manifestation of a very human, albeit amazing, ability of mental telepathy. It might, on the other hand, have been the effect of a combined and powerful psychic energy. Or maybe . . . it was contact with the beyond.

MATERIALIZATION

There is ample proof that experimental materialization . . . should take definite rank as a scientific fact. Assuredly we do not understand it. It is very absurd, if a truth can be absurd (Richet 1923, 112).

We have finally come to my most favorite topic of all. I am preoccupied with materializations not only because of my grandfather's failure to achieve them, but also because of a long-held and frustrating lack of a conceptual framework within which to consider reembodied spiritual entities.

In an attempt to provide such a framework, it may be worthwhile to view materializations as only one manifestation of the larger class of phenomena that fit under the umbrella of apparitions, a taxon that includes such occurrences as hallucinations, deathbed appearances, and collectively witnessed visions.

In psychology and parapsychology, an apparition is defined as an anomalous, quasi-perceptual experience of something that is not really there. The idea that the apparition is "not really there" suggests that all such phenomena are illusions, and in that suggestion alone, perhaps, we will see our first dilemma.

Apparitions can be clearly illusion, and some are readily admitted to be such by those who experience them. Hallucinations are usually alarming experiences that may involve not only visual effects but also, at times, powerful tactile and auditory sensations. But hallucinations can routinely be traced back to an explicable origin, whether illness, fatigue, or the ingestion of a toxic substance, and can in no way be considered evidence of a psychical experience. Other apparitions, such as the high volume of spirit appearances in Thailand after the 2004 tsunami, seem to be more complex phenomena. They are usually considered by those who experience them to be anything but illusion.

Deathbed visions, and their close cousin near-death experiences, are among the more puzzling apparitions. For one, they are typically described in a similar fashion. Secondly, deathbed visions are seen not only by the dying person, but also occasionally by onlookers.

Sir William Fletcher Barrett (1844–1925), an early psychic researcher, was one of the first to systematically study deathbed phenomena. In 1924, Fletcher's wife, an obstetric surgeon, described a patient of hers whose deathbed visions "transformed her into a state of peace and radiance before she died" (Guiley 1991, 142). Following in the footsteps of earlier psychic researchers such as James Hyslop, Fletcher made a well-ordered and thorough analysis of visions experienced by dying people, which culminated in the 1926 publication of *Death-Bed Visions*. His results, in turn, led others like Karlis Osis

(1917–1997) and, more recently, Elisabeth Kübler-Ross (1926–2004) to continue such research.

From 1959 through 1973, Karlis Osis, under the auspices of the ASPR, collected data in both the United States and India on tens of thousands of cases of deathbed visions and near-death experiences. Kübler-Ross, a Swiss-born psychiatrist whose early studies with dying patients in New York yielded an enormous volume of work, published her findings in 1969 in her watershed book *On Death and Dying.* Her theory outlining the five-stage process of grieving is the basis for much of the policy and practice at work today in the field of palliative and hospice care.

Kübler-Ross stands as one of the most famous modern theorists of the science known as thanatology, the scientific study of death. Interestingly, her theories, combined with consideration of a modern practice known as visualization, may help to explain, at least in part, the phenomenon of deathbed visions.

Visualization is a useful tool practiced by athletes and perfected by the elite among them. In visualization, the desired effect is imagined, whether it is six perfect carves in succession on the giant slalom ski course, a tennis lob whose "sweet spot" ping on the racket reverberates into the stands, or winged feet taking one across the marathon finish line. A similar kind of visualization has been extremely useful in health care, where patients, particularly those with cancer, are encouraged to picture in their minds their bodies seeking out and confronting the disease that is attacking them.

As strange and simplistic as these practices may seem, they have been found to be amazingly effective. In essence, the person mentally pictures and focuses on the desired effect, and if the projection of the image of the desire is strong enough, it can become a reality. As June Bletzer explains in her 1998 *Encyclopedic Psychic Dictionary:* "one sits and images the end result of the request in mundane form; the picture will eventually become a thought-form strong enough to manifest in the outer world" (Buckland 2006, 424).

Although the precise process is not understood, there has been speculation that the ability of some people to heal their own bodies by visualization is the result of a biochemical reaction to optimism.

Endorphins and other chemicals are released into the system, resulting in a retreat of the invading cancer cells.

Elisabeth Kübler-Ross's research led her to believe that "Dying is nothing to fear. It can be the most wonderful experience of your life."[31] Who can say that the dying person who wishes to have a preview of what the next world is like could not experience it by visualizing his or her own concept of it? Furthermore, if some people can project images strong enough to affect the body's performance, then who is to say that a person who so strongly desires a recently deceased loved one to return to say good-bye or to give a few moments' solace cannot achieve it?

Spiritualists and others who believe that the soul lives on in a physical form would give a different explanation for deathbed visitations. They might suggest that an apparition seen at or around the time of death is the loved one's astral body making its final departure from the physical body. In his 1946 book *God's Magic*, Lord Dowding, a spiritualist and senior officer in Britain's Royal Air Force during World War II, wrote: "This body is actually material, though invisible and impalpable. In a normal 'natural death,' the etheric double and higher bodies are slowly withdrawn from the physical, a process which can be seen by some clairvoyants" (Buckland 2006, 19).

This explanation may ring plausible to anyone who has ever been present at the passing of a loved one. Many of those who have describe a point after which they were aware, with a clear, unambiguous, and palpable sensation, and regardless of the physical aspect of the dying person's body, that the moment of death had occurred: the moment when their loved one's being—their loved one's soul—was no longer there. Some, perhaps, simply experience this moment more fully than others.

Group-Witnessed Visions

Sometimes referred to as "collective veridical hallucinations," these apparitions are perceived by a number of people at the same moment in time. Although some prehistoric phenomena of this kind were suggested by cave drawings and other artifacts, the first witnessed and recorded events including apparitions appear in the Bible.

Of all the instances of such apparitions in recorded history, none are more striking than the post-resurrection appearances of Jesus as chronicled in the New Testament. Although many of these appearances were to individuals, a significant number were perceived by multitudes. Post-resurrection appearances have been examined, analyzed, and explained away by successive generations of New Testament scholars and critics. Yet the stories of the documented appearances of Jesus in the weeks following his resurrection from the dead form a compelling backdrop for the consideration of apparitions as possible evidence of contact with the next world.

Days after his death on the cross, Jesus appeared to two disciples who were on their way to the town of Emmaus: "And it came to pass, that, while they communed together and reasoned, Jesus himself drew near and went with them" (Luke 24:15). Other accounts of collective sightings of Jesus after his death include the appearance on the shore before Peter, John, Thomas, and four disciples as they were fishing at the Sea of Tiberias—"But when the morning was now come, Jesus stood on the shore" (John 21:4)—and the appearance of Jesus to a multitude on the mountainside, as reported in 1 Corinthians (15:6)— "he was seen of above five hundred brethren at once."

Myriad reports of these "Christic visions" are examined by Phillip H. Wiebe in *Visions of Jesus: Direct Encounters from the New Testament to Today,* his comprehensive 1997 book on the topic (see Comments, Chapter 4, iv, for more on Christic visions).

The Phenomenon of Marian Apparitions

Miraculous apparitions have not been confined to visions of Jesus. The phenomenon of the Marian apparition has in itself provided lifetime work for the thousands who tend the shrines and produce the paraphernalia that are the aftermath of such miracles. In Lourdes alone, where the Virgin Mary appeared to a young peasant girl named Bernadette Soubirous in 1858, an average of 5 million pilgrims and tourists visit every season.[32] It is estimated that 200 million of the faithful and the curious have visited the world-famous grotto since the apparition took place, and 68 documented miraculous healings have been attributed to the curative properties of the grotto's bubbling springs.

Lourdes is not alone. The shrine in the village of Knock, Ireland, draws multitudes every year to the small church that was the site of an August 1879 apparition of Mary. The percipients numbered 15: members of the Byrne family and some of their neighbors. According to testimonials, all who witnessed the vision said the area outside the church was bathed in luminous light, like nothing they had ever seen, and they spoke of balls of brilliant, white light appearing to float through the air. Three more similar apparitions were reported within the next few months: On January 2, 1880, one was reportedly witnessed by 20 people, including the county's archdeacon; 3 nights later, another vision was seen by a large crowd, including the two police officers who had been sent to keep order; then on January 6, the same vision was seen again by a much larger crowd that included people from neighboring towns and villages.

The apparitions had an almost immediate and positive effect on the famine-ravaged region. Pilgrims who came from faraway places were appalled at the conditions under which the Irish farmers were forced to live and implemented famine relief, saving many lives with food and supplies sent from afar. A thriving tourist trade began, and the economy of Knock has not suffered since. But the success has not been solely financial. According to Swann (1996, 103) more than 300 cures have been reported at Knock since that first apparition.

Dozens more accounts such as these have been reported and documented. Readers may be familiar with Our Lady of Guadalupe, the Virgin who appeared to Juan Diego in 1531 near the Mexican village of Tlaltelolco, or the Blessed Lady of Fátima, Portugal, who made herself visible to three small shepherd children on six successive occasions between May and October and promised to reveal her power to a multitude. On the specified day of October 13, 1917, a rainy day, thousands watched in utter amazement as the clouds parted to reveal a sun shining so brightly it dazzled them. Even the disbelievers saw the sun appear to whirl like a giant pinwheel and then plunge toward the earth while red and orange streamers of light shot through the sky.

Again, whether or not these remarkable sights were witnessed or simply imagined is open to debate, but later testimony indicated that people from as far away as 30 miles reported the same sights in the sky. Even those who claim to have seen nothing at all admitted that the surrounding area, which had been soaked with rain, was suddenly and inexplicably dry.

Reports of documented and bona fide incidents of collective veridical theophanies[33] continued through every decade of the 20th century and into the new millennium: the 1930s in Belgium and France; the 1940s in the Philippines and the United States; the 1950s in Israel; the 1960s in Spain, Egypt, and Italy; the 1970s in the United States; the 1980s in Yugoslavia and Rwanda; the 1990s in Germany and the United States; and 2000 in Egypt. What can account for such visions? If they are produced by powers in the next world, what is their purpose?

Although the Catholic Church considers these apparitions apocryphal and has failed to endorse the validity of any of them, it recognizes them for their power to reinforce faith. Apparitions reported at séances were also, from the very beginning of the spiritualist movement, seen as reinforcements of faith. They were affirmations of not only the continuation of the spirit into eternal life, but also its ability to communicate with the living.

Séance Apparitions

The word "materialization" was first used in 1873 in the United States to replace the term "spirit-forms."[34] Materializations, as they occur during séances, typically produce figures that appear and disappear behind a curtain or in the dark. Reports of the materialization phenomenon describe an ethereal form floating or hovering near the sitters, appearing weightless and mobile.

In many instances, the materialized spirit appears to be little more than insubstantial vapor. In other instances, those who claim to have touched or been touched by entities during a séance report that they are warm and feel as if they are made of flesh and blood. Although many theophanies describe ethereal beings, such accounts of flesh and blood apparitions, although rare, are not inconsistent with the description of Jesus as he was when he appeared to the disciples soon after his resurrection:

And while they were telling these things, he himself stood in their midst. But they were startled and frightened and thought that they were seeing a spirit. And he said to them, "Why are you troubled, and why do doubts arise in your hearts?

"See my hands and my feet, that it is I myself; touch me and see, for a spirit does not have flesh and bones as you see that I have."

And when he had said this, he showed them his hands and his feet. And while they still could not believe it for joy and were marveling, he said to them, "Have you anything here to eat?" And they gave him a piece of a broiled fish; and he took it and ate it before them (Luke 24:36–43).

The sudden appearance of Jesus among the apostles, in a room with a door that had been locked from the inside, was astonishing. It was no wonder they doubted not only whom it was they were seeing, but that they were experiencing the vision at all. It was their faith, ultimately, that permitted them to accept it. Since the search for truth requires imagination and faith as well as science, perhaps it is enough to apply a certain *fides humana* to the whole study of apparitions. I am, nevertheless, a believer seeking knowledge, and so my journey continues. Let us return to Wiebe for some well-researched findings that inform us of St. Augustine's explanations for visions—explanations that have, for centuries, formed the basis of a classical interpretation of them.

Augustine (354–430) maintained that it was not specifically the eye that saw these apparitions, but rather the soul permitting the body, with its organs of sense (including the eye), to experience the image. Augustine fails to give us an explanation of *how* visible manifestations are achieved, but suggests that angels play a large part in their presence, although, again, he doesn't explain how the angels achieve them. In *The Care to Be Taken for the Dead*,[35] Augustine suggests that manifestations of God are mediated by angels, which is not surprising since angels, apparitions themselves, have long been accepted in various religious traditions as holding a medial position between God and man.

A Question of Angels

The entire subject of angels could occupy a lifetime of research, and it certainly deserves a nod in this discussion of apparitions. Beings that have appeared to untold numbers of people over the centuries yet that never really existed corporeally, angels are among the most mystical and least understood of spiritual concepts.

In *The Great Code,* Northrop Frye describes angels as being metaphorically associated with the sky and occupying the world above the human world. He refers to them as "creatures of God and fellow servants of man" (1982, 161), available to help humans when the need arises. St. Thomas Aquinas suggests how that help can be achieved: "Humans can become more susceptible to the influence of angelic ministries by reducing their preoccupation with sensible and corporeal objects" (Wiebe 1997, 25).

The assistance of angels would seem to be a valuable commodity for helping communication with the unseen world take place successfully, and yet séance sitters typically ask for and receive help from disembodied mortal souls, not from their angelic counterparts. If, as St. Augustine so vigorously taught, angels are closely linked with God's plan of salvation for us, then why are they not involved in man's plans to communicate with the afterworld? Perhaps, as Dionysius Exiguus (ca. 500–ca. 560) observed,[36] angels are "beings so simple that we can neither know nor contemplate them." Perhaps they are working in ways we will one day be able to understand.

The presence of angels notwithstanding, if we put together these two ways of thinking, Frye's idea of spiritual helpmates and St. Thomas Aquinas's attitude of mind, we come very close to the conditions required by mediums to produce a materialization: assistance being received from the spirit world in the first instance, and the mind being allowed to drift away from the workaday world into a more relaxed (i.e., trance) state in the second.

There is one basic difference however, between post-resurrection and Marian apparitions and the materializations produced in the medium's cabinet. There have been no records to date of Christ or God in any of his forms, Mary, or any of the saints appearing during a materialization séance. In fact, the whole question of being able to "see" God once we are dead hangs in the air of séance rooms. As one medium, Mary J. Langley, aptly put it in the *Progressive Thinker* of June 23, 1928: "We have talked to one who said he has been a spirit for 600 years, and he has never seen 'God.'"

The question that arises is whether or not Augustine's thesis about assistance from the saints also holds true for materializations through a medium, and if so, how does a medium elicit such cooperation? Are spirit guides and controls being helped by the angels? Could spirit guides and controls who do not reveal their former earthly identities be angels themselves, spirits who cannot reveal an earthly identity because they never had one? And if materializations are indeed performed using assistance from the next world, what is their purpose?

Perhaps the difficulty is not with who is assisting, but with the nature of the manifestations. We must consider the possibility, however remote in the minds of believers, that some of the mediums we have been discussing were suffering from some underlying mental conditions. Mrs. Eileen Garrett was one of the first of the "famous mediums" to accept that this might be the cause in her own case.

Mrs. Garrett and Uvani

All the psychological tests administered to Uvani and Mrs. Garrett are classified as projective techniques. It is important to mention the widely held view in the psychological community that projective measures are among the least reliable of psychological tests. One can understand, however, the reasons for investigators wishing to use them on Mrs. Garrett and her "control."

There was an underlying suspicion (or at least an acceptance of the possibility) that Mrs. Garrett was suffering from what is now called dissociative identity disorder (DID). More commonly known as multiple personality disorder, DID is a psychological condition characterized by the existence of two or more distinct personalities in one individual, each personality having its own pattern of perceiving and interacting with the environment. To qualify as DID, at least two personalities must routinely take alternate control of the individual's behavior, and there must be a loss of memory that goes beyond normal forgetfulness.

Mrs. Garrett's "Uvani" and the forgetfulness that she experienced after a visit from him could certainly qualify her as suffering from DID. Indeed, Mrs. Garrett herself was not resistant to the suggestion that the personalities she encountered while in a trance were simply figments of her own mind.

Mental disease—and the similarities between theophanies and mediums' materializations—aside, some of their differences suggest that we may be dealing with two separate phenomena.

First and foremost of these differences is the unusual structural element of materialization. There has never been a suggestion that ectoplasm, or any other substance, was ever required in order for post-resurrection or Marian appearances, yet production of ectoplasm is considered a necessity before materialization can take place.

Secondly, there is the question of environment. In the ongoing dialogues between the various mediums and the entities with whom they purport to communicate, there is repeated mention of the atmosphere in the room, the attitudes of the sitters, and cooperation from the spirit side, all of which must converge in their proper states in order to permit a materialization. Theophanies, on the other hand, have often been experienced in open, uncontrolled environments, in sometimes inhospitable surroundings, and occasionally before suspicious onlookers.

Lastly, the messages that the spirits bring into séances are vastly different in significance and scope than the messages that have been brought via theophanies. At Lourdes, Saint Bernadette relayed messages for those crippled by illness and disease; at Knock, starving people were saved; at Fátima, hundreds were cured; at Guadalupe, churches were built. And the list goes on. With the startling revelations that have been made over the years through such visitations, it is difficult to picture spirits with nothing better to do than sit on the other side of the great spirit divide just waiting to materialize a figure as comic as Bien Boa with his three curtain calls! And Bien Boa is not unique. As we have seen in previous chapters, the messages brought even by modern-day mediums tend to be completely mundane.

Let us assume for the moment, then, that we are dealing with two separate, though similar, phenomena: theophanic apparitions on the one hand and materializations on the other. Of all the scientists who researched materializations, it is perhaps Géley who gives us the most scientifically based and emotion-free reportage. Gustave Géley (1868–1924), former director of the Institut Métapsychique International in Paris, was primarily a researcher, as opposed to an investigator, of psychical events. This fact may have made it easier for him to study the phenomena objectively, without the interfering baggage that having personal relationships with the mediums may have produced.

In any event, his descriptions of materializations (and other paranormal phenomena) are among the most clearly scientific on record. Géley's experiments led him to theorize that materializations were, in fact, duplications of the medium. In an endeavor such as this, in which one mostly hears about materialized entities that closely resemble the medium, there is good reason to lean close when Géley speaks.

Doppelgängers

Géley maintained that during the trance state, a portion—sometimes small, sometimes considerable—of the medium's organism is externalized. This theory is consistent with an idea found throughout human history of the existence of a "soul double," also known by the German term "doppelgänger" ("double goer"). It is supposed that each human has an ethereal self that may be seen at various times distant from the physical self. The double appears as a solid, flesh-and-blood being and occasionally acts strangely. People have reported seeing their own doubles, but the folklore of various countries typically suggests that such apparitions are bad omens.

Géley believed that the organism known as ectoplasm is observed as "an amorphous substance which may be either solid or vaporous" that quickly becomes organic, condenses, and is seen as a distinct form, "having all the anatomical and physiological characteristics of human life" (1975b, 176). The solid form of the ectoplasm he describes as an amorphous protoplasmic mass, usually white but occasionally gray, black, or flesh colored, emanating from the natural orifices of the medium. The vaporous form he describes as a faintly luminous, visible mist that usually emanates from the region of the medium's head. A smell of ozone sometimes accompanies the appearance of ectoplasm.

Other of Géley's observations indicate that this substance, if produced at all, may simply be a natural by-product of our bodies. He reports that when it is produced, it is usually slow and deliberately mobile, in the fashion of invertebrate animals, yet able to react instantaneously to return to its host (like an invertebrate) when it is threatened, as when someone attempts to touch it. Géley himself admitted that he had never seen the materialization of a complete body, however:

> I have seen admirably modelled fingers with nails; I have seen complete hands with their bones and joints; I have seen a living head and felt the skull under thick hair; I have seen well-formed and living faces—human faces. In many instances these representations have grown under my very eyes from the beginning to the end of the phenomena (1975a, 186).

By far the most astounding of Géley's experiments were those he conducted with the Polish medium Franek Kluski at the Institut Métapsychique International in Paris in 1920, during which he was able to obtain wax molds[37] of materialized hands. In order to conduct the experiments, Géley set out near the medium a tank containing paraffin wax, which was kept at melting point by a small heating unit. When the entity (or portions thereof) materialized, it would be asked to cooperate by plunging its hand several times into the warm paraffin. The warm wax would form a thick, close-fitting skin, like a glove, that would solidify when it came into contact with the colder air. When the hand was dematerialized, the wax form was emptied, allowing the experimenter to fill it with plaster to create a mold.

The molds were verified by, among others, the head of the Identification Department of the Service of Criminology for the French National Police's Prefecture of Police. Detailed examination indicated that the molds could not have been made by any of the living people present in the room during the time of the materialization.

Of course, materializations performed onstage were more than likely the products of one of the cleverest, and most popular, tricks used by stage mediums in the 19th century: the materialization of a spirit before hundreds of pairs of eyes. Two sheets of clear glass were positioned so that one was above the stage, in front of the medium, while the other was below stage level. The sheets of glass were angled so that when a strong light was shined on an actor standing below stage level, the reflection would be projected from the lower piece of glass onto the one onstage, giving the appearance of a "spirit" materializing there.

Fraud and its implications were the downfall of even the most enterprising and resourceful of the mediums. It also proved to be just as damaging to the investigators, and W. J. Crawford, whom you have already met, is a sad and sobering example. In 1916, Crawford became involved in the investigation and subsequent promotion of a young Irish medium named Kathleen Goligher, who came from a mediumistic family. After observing Goligher produce levitations, table rappings, and ectoplasmic structures, Crawford published a paper proposing that certain well-known engineering principles such as the cantilever and mechanical leverage were responsible for producing what he called "psychic rods" constructed from ectoplasm. The paper was an overnight sensation and, given the public's hunger for anything that even hinted at spirit contact, it made him and his medium celebrities.

Sadly, Goligher's skills appeared to diminish over time, and in 1920 she was caught in a fraud by another researcher. Crawford suffered a nervous collapse and committed suicide on July 30, 1920. Before his death he sent a letter to *Light*[38] that not only affirmed his belief in the hereafter, but also made it clear that the existence of unexplained phenomena at séances mattered not at all to his expectations for the next world.

E. E. Fournier d'Albe (1868–1933), the French researcher who ultimately caught Goligher in the fraud, later published in the same magazine a letter that should have been a warning to other investigators not to underestimate the people they were investigating.

> I expected a gifted medium surrounded by her honest folks, but then came the blows. . . . The sight of the "medium" raising a stool with her foot filled me with bitter disappointment. The

simple, honest folks turned out to be an alert, secretive, trouble-some group of well-organized performers (Jolly 2006, 85).

A NEW PARADIGM

Where does all this leave us in our search for truth? We have seen how skills, whether demonstrated by talented mediums or by the disembodied spirits they commune with, have enabled various people to feel that they have contacted the mysterious "other side."

Some such manifestations may have been caused by a phenomenon similar to the deathbed experience in which an etheric double is somehow "let loose" and manages to be heard or seen by the more sensitive sitters. Still others may be the result of collective psychic energy recreating a life force that can make its presence known in concrete ways. Graham Hancock has made an exhaustive study of the supernatural and its various manifestations throughout man's history. Of these and the other extraordinary skills we have seen, he suggests: "Isn't it logical to conclude, since evolution has bestowed these peculiar and distinctive abilities on the human race, that contact with the supernatural must have offered some profound adaptive advantage to our ancestors and could, conceivably, continue to do so today?" (Hancock 2006, 281).

Psychical manifestations as they occurred during séances may have been the result of participant hallucinations. Indeed, many such situations carry with them all the hallmarks of the classic hallucination scenario: sitters in a state of altered consciousness that has been promoted by semi- to complete darkness, combined with a mood of expectancy fueled by past successes and stories of the successes of others. Could such psychical manifestations, then, be all in the mind? Richet certainly thought so, initially at least. And what, after all, is imagination but the conjuring up of some idea, whether visual or verbal? And why, even in today's modern, technical world, are people still imagining ghosts and wondering about existences beyond our reality? Perhaps we are programmed to. Perhaps there is some mechanism inherent in the human brain that makes us believe that there is more out there, more than can ever be imagined.

Many of the psychical manifestations are clearly fraud and others are suspect, and there is no doubt that a great many mediums have gone down the road of deception. But a fascinating fact is that scores of people, even after facing proof of fraud, continue to believe that what they experienced was real. So many, in fact, have exhibited this behavior that it has been given a name. "True-believer syndrome" is a term coined by M. Lamar Keene in *The Psychic Mafia* (1976) to refer to what he considers an irrational belief in paranormal events even after they have been proved fraudulent.

If the will to believe can be so strong that it withstands evidence of fraud, then perhaps some of the occurrences resulted from mass hysteria, or from the power of suggestion. Or, perhaps they really occurred. At this point, it is all speculation, and certainly worthy of ongoing study. But what kind of study?

What a pity that psychic phenomena became synonymous with fraudulent mediums such as the Golighers and others who, although possibly authentic, found it necessary to resort to fraud in order to satisfy the public's appetite for increasingly marvelous and tantalizing performances. They may have found momentary fame for themselves, but they ultimately succeeded in driving the study of psychic phenomena into the realms of the occult, perhaps forever preventing such investigations from becoming a topic of serious consideration for mainstream society. But this may not be the end of the road.

Psychic investigator William James clearly understood that our perceptions are largely determined by the context in which they are experienced. In 1890, James cited the meaningless French phrase *pas de lieu Rhône que nous*. As Nikos Logothetis suggests, you can read the phrase again and again, yet you will still be unlikely to make any sense of it.[39] While viewed in the French context and in written form, they are real words, yet the phrase as a whole is meaningless. If, however, it is suggested that you think of it as an uttered English phrase, meaning is suddenly achieved. The phrase sounds like "paddle your own canoe."

In such a light, serious scientific investigation may not, after all, be the answer. Perhaps the strange and curious phenomena that have been experienced over the centuries simply need to be viewed in a totally different context.

Chapter 5

From Séance to Screen

All the world's a stage,
And all the men and women merely players:
They have their exits and their entrances;
And one man in his time plays many parts.

—*William Shakespeare,* As You Like It

Near-materializations, voices hovering in the air around the sitters, spirit faces in photos alongside living ones, messages in red chalk. Were Dr. A. and the sitters in the Aykroyd circle simply deceived? Were other séance-goers around the world led to believe in the reality of things that did not exist? Was it all trickery, empowered by true-believer syndrome? If it was trickery, for what purpose? If it was not trickery, but in fact was created by sprits, why would they go to such lengths to let us know they are there and able to communicate? Perhaps we will never know the answers. But E. E. Fournier d'Albe's letter of warning to psychic investigators after his discovery of fraud by Kathleen Goligher may point to a possibility that has yet to be considered, with the phrase "The simple, honest folks turned out to be an alert, secretive, troublesome group of well-organized performers" being the key.

A thought has been in the back of my mind over the years as I've gone through these files and heard these stories: Whether they were believers or skeptics or somewhere in between, those who have experienced psychical phenomena have been entertained. Frightened, amused, touched, moved. And aren't these precisely the emotions we want to experience when we attend a play, or see a movie, or go to a ballet?

We want our everyday lives to be put on hold for that brief period of time and to be transported—into another town, another time, or another reality. We will, for those few minutes, permit ourselves to be bombarded with sounds and visions and ideas that may change our perceptions, our minds, perhaps our lives. Or the event may change nothing at all, except for the brief time we allow ourselves to experience *the willing suspension of disbelief.*

Géley, whom you will remember to be the creator of the wax molds of materialized hands, was, in fact, one of the greatest defenders of "private mediumistic séances," but it appears as though he thought that the greatest worth in the public displays (which he felt were like an epidemic) lay in the entertainment they provided.

> The scene . . . is always the same . . . a more or less numerous circle assembled in a totally dark room; in front and in the middle stands the hypno-organizer. In one corner of the room, on a sofa and always at some distance from the audience, is a hypnotized subject. . . . This person is usually placed behind the curtains of a dark cabinet, which latter is obviously unnecessary since the whole room is quite dark.
>
> By the side of the subject are placed some flowers, some sheets of paper and pencils on a small table, and at his feet two luminous screens, face downwards. A music box lulls the audience, while subtle perfumes pervade the room.
>
> The hypnotizer puts his subject to sleep and leaves him, and the results are patiently awaited. When the trance is deep enough (and, incidentally, when the phosphorescence of the screen is sufficiently weakened) the performance begins (Géley 1975b, 391).

Performers? Performances? Created characters? Could these phrases be keys to the phenomenon of spirit contact?

THE SÉANCE AS PERFORMANCE

The idea of the séance as performance was originally postulated by George Nugent Merle Tyrrell (1879–1952), a psychic investigator who became president of the SPR in 1945. Tyrrell spent a good deal of his life studying psychic visions, and his unique take on the topic is quite refreshing.

In his book *Apparitions,* published posthumously in 1953, Tyrrell postulated the existence of layers of unconscious creative potential in the minds of sitters. When working together, he suggested, the minds were capable of producing an "apparitional drama." Tyrrell referred to sitters as producers and stage carpenters, and any lack of success during a séance he blamed on weaknesses in stagecraft.

Stagecraft notwithstanding, it isn't inconceivable to think of séance sitters as a dedicated group of regular theatergoers who congregate weekly at the local theater to attend the performance of a monologue by one of a variety of well-known actors. In a clear departure from public theater, our audience members do not know who the performer will be, or indeed whether or not one will be appearing at all. But all the rest has a parallel in popular entertainment.

Stage, Set, and Props

Our psychic theater, of course, is the Victorian house. Home circle séances, often referred to as "amateur séances" to distinguish them from the séances people paid to attend, were usually held in the parlors of private homes, which can be linked to the stage in our performance analogy. Center stage is our séance table.

Regardless of its solidity, or whether it has ever been involved in telekinesis, the table is the area upon which much of the action, and most of the attention, is typically focused. As in theater, how audience attention is drawn to the stage is an art in itself—the art of clever lighting.

Most séances are held in the evening, a fact that has been the cause of some debate, particularly among skeptics who observed that it was easier for frauds to perform convincing feats under the cover of darkness or semidarkness. There may be a justifiable aesthetic reason, however: to provide ambiance by taking advantage of the peace and stillness that time of day provides.

Paul Allain and Jen Harvie in the *Routledge Companion to Theatre and Performance* (2006, 206) advocate a consideration of theater space in terms of how it may limit or facilitate movement and how it may affect interaction. Taking the parlor as the theater in which the séance is performed, one can see that the sitters are not free to move about.[1] When table tipping is not an objective, sitters usually hold hands to form a complete "circle of energy." Interaction during a séance—physical interaction, at least—is virtually impossible, and the skeptics pounce on this, saying that the frauds don't want their audience to see what they are doing behind the scenes!

The skeptics may have a point. Asked to remain seated, with their feet planted firmly on the floor, their eyes closed, and their hands resting on the tabletop or firmly clasped with those of their neighbors, sitters are hardly in a position to be keen observers of the situation. But we must go to the spiritualists themselves to discover their reasons for the established séance routine, and as we shall see, it is all about atmosphere.

Ambiance

The silence, or near silence, in the room, the eagerness of the audience, and the general atmosphere (room temperature, comfort level, lighting, etc.) are said to assist the medium in acquiring the altered state of consciousness necessary for a successful séance. It is the same general ambiance required for a successful performance in a theater.

Think of a modern theater just as the play begins. The house lights dim. A hush settles over the audience. A stray cough here and there. The rustle of silk. The faint smell of perfume in the air. The anticipation is palpable.

When the actors take the stage, we are no longer sitting in the theater seats, wondering how traffic will be on the drive home. We no longer care about the dirty dishes in the sink at home. We are one with the action, waiting for the tempest that we know will come. We are aware, intellectually, that the thunder is nothing more than a drumroll from the hidden orchestra pit. We know that under that black wig the actor is bald. But we are willing to be part of the moment because of a brilliant piece of staging, and, more importantly, because of our willingness to radically suspend disbelief.

Spiritualists insist that a successful séance is the coming together of willing minds. Any negativism in the room is anathema to spirit contact. Sitters must be willing to consider that they can achieve whatever it is they, as a group, are seeking.

Skeptics, according to the spiritualists, break the circle of energy. Atmosphere is important in allowing sitters, the séance audience, to be in the relaxed, introspective, meditative state that is more welcoming to spirits. As important as atmosphere is to the sitters, it is absolutely essential for the medium.

Likewise, in a modern theater, a few bored or disrespectful audience members can turn a performance into a fiasco. Muttering, coughing, or squirming attendees can distract the rest of the audience sufficiently that people in close proximity to them can never get the sense of being transported to Dunsinane or feeling the passion in the dying Aida's last breath. The effect on the performers can be every bit as profound, a fact readily attested to by anyone who has been present, as I have, when an actor refused to continue until "that gentleman with the cell phone leaves the house!"

The Players

The medium could be considered the star performer at a séance, for it is on the medium that the sitters focus their attention, and it is the medium who acts as an intermediary between the physical world and the world beyond. Whether on the stage alone delivering a monologue (as the trance medium does when his or her vocal apparatus is taken over by the etheric visitor) or sharing the stage with others (as on those occasions when the spirit guide permits other characters to come through by direct voice), the parallels between the psychic instrument and the actor are intriguing.

On the other hand, the spirit could be the star, practicing a bit of dramatization. But why? In the words of Graham Hancock, who has made a study of spirit visitations across many societies and countless time frames: "What business do they have with us? Why are they here? What do they want? What's in it for them?" (Hancock 2006, 337).

Was Bien Boa, Marthe Béraud's spirit entity, simply having some fun when he took three curtain calls, or was he testing the sense of humor of the living? Do the entities purported to have brought earth-shattering news or revelations at Fátima and Lourdes have a higher calling than those who talk to percipients about mundane matters?

FROM SÉANCE TO THE BIG SCREEN

In considering séances and their public counterparts as performance, I needed to fit together several pieces of a curious puzzle: my and my sister's recollections of séances we attended, along with accounts both written and verbal from experts in the field. And I needed to talk to the next generation, my sons Dan and Peter, about the influence that their great-grandfather, Dr. Samuel Aykroyd, had on them. They had, I was sure, gotten their inspiration for the marvelous entertainments they have created from the very source I have been writing about.

I caught up with Dan and his wife, Donna, at the same farmhouse where Dr. A.'s séances were held during the '20s and '30s. He has his own house on the property now and uses the farmhouse as an office and a guesthouse.

Warmed by a crackling fire in the huge fireplace and nourished by steaming mugs of tea and bowls of Donna's tasty, fruit-laced oatmeal, we discussed science and crop circles, childhood and memories. Then we talked about *Ghostbusters* and its genesis. It was an easy birth: one that had occurred right where we sat.

Dan Aykroyd: On the Genesis of *Ghostbusters*

"The first story I remember hearing about this stuff was from my grandmother Gougeon [Dan's grandmother on his mother's side] about sleeping in the little bedroom[2] and having covers pulled off her. She thought it was my grandfather, but the same thing had happened to him too. He was even pushed to the floor once.

"Another time, my mother was sitting in the rocking chair in that room nursing me and saw aboriginals walking in the yard. Likewise, John Gerdy, the architect who reconfigured America's concept of malls and outdoor/indoor spaces, said he heard Mississauga Indian voices outside. Come to find out, it was a running ground for the Algonquin Indians. The whole place must be charged.

"And of course there are the stories about the séances with Dr. A., my grandfather, and my father. While the sitters were talking about radio diagrams and fission and Steinmetz and stuff, they were also trying to offer some tangible evidence that something else was out there. But ultimately, what, other than entertainment, did people get out of the séances? No great, earth-shaking revelations or prophecies were made. But don't tell me that a trumpet floating around the room with voices coming out of it isn't entertainment.

"And so I combined some of these real stories and stories from the séances with my love of comedies to make a script. *Ghostbusters* was a marriage of Bob Hope, Abbott and Costello, and the Bowery Boys—the whole '30s thing—and the articles in the ASPR journal about quantum physics, parapsychology, and readers' stories.

"My original script was much darker—the work the Ghostbusters were doing was much more dangerous—but changes were made to take out some of the darker elements. I could live with those changes because the movie was always meant to be a satire, a take on the old ghost chasers with the understanding that there really is a science here. Not a pseudoscience. It's the science of paranormal exploration.

"Now there's so much on screen about this stuff—*Medium, The Unexplained, Psi Factor,* a travel show with ghost busters, and another with mediums. There are enough shows for a whole paranormal channel!

"With *Ghostbusters,* I wasn't thinking in spiritualist terms; I was thinking in paranormal terms—the science of dealing with disturbances. By mentioning things like deep-trance mediums and ectoplasm in the movie, I could address the science part of it. The characters took a defensive, coping posture in the face of the entities, not a welcoming one. I wasn't so much concerned with the spiritual aspects as with the psychology of dealing with something extra-dimensional that interrupts the land of the living.

"I, myself, haven't had any extrasensory experiences, but I've had dreams about people who have passed on and said good-bye to me. My grandpa Gougeon, for example. I had a dream that he was on our property, walking down to the lake, waving good-bye to me. When I woke up, there was a telegram saying that he had died.

"Another time, I was talking about leveling this old farmhouse and putting up my new place on the same spot. Someone said, 'It's the most perfect site on the whole property, looking south across the lake where the sun can pour into the windows. Just go for it!'

"After that conversation, I sat out on the old, dilapidated porch on a perfectly sunny day, thinking, 'Okay, Dr. A. Is it okay for me to get rid of this? Why should I spend money to restore something so run-down?' Suddenly I heard three snaps and everything vibrated like there was electricity around the whole area where I was sitting.

"At that moment, I thought, 'Scraping Dr. A.'s house away? I can't do that.' So we restored the farmhouse back to what it was in those days and put on an addition. And here we are.

"I know Dr. A. had a hand in that. He also inspired me to do *Ghostbusters* so that I could keep this place as a shrine to a great Canadian spiritualist—my great-grandfather—and to his son and grandson."

FROM SÉANCE TO THE SMALL SCREEN

As a screenwriter, actor, television scriptwriter, and paranormal investigator, my son Peter is in the unique position of seeing the effects of alternative realities in a variety of media.

He has said that he believes, as all our family does, that the universe is a result of some kind of divine intelligence. His explorations into the unknown, like mine, have been an attempt to see the universe in more or all of its variations, characteristics, and colors. His insights are a powerful justification for believing that our awareness and consciousness are filtered heavily by internal mechanisms, and that he, too, was inspired by his great-grandfather.

Peter J. Aykroyd: On *Psi Factor* and More

"While I was growing up, the bookshelves at home were not by any means filled only with stuff on spiritualism. Nor was the paranormal a subject of discussion that was foisted upon us. But there is no doubt that my father's beliefs and experiences justified and fueled both my brother's and my interest in the subject. Folks like the Amazing Kreskin and Uri Geller helped to add credibility to the subject of human potential. My mother was accepting of the whole thing, but she was more grounded and frequently would remind us that at the end of the day, we all had to attend to the things in the real world.

"My paranormal experiences at the farmhouse have been waking up to a mirror bouncing in place near the bed; hearing an odd, crunching noise from the ceiling, like crushing thick cellophane; the sound of something sliding off the roof during the winter when there was no ice or snow on the roof. Another time, I heard two females chatting happily as they went in the direction of the lake. They were speaking in what I am convinced was a North American Indian dialect or language.

"My father was a member of the ASPR, and he used to receive their quarterly journals. It was kind of boring reading for a young teen; however, it did lend an element of credibility to the whole subject and contributed to my belief in much of this stuff.

"I accepted the family history in that arena as being true and probably didn't realize that at the very least, I risked appearing to be an eccentric. For the most part, though, my friends were not skeptical and accepted the possibilities that I said the subject implied. Maybe they didn't have the heart to tell me if they thought I was being hoodwinked by my family.

"The fact that the subject of the paranormal was not taboo in the family, and was part of the constituent makeup on the Aykroyd side, opened my mind to the idea that there were alternate approaches to perceiving and understanding consciousness and reality. Even though *Ghostbusters* and *Psi Factor* would appear to be natural outcomes of this worldview, they both came after years of writing and performing comedy using material that was based on normal situations and premises rather than the supernatural. Still, the subject matter crept into my work, perhaps more as a reflection of the growing interest in that area and its use in entertainment (*The Birds, Poltergeist, The Exorcist*) than as an inevitable outgrowth of my family's history.

"My friend Chris Chacon, who was working with the Office of Scientific Investigation and Research (OSIR) [see Comments, Chapter 5, for more information], gave me the opportunity to join his group of researchers in some on-camera investigation work, which resulted in my appearing with Chris on various news shows including *Dateline, National Geographic Explorer, Hard Copy,* and *Eye to Eye with Connie Chung.*

"Upon my initiation into OSIR, I was allowed to go to active locations where I witnessed objects flying through the air, doors closing inexplicably, water spurting out of plumbing fixtures, a can rolling across the floor by itself that was accompanied by a head-and-shoulders shape seen on an Aegema heat-sensitive camera. I also saw an ashtray fly off of a shelf and break into uniform cubes that landed on the floor in a perfect circle.

"I have read the transcribed notes of [my great-grandfather's] séances, and I was particularly intrigued by the repeated communications with someone who called himself Blue Light. When I was 5, I had a dream wherein I was near the presence of blue light that emitted what I can only describe as infinite love. I didn't want to leave the dream, but I was only there for what seemed a moment in time.

"It was one of the most, if not the most, profound experiences I have ever had. You might say it was my first paranormal experience, and perhaps my first look at the underlying substance of the universe. During and after the dream, I got the distinct impression that it was from whence I came and is to where I will ultimately return. This impression has remained unaltered in the 45 years since. And even though the intensity of the dream itself has faded somewhat, my memory of it as having been intense and profound has never dwindled."

And This Is What Dr. A. Had a Hand In

Ghostbusters, released in the United States on June 8, 1984, was written by Dan Aykroyd and Harold Ramis and starred Bill Murray, Dan Aykroyd, Harold Ramis, Rick Moranis, Sigourney Weaver, Annie Potts, and Ernie Hudson. The $30 million movie grossed approximately $240 million in the United States and more than $50 million abroad, making it the most successful film the year it was released and the most successful comedy of the 1980s.

Psi Factor[3] was a phenomenal television series cocreated by Peter Aykroyd and Chris Chacon and hosted by Dan Aykroyd. With an emphasis on actual cases investigated by the OSIR, this dramatic thriller series produced 88 episodes that are still being broadcast in more than 30 countries worldwide.

EPILOGUE

The universe that is opened up when considering *A History of Ghosts* is full of fascinating observations, mysteries, and complex issues. Dr. A. was a man of science, but he had the open-mindedness to accept that science may not have all the answers. He acknowledged that it was not necessary for there to be scientific evidence for people to give themselves permission to believe in certain spiritual phenomena. I have chosen to dwell on a small fraction of these phenomena—in my judgment, an important fraction.

When I first read Dr. A.'s journals from start to finish, I was disappointed by the lack of evidentiary weight for the survival hypothesis, which is at the core of spiritualism.

But after looking at all the evidence presented throughout this book, a jury, were this a case being made in a civil court, might say that, "on the balance of probabilities," something survives bodily death. If there were evidence enough for a jury to say "it is certain," then we would have to conclude that if one person survives, all survive. It is the "one white crow" again!

What is it, however, that survives bodily death? The human personality? The soul? The spirit?

What would we want to survive? The person in adolescence who doesn't know much? The person in decrepit old age who really isn't good for anything anymore?

Dr. Carl Jung did some very clear, original thinking about this, and in a remarkably lucid essay, he posited that the human consciousness survives bodily death. This resonates well with his widely accepted

theories on the nature of the collective human psyche, and also resonates with the various tantalizing glimpses of the unexplained that *A
History of Ghosts* has brought us.

A reinforcement of this postulation appeared in an article by Lar-
issa MacFarquhar published in the *New Yorker* on February 12,
2007, describing the work of two academic philosophers, Paul and
Patricia Churchland, professors of philosophy at the University of
California, San Diego. They postulate that time and space are abstrac-
tions and yet, at the same time, they are realities, because we experience time and we experience space. They believe that human
consciousness has an infinite dimension, as well.

Although the infinite dimensions of time, space, and human consciousness are beyond the capacity of the mind to fully understand, I
will join the chorus. I will take my stand with Dr. Jung, the Church-
lands, and others and say, "Human consciousness survives bodily
death."

But this is not quite right. I would add "aspect" to the statement:
"Some aspects of the consciousness of humans survive bodily death."
Thoughtography, the ability to psychically "burn" images from one's
mind onto surfaces, explains that in spirit photography, spirits always
appear in the prime of life, dressed in their Sunday best. I believe that
we are able to tap into part of the infinite human consciousness during
a particular time and place—not to the totality of the human consciousness.

Perhaps a survival hypothesis is at odds with science. If our brains
have been given this overwhelming desire to explain the inexplicable,
surely there is more to the natural world than we can see or feel. If we
are going to even consider the possibility that something other than
just the natural world may be at work, then surely we must consider
what that other world might be and what our relation to that world
will be when we die.

This leads us directly to consideration of God and heaven. I will
resist the temptation to indulge in vain discussion of the philosophies
triggered by these two words.

Often during the séances of Dr. A.'s circle, the sitters would ask the
spirits if they had seen God. The same question was asked many times

in the open literature of spiritualism, and the answer in every case was no.

I hope that God and the concept of God are ineffable. In Sunday school, we were taught that God is omniscient, omnipotent, and omnipresent. I will leave it there.

Heaven, paradise, and Valhalla are all words that relate to an invisible space full of unknowns. The study of this subject reveals that heaven is a very subjective concept. To the Eskimo, heaven is a perpetually warm place. To the Bedouin, heaven is a sheltered oasis surrounding a perpetually flowing stream.

And so, as we near the end, I turn to the sacred literary work.

> Whosoever shall not receive the Kingdom of God as a little child, he shall not enter therein (Mark 10:15).

Whether we consider the kingdom of God to be a present concept of the present time or to be of some future time, it is clear that Jesus was exhorting us to emulate the attitude of a toddler.

And what is that attitude?

Trust.

So in this epilogue, and as I get ready to "shuffle off this mortal coil," an attitude of trust prevails.

ACKNOWLEDGMENTS

My principal research assistant throughout this project has been Lindsay Ann Cox, whom I found at Queen's Theological College in Kingston in 2003. She was completing undergraduate courses in comparative religion, and subsequently has gone on to earn postgraduate degrees in theology. Scholarly, prompt, and a prodigious worker, she earned my gratitude for her extraordinary assistance. Kim Steacy, my faithful administrative assistant (much more than a secretary), has helped me in so many ways over these lo 17 years, starting with the tedious job of reading all 83 of Dr. A.'s handwritten journals and producing a typescript.

Barbara Sears, longtime research assistant to Pierre Burton, gave me valuable advice in the beginning with regard to the possible structure of the work. She in turn led me to the Writers' Union of Canada.

The Writers' Union of Canada maintains a roster of professional writers who are available to assist others who are trying to complete a manuscript and need collaboration or a "ghostwriter" (an unfortunate appellation). The Writers' Union turned up Angela Narth, without whom there would be no *History of Ghosts*. Angela, a published author and a literary reviewer and critic for national newspapers, caught my mind and my voice, and, using my six drawers of research notes and my extensive library, together with numerous interviews, she assisted me in completing the manuscript in its present form.

I had 17 replies to my appeal for a collaborator. Among my unstated specifications were that the person should be a male and should live close to my place of writing. In telephone interviews with Angela, I learned that she was from Winnipeg (far away), the site of Dr. Glen Hamilton's wonderful work, that she was originally from near Ottawa—in fact, Gatineau Quebec—and that she was a practicing Roman Catholic, which meant we could dialogue easily. She was the clear first choice, and on top of all this, her name was Angela, and I knew the definition of "angel" to be "God's messenger."

In a section of acknowledgments, it's not usual to include an ephemeral personage, but I have made reference in the text to the Holy Spirit, sometimes referred to as the Pneumatos. "Pneumatos" means "one who breathes in," and in this case, it's the breathing in of inspiration, and, again characterizing this in another way, it is the "still, small voice" that speaks to me when I am worrying through what to write. I suppose for better or worse, one might refer to this as my muse.

Lorraine Heléne Gougeon, my wife of 58 years, would so often come to me and say, "What are you doing?" And I would say, "I'm writing." She would say, "No, you're looking out the window." And I would say, "Well that's true, but you know I'm thinking, and thinking has to precede writing." She would encourage me to continue, to keep up my work.

Shelley Sweeney is head of Archives and Special Collections at the University of Manitoba Libraries. The University of Manitoba and the University of Waterloo in Ontario are the two places where material relating to psychic phenomena in Canada is nucleating. The University of Manitoba has graciously agreed to accept Dr. Samuel Augustus Aykroyd's original journals in both handwritten and typescript forms. They will be on deposit for future generations to refer to on any detailed subject that might be of interest to researchers.

Toward the end of this project, my vision unfortunately deteriorated to 10 percent (legally blind), and the services of Anne Chiarelli, RN, specialist in low vision for the Canadian National Institute for the Blind, have been extraordinarily helpful in assisting me in coming to terms with this new reality.

The skill and experience of the Rodale editorial staff under the supervision of Shannon Welch contributed greatly to the evolution of the manuscript at every stage.

COMMENTS

This additional information supports, in one way or another, the text within each chapter. We did not wish to be pedantic, but we realize that with a subject so vast and so controversial, there will be numerous unexplored avenues that readers may wish we had taken. The information, along with our comprehensive list of sources, should enable those who are interested to pursue any number of explorations into the vast and fascinating world of spirit communication.

Included in these comments and the following endnotes is mention of a number of additional personages who are not discussed in full form in the text, where the mountain-peak mediums tower above the less-prominent ones. Because the greatest mediums were extraordinary psychic instruments (EPIs), they were experimented and reported upon and, in a sense, discovered. Like movie stars plucked from service behind drugstore counters to loom larger than life on stage and screen, the names of these EPIs have been enshrined. Although an exhaustive summary would undoubtedly include many, many more EPIs, we have chosen to concentrate on a limited number in the text and to nod in these notes, as a kind of honorable mention, to a few others.

Within the spiritualist movement, there must also have been hundreds of credible mediums who were operating in many home circles. Their names are lost because their handlers did not take the trouble to describe their activities. Walter Ashurst would surely have been one of those had it not been for Dr. A.'s curiosity and scientific disposition. Although we do not know the names of the others, there is no doubt that their work was of great assistance to those involved in the study of psychic phenomena.

CHAPTER 1. GHOSTS AT HOME: THE HOME CIRCLE

i. A cast of featured spirit regulars appeared. There is something fascinating about the omnipresence of some of the spirit visitors: Sir Arthur Conan Doyle, David Livingstone, and Walter T. Stead seemed to be favorites, appearing again and again at various unrelated séances throughout the world. Almost like famous film stars, audiences couldn't seem to get enough of them at the height of their popularity. The pirate who called himself John King (presumed to be the spirit of the Welsh buccaneer Henry Morgan) was also a regular, along with a number of his relatives.

King/Morgan's daughter, Katie King, became famous in her own right and evolved as time went on, something that the other spirits did not seem to do. It was said that in her early séances, she spoke with a common accent and in a shrill voice. Several years later, after working as Florence Cook's spirit guide, she became much more socially refined.

ii. Florence Cook (1856–1904) was a British medium who became famous for spirit materializations, but was later exposed as a fraud. At a time when most séances were being held in almost complete darkness, Florence Cook managed to materialize Katie King with the lights on, but over time her séances became more like theatrical spectacles than spiritual sittings. Cook would be tied hand and foot in the medium's cabinet, then Katie would appear and float around the room, smiling, nodding, and looking, as it happened, very much like the lovely medium herself. When the spirit at last disappeared, the cabinet doors would be opened to reveal an exhausted but still securely tied Florence sitting in the cabinet where the sitters had last seen her.

When she was still in her teens, Florence managed to attract the attention of the famed British physicist Sir William Crookes (1832–1919), one-time president of the Royal Society.[1] Despite Florence's being exposed in numerous incidents of fraud, Crookes's support of her seemed undaunted. He employed only the most basic antifraud measures and ignored instances where fraud was obvious to other sitters, such as occasions when a sitter would grab hold of a spirit only to find when the lights came back on that he or she was holding Florence's hand, and times when a sitter would sneak a peek into the cabinet when the spirit was manifesting and find the medium's chair empty. Crookes explained away the "misunderstandings" by claiming that Cook was somnambulistic and never intended to deliberately deceive sitters.

Crookes began intensive testing of Florence in 1874, when he was 42 and she was just 18 years old. He published a series of reports outlining his findings, but they met with much derision. It was whispered that the confused Crookes was completely captivated by the comely but conniving Cook. Although he has remained somewhat of an icon among fellow psychic investigators, Crookes never regained much of a reputation for sanity after that.

iii. The Reverend George Vale Owen (1869–1931) was a British-born ordained minister who began to experience psychic manifestations while in his forties. Owen felt impelled to produce a book of inspired writings that purportedly came through his deceased mother and other spirits. *Life Beyond the Veil,* a five-volume account of life after death, was published in the early 1920s. Its publication and the resulting furor in the Anglican Church led to Owen's resignation. A lifelong friend of Doyle's, Owen became interested in the spiritualist movement and eventually took the role of pastor at a London spiritualist church. He spent the remainder of his life lecturing and writing about spiritualism.

CHAPTER 2. GHOSTS ABROAD: THE INTERNATIONAL STAGE

i. William Eglinton (b. 1857) was a young boy in London when he discovered his psychic abilities. His mediumship, which had its zenith in the late 1870s, was largely one of professional stage performances in various parts of the world, including South Africa, India,

Denmark, Germany, and Russia.[2] Eglinton's psychic career echoed that of D. D. Home's in that

> his séances were usually held in the light, and he always agreed willingly to any proposed tests. A further point of similarity was the fact that his results were observed and recorded by many eminent men and by good critical witnesses (Doyle 1926, 2:44).

Over a period of 12 years, Eglinton was tested by members of the Society for Psychical Research, by Charles Richet, and by a magician by the name of Harry Kellar, who said of his session with the young stage medium: "I went as a sceptic, but I must own that I came away utterly unable to explain by any natural means the phenomena that I witnessed" (Shepard 2002, 283).

One of Eglinton's most astounding feats was the performance of materializations in the open air. An account by Epes Sargent, reported in his book *The Scientific Basis of Spiritualism*, published in Boston in 1881, elaborates: "Mr. Eglinton lay on a garden bench in plain sight. We saw the bodies of four visitors who formed themselves from a cloud of vapour and then walk about robed all in purest white, upon lawns where no deception was possible." According to the reports, Eglinton was in full sight throughout the materialization, and there was no possibility of an accomplice entering the area without being seen.

The March 22, 1878, issue of *The Spiritualist* reported a séance held on March 16, 1878, at the London home of Mrs. Makdougal Gregory during which Eglinton transported himself from the séance room into a room on the floor above. The act was close to a carbon copy of the one performed by D. D. Home almost 10 years before.

ii. William Stainton Moses (1839–1892) was among the earliest British spiritualists. Discovering his psychic powers at the age of 32, William found he was able to levitate, manifest apports, and produce spirit lights. The majority of his manifestations tended to be physical in nature, including musical sounds made without instruments and scents, such as musk and newly mown hay. He is best known for automatic writing, which he was able to produce without going into the trance state. Forty-nine spirits communicated through him in this way, including three who called themselves the imperator, the rector, and the preceptor. His manifestations never garnered the kind of negative press or accusations of fraud that those of other mediums did, and his philosophies and spirit communications were shared with the world in his four published books.

Current research examines ESP functioning in an altered state of conciousness. New case reports of personal experiences include premonitions of 9/11, as well as reports bearing on the survival hypothesis from a survey of near-death experiences, apparitions, awareness of death at a distance, and unusual experiences in the presence of dying.

The ASPR library and archives constitute a leading repository of significant works of American and scientific history, including the earliest history of psychology and psychiatry in the United States; early studies of multiple personality disorder; works chronicling the evolution of mind-body medicine; and publications on Eastern and Western religious philosophy, the mental healers movement, and American visionary traditions. They include rare manuscripts that date back to the 1600s, case reports, correspondence (by William James, Henry James, W. B. Yeats, Sir Arthur Conan Doyle, Harry Houdini, and Upton Sinclair, to name a few), and thousands of periodicals, books, and pamphlets—the majority out of print and extremely rare. In addition to works of scientific value, the ASPR archives contain rare examples of fine art, including "spirit" drawings and photographs and a significant collection of Shaker manuscripts relating to their members' visionary experiences. The archives also include a continuously growing collection of audio- and videotaped interviews and lectures by leading contemporary scientists. The library is constantly growing as new collections are added. The archives are a priceless, irreplaceable treasure that must be preserved and protected for future generations.

In recent years, the ASPR has participated in groundbreaking exhibitions of rare photographs at the Metropolitan Museum of Art in New York City and the Maison Européenne de la Photographie in Paris. It also participated in exhibitions at the Hammer Museum in Los Angeles; the Shelburne Museum in Shelburne, Vermont; the Bard

Graduate Center for Studies in the Decorative Arts, Design, and Culture in New York; and the Drawing Center in New York.

The ASPR is in the process of developing a special exhibit from its archives that was initially funded by a grant from the National Endowment for the Arts.

With sufficient support, the ASPR will protect and preserve its existing historical legacy. The society will also continue to stimulate modern thinkers representing a variety of mainstream disciplines, including physics, psychology, biology, medicine, religion, and philosophy. The ASPR will continue its tradition of sponsoring top-level, interdisciplinary scientific conferences with the best minds in their fields. It will facilitate among leading scientists conversations about the nature of reality that incorporate a century of evidence from psychical research and modern research from mainstream science—evidence that suggests an interdependence and connectedness of conscious beings and the physical world.

The ASPR is a primary contemporary force for advancing our understanding of the far-reaching scientific and spiritual questions raised by the mysteries of consciousness. The ASPR is a 501(c)(3) tax-exempt nonprofit organization that has served public and professional audiences for more than a century.

iii. Sir Arthur Conan Doyle led a very public private life. In the years following his conversion to spiritualism, Doyle spent much of his time attempting to educate the public about the need for ongoing study of the phenomena associated with spirit communication. His life after 1916 was spent almost exclusively on the promotion of spiritualism, and his numerous speaking engagements took him around the world. During these very public performances, Doyle routinely showed projected images of photos taken during séances, allowing his audiences a glimpse into what Doyle felt was the unseen but parallel world of the beyond.

CHAPTER 4. EXTRAORDINARY SKILLS

i. Leonora E. Piper (1857–1950) was an American from Boston who discovered at the age of 27 that she had psychic powers. Her control, who from the beginning identified himself as Dr. Phinuit, purported to be the spirit of a deceased physician from France, although records indicate that Dr. Phinuit neither spoke French nor had much knowledge of medicine.

Mrs. Piper came to the attention of researcher William James, who pronounced her genuine after testing her over a period of 18 months. Spirits with deep men's voices spoke through her when she was in a trance, and she had no recollection of what had transpired once she left the trance state. Piper was a mental medium (like Walter Ashurst) who did not manifest any physical phenomena such as table tipping or materializations, but worked strictly as a conduit for verbal communication from the spirits.

Over the years of her mediumship, between 1885 and 1915, she was investigated at one time or another by a host of well-known and well-respected investigators. In addition to James, she was tested and pronounced genuine by Sir Arthur Conan Doyle, Sir Oliver Lodge, and, eventually, by Dr. Richard Hodgson. At first suspicious of Piper's ability to give accurate details of deceased strangers while she was in a trance state, Hodgson devised some extreme measures to prevent fraud during the 88 sittings he had with her. He hired detectives to follow her to ensure that she was not picking up information about the deceased people. He had the staff at the house where she was staying changed regularly so they would not become friendly with and try to help her. He prevented Piper from reading newspapers for 3 days prior to each sitting so that she could not pick up any information that might influence what she would say in the trance state. His precautions appear to have been prompted, at least in part, by the controversy that was raging (and rages still) about whether mediums are communicating with spirits or mentally receiving telepathic messages from the sitters. A very candid opinion in this regard is from Dr. Hodgson himself. In a statement published in the 1897 *Proceedings of the Society for Psychical Research,* he makes it clear what he believes is occurring:

> I cannot profess to have any doubt but that the "chief communicators" . . . are veritably the personalities that they claim

to be; that they have survived the change we call death, and that they have directly communicated with us whom we call living through Mrs. Piper's entranced organism. Having tried the hypothesis of telepathy from the living for several years, and the "spirit" hypothesis also for several years, I have no hesitation in affirming with the most absolute assurance that the "spirit" hypothesis is justified by its fruits and the other hypothesis is not.[3]

ii. Yet another Walter? Among the numerous Walters whose names invariably spring up during discussions of research into psychic phenomena we must include Walter J. Meyer zu Erpen, president of the Survival Research Institute of Canada (SRIC), a charitable organization researching survival of the human personality after death. Walter is the author of a number of articles on survival research. He has collected a wealth of information on Dr. Glen Hamilton's work in Winnipeg and is frequently called upon to give lectures and presentations on various aspects of the work of the SRIC.

iii. Madame Helena Petrovna Blavatsky (1831–1891) was born in the Ukraine. Madame Blavatsky, or HPB, as she preferred to be called, came out of the spiritualist movement, where she had exhibited manifestations such as levitation and automatic writing. A talented musician and artist, she was an unorthodox blend of madcap traveling circus performer and serious psychic. As the former, she confirmed many of the beliefs about public mediums. As the latter, she neutralized much of the suspicion previously held about mediums and brought many people to new understandings of the spiritual world. A sort of early hippie, she is considered by many to be the inspiration behind what we now view as New Age belief systems.

HPB spent much time in Tibet and had a lifelong desire to synthesize Eastern and Western religions with manifestations of the science of her day. There were reports that her somewhat erratic powers were feeble at times and that she helped them out by resorting to trickery. Her reputation as yet another likely fraudulent medium stuck until 1874, when she met Colonel Henry Steel Olcott, an American lawyer, freelance journalist, and Civil War veteran. Within a few weeks, he was supporting her in a little apartment in New York. One year later, they were living together in Manhattan and had joined a group of like-minded people to explore unexplained events in nature and human latent psychic abilities. Together they formed the Theosophical Society in 1875, a group that in turn led some members to form the Order of the Golden Dawn.

Although the Theosophists conducted their search for the truth in practices such as vegetarianism, meditation, astrology, and astral travel, the Order of the Golden Dawn inserted occult rites and practices into their belief systems. Among the most prominent members of Golden Dawn were William Butler Yeats,[4] Algernon Blackwood,[5] and Florence Farr, an actress who assisted the order in developing rites that included a variety of theatrical elements. The Golden Dawn persisted for a few decades, but internal bickering finally led to its demise, with members either losing interest or branching off into various splinter groups.

The Theosophists, however, remained a strong force in the spiritual movement, and indeed, Theosophy became a worldwide phenomenon with specific and long-lasting influence on art. Among the Theosophist artists was Piet Mondrian, a Dutch painter who joined the Theosophists in 1909 and spent his career pursuing a way to render on canvas the universal truths of spirit, force, and matter, the three basic Theosophy principles. Russian-born painter Wassily Kandinsky was also a Theosophist. His works displayed the Theosophist notion of "thought vibrations," the idea that works of art are shaped by vibrations of the artists' thoughts.

iv. Modern-day Christic visions: Phillip Wiebe's firsthand interviews[6] identified some startling, although unverifiable, stories of modern-day apparitions. In 1958, John Occhipinti, now a counselor, evangelist, and musician living in Scranton, Pennsylvania, experienced what he reported as an encounter rather than a vision. He was tending to his college roommate, Nathan, who had come down with a virus. As he was praying for Nathan one night, he opened his eyes to find a stranger standing about 8 feet away, beside Nathan's bed. The figure appeared as Jesus is portrayed in pictures, with a long, flowing robe, long hair, and a beard. Although the figure appeared out of nowhere, it seemed to be solid flesh and blood, like an ordinary person. John says he knew the figure was Jesus not so much because of how he looked, but because of how it felt to be in his presence. The figure slowly reached out and placed his hand on the sleeping Nathan's forehead, then disappeared. A moment later, Nathan got out of bed and announced that he had felt a soothing hand on his forehead and had been cured.

Robin Wheeler, of Abbottsford, British Columbia, experienced a series of visions in 1984 of a frightening creature that was shortly joined by a sackcloth-clad figure whom Wheeler assumed to be Jesus. Each time the frightening creature approached Wheeler, he managed to use the tie around Jesus's waist to subdue it. The visions finally stopped when, one night, Wheeler was unable to subdue the monster himself and begged for Jesus's help. He accepted this as a sign of the need for Christ in his life and promptly returned to the religion he had forsaken.

In 1993, a woman named Marian Gallife was living in London with her husband and their children. Marian had fallen into a dreadful depression after the sudden death of the couple's 18-year-old son, Joe. Marian had turned against God for what had happened. One evening, while she was fully awake, Jesus appeared to her in the midst of a light brighter than anything she had ever seen before. As she reached out to touch him, he gradually began to disappear until only his hand was visible. She gazed into the hand and could see off in the distance a grassy hill where Joe and three other children were running toward her. With prompting from Jesus, she realized the children were her own children who had died while young, and who now appeared at the ages they would have been had they lived. Marian immediately recovered from her depression and announced to everyone who would listen that Joe was alive and that they would be together one day.

INFORMATION ON SOME ADDITIONAL EXTRAORDINARY PHENOMENA

Because of the sheer volume of material we encountered in researching this book, we were unable to include discussion of a number of additional extraordinary phenomena even though they have been studied and their incidence recorded. Phenomena such as weeping statues, paintings that ooze blood, crop circles, visits by fairies and little people, documented appearances of lake monsters and high-altitude snow creatures, UFO sightings, and alien abductions have all been featured in the panoply of events experienced by humans over the centuries, and many individuals have made a conscious effort to investigate them.

Among those whose work might interest readers is Charles Fort (1874–1932), an American journalist who is often called the father of modern phenomenism. After an inheritance he received at the age of 42 enabled him to quit working as a journalist, Fort began collecting and cataloguing thousands of reports of unexplained and unusual phenomena. Most of this material he found by poring over scientific and popular journals in the British Museum and the New York Public Library.

The collecting proved to be so absorbing that Fort dedicated the remaining years of his life to it. He never attempted to explain the phenomena, but used the examples to point out the limitations of scientific knowledge. He published his research in four separate books: *The Book of the Damned* (1919), *New Lands* (1923), *Lo!* (1931), and *Wild Talents* (1932).

Among the unexplained phenomena that Fort found most fascinating was spontaneous human combustion, an event also known as auto-incineration. In typical cases of spontaneous human combustion (if any such sensational events could be considered typical), human bodies are burned to ashes by sudden, intense heat that has no apparent source. In many cases, flammable objects in the body's immediate vicinity, such as furniture or structures, are not even scorched. Although incidents of spontaneous human combustion continue to be reported even today, modern science has no explanation for them.

Fort's work eventually caught the interest of others, and in 1965 the International Fortean Organization was founded. Based in Arlington, Virginia, it sponsors investigative teams and provides programs for education and research. As yet there is no generally accepted theory linking these phenomena with any of the psychic occurrences we surveyed in Chapter 4. The subject of unexplained phenomena nevertheless continues to be an area holding great fascination for the general public, many of whom appear to have a healthy appetite for attempting to solve the apparently unsolvable.

CHAPTER 5. FROM SÉANCE TO SCREEN

A word about the Office of Scientific Investigation and Research (OSIR) and my son Peter's role vis-à-vis the agency: The organization is a US-based private agency that was created in the 1940s. Its special division, which went under the title of Phenomenology, focused entirely on the investigation, researching, and application of anomalous phenomena, occurrences that the general public tends to consider to be paranormal, supernatural, or metaphysical. With unlimited resources and budgets, hundreds of trained scientists and researchers, and specialized global networks of logistics and communications, the division was able to monitor, contain, and conduct ongoing investigation, research, and experimentation on every type of supernatural and anomalous phenomena imaginable, all while maintaining a clandestine status.

In the early 1990s, the OSIR created a Public Affairs Department for the stated purpose of disseminating information on paranormal phenomena by utilizing an objective scientific approach, rather than one that relied on either blind belief or skepticism. A handful of veteran field operatives and case workers were declassified and installed in the Public Affairs Department to interact directly with the media and general public. This created a massive surge in interest from media and news organizations desiring to get a glimpse not only into the world of such an elite organization, but also into "documented" accounts of phenomena that had, to date in Western science, been considered too elusive to document.

Among the operatives representing the agency during this exciting time was Chris Chacon, who had already been involved in thousands of cases dealing with all types of phenomena, including possessions and miracles, UFO close encounters and abductions, miscellaneous

anomalies (worm rainstorms, time/space distortions, etc.), haunts/pol-
tergeists and witchcraft, encounters with strange creatures, and para-
psychological phenomena such as psychokinesis, clairvoyance,
reincarnation, and astral projection.

Inundated with media requests and desiring to make their scientific
approach less cumbersome as well as more compelling and entertaining to the general public, the Public Affairs Department
approached Peter, who was brought on as an "unofficial spokesperson" for the agency. Although he did not go through the OSIR's
rigorous training program, Peter was granted an exceptional security
access status and allowed to observe several unofficial case investigations, as well as to serve as spokesperson for the agency and its
research. Peter's levity and brilliant insights added to Chacon's showmanship as they educated the world about scientific explorations into
the paranormal and anomalous phenomena.

The OSIR went by its public name from 1990 through 2000, but
subsequently closed its Public Affairs Department, terminating
all contact with the general public and apparently dissolving the
organization.

ENDNOTES

CHAPTER 1

1   This ability to see through the skin to the affected organs was not
    unique to Davis. The remarkable gifts of Kentucky-born Edgar Cayce
    (1877–1945) to envisage internal human physiology and to diagnose
    medical problems at a distance are well documented. Barely literate in
    his early life, Cayce was known as the Sleeping Prophet for his ability to
    recite the contents of books he had not read, but only laid his head on
    while sleeping.

2   Slate writing is the ability that some mediums have of facilitating
    writing by the spirits on slates that have been bound together face to
    face.

3   Etta Wriedt was one of the many mediums who was later consulted
    by Canadian prime minister William Lyon Mackenzie King. Her first
    séance for him was held in 1932 at his summer residence at Kingsmere
    in the Gatineau Hills, the PM's summer residence in Quebec.

4   Trumpet séances are those in which the spirit speaks through a conical
    device similar to a cheerleader's bullhorn. Séance trumpets are usually
    made of copper or a light copper alloy. When being used by a spirit for
    communication, the trumpet appears to levitate in the air above the
    heads of the sitters.

5   Also referred to as the "control," the spirit guide is, according to
    Buckland (2006, 382), the entity from the spirit world who acts as a
    gatekeeper or as a master or mistress of ceremonies, contacting other
    spirits and arranging their access to the medium. A control typically
    remains permanently with the medium.

6   Most séances are held over 1- or 1½-hour sittings. Trumpet séances tend
    to be longer, between 2 and 2½ hours long.

7   I have coined the term here to refer to what was described as a state of
    energy exhaustion that Carol Andrew was experiencing. In October
    1921, the other spirit visitors explained that his energy was being
    absorbed, that soon he would be no more and go completely out of
    existence as an individualized being. His appearances at Dr. A.'s séances
    ceased shortly thereafter. The other spirits did not seem to either trust
    or admire Carol Andrew.

8   Most of the Sydenham séances were held in the original farmhouse, but some were held in Elsam cottage. "Elsam" is a combination of the names "Ellen Jane," Dr. A.'s wife, and "Samuel," and it was built in 1922 by Dr. A.

9   The device referred to as a medium's cabinet can be anything from a simple, curtained-off area in the séance room to a wooden structure similar to a large cupboard with doors. The cabinet is an important part of séance manifestations because it apparently serves to condense the available energy into a confined space, thus strengthening and focusing it. Dr. A.'s circle never used a cabinet for its séances.

10 Although Hamilton was usually known as Glen, he was frequently called TGH.

11 Telekinesis is the movement of objects without any physical contact by the medium. It is sometimes referred to as psychokinesis.

12 Although the trance state sometimes requires an external stimulus such as hypnotism or meditation, it may also occur spontaneously, as in the cases of Elizabeth M. and Walter Ashurst.

13 A trance personality is the manifestation of the voice, sometimes along with a clairvoyant image, of a deceased person.

14 Walter King claimed to be the brother of Katie King, a well-known trance personality who had been appearing regularly through the famous medium Florence Cook (see Comments, Chapter 1, ii).

15 The cabinet used in Dr. Hamilton's séances was a three-sided wooden structure with one lockable door and two windows that could be boarded over from the inside when necessary.

16 Although "ectoplasm" is the commonly accepted term for this substance, Dr. Hamilton's notes consistently refer to it as "teleplasm." It is believed Hamilton used the term to suggest that manifestation was created by the medium's thoughts.

17 Walter, the spirit control, always announced when a materialization was imminent.

18 Despite searches done through various sources, confirmed dates of birth and death for Thomas Lacey have not been found. It is known, however, that the séances held under his auspices took place between 1931 and 1951. One could assume then, that he was born no later than 1910 or 1911. Date of death, of course, is more difficult to guess.

19 What is with the ubiquitous Walters? Walter Stead was a frequent spirit visitor at séances; Dr. A.'s medium was Walter Ashurst; the controls for both Dr. Hamilton and Thomas Lacey were named Walter, as was the control for Margery Crandon (see Chapter 4). There may be more to this than meets the eye.

20 William T. Stead was a British journalist, editor, and psychic whose writing was an ardent promotion of spiritualism. *After Death, or Letters from Julia* was a diary written by Stead through automatic

writing from a young girl apparently communicating from the spirit world. In an ironic twist of fate, Stead, whose newspaper articles warned repeatedly of the dangers of icebergs to trans-Atlantic ships, was one of the more than 1,500 passengers lost when the *Titanic* went down on April 15, 1912.

CHAPTER 2

1   Home was a consumptive. He suffered all his life from the rampant 19th-century ailment tuberculosis.

2   Doyle's knighthood was conferred not for his literary prowess, but rather for his medical work with the Langman Field Hospital in Bloemfontein and for his patriotic vindication of the British army for its activities in the Boer War. After he retired from medicine, he became very involved with the Congo Reform Association and did significant work in the area of tariff reform. Although the modern public remembers him chiefly for his Sherlock Holmes creation, he himself felt that the detective series constituted a very insignificant part of his life's work. For more on Doyle's life, see Comments, Chapter 2, iv.

3   Mrs. Eleanor Sidgwick was the wife of Henry Sidgwick and a psychic investigator in her own right. She was at one time president of the SPR, as were her husband and her brothers, British prime minister Arthur Balfour and Gerald Balfour.

4   *The Progressive Thinker,* published in Chicago, was a major spiritualist newspaper in circulation during the 1920s and '30s. Dr. A. was a subscriber.

5   "Poltergeist," from the German, means literally "noisy ghost." A poltergeist is a spirit, usually mischievous and sometimes malevolent. It attracts attention by moving objects and making noises, usually knocking and pounding. It sometimes assaults people and animals, often pushing or tripping them or throwing stones or sand at them.

6   Items teleported out of the séance room are known as asports.

7   Phantom limbs produced by mediums are called pseudopods. In Eusapia's case, they sometimes developed into almost full forms after detaching from her body.

8   Lombroso, a professor of psychology and anthropology at the University of Turin, was also director of an insane asylum. Among his theories: that human anatomy is an indicator of one's potential for criminality, and that left-handed people possess an innate criminal instinct.

9   Richet is credited with coining the term "ectoplasm" (from the Greek meaning "exteriorized substance"). In the interest of accuracy, however, it should be noted that Gustave Géley, a French physician, psychical researcher, and director of the Institut Métapsychique International in

Paris, who was present when the term was coined, claims that Richet used the plural form "ectoplasms" and was not naming the substance at all, but the forms created from the substance (Géley 1975b, 177).

10 Baryta water is an alkaline solution of barium hydroxide used for measuring the production of carbon dioxide from respiration.

11 Some accounts, including those of Doyle himself, refer to Madame Bisson as the wife of Adolphe Bisson, a wealthy French Algerian businessman. Other accounts refer to her as the wife of sculptor André Bisson. Schrenck-Notzing identifies the husband as Alexandre Bisson. Whatever his name was, he passed to the spirit world in 1912. Now, will the real Monsieur Bisson please make his presence known?

12 Madame Bisson frequently reported that during their private sessions, the veil-like mass was expelled through Eva C.'s vagina, giving rise to the theory that the medium was experiencing a pseudobirth.

13 When I read Schrenck-Notzing's book, I was really struck by the photographs. It seemed to me that they were in the realm of "thoughtography": thought-as-energy projected to the point of being recordable by the photographic film.

14 The powers of physical mediums appear to dull over time, apparently due to the enormous toll exacted by the energy required for manifestations.

15 Even though Schrenck-Notzing reported that Eva C. was always visible during a séance, it is quite clear that she was never wholly visible. His notes indicate that Eva's head could be seen through a narrow gap in the curtain, but that the rest of her body was hidden from view.

16 I was in New York a few years ago doing research at the ASPR's library. When I asked the librarian about materialization, he disappeared into the back and emerged with Schrenck-Notzing's book, which I subsequently bought. It was clear that, in the mind of that librarian, any discussion of materialization starts with Schrenck-Notzing.

17 Mental mediums are also known as trance mediums.

18 The young spirit's name was apparently quite long and unwieldy and Mrs. Leonard simply selected random letters from the name to form the name Feda.

19 See Chapter 4 for details on proxy sittings.

20 Schizophrenia is a mental disorder characterized by withdrawal from reality and deterioration of personality. The condition is usually accompanied by the presence of mutually contradictory character qualities. The term "schizoid" was used in the past to refer to a mildly schizophrenic personality.

21 From Shakespeare's *Hamlet* (1603): "What dreams may come, / When we have shuffled off this mortal coil, / Must give us pause."

22 This finding is consistent with other spirit communicators, who maintain that names are unimportant in the spirit world.

23 Author Jane Austen, who was Charlotte's dear friend on earth, seems to have remained a close friend in the next life.

CHAPTER 3

1 Monism is the doctrine that holds that in the universe there is only a single element or principle from which everything is developed (i.e., we are all one with the universe). In addition to being an essential feature of many Eastern religions, this doctrine was also preached by Jesus: "All things were made by him; and without him was not any thing made that was made" (John 1:3); and "Now they have known that all things whatsoever thou hast given me are of thee" (John 17:7).

2 Eckankar, which now boasts a following of 50,000 people in more than 100 countries worldwide, became a religion in 1990. Based on the idea of the spiritual journey as a direct approach to consciousness and knowingness about God, it is a religion of personal experience and self-exploration that holds belief in reincarnation as a basic tenet.

3 It may appear that there are no spiritualist churches in states/provinces not listed. That is not the case. The summary indicates only that no responses were received from them. For the sake of brevity, we have not included them in Table 1.

4 *Encyclopedia Britannica*, 14th ed., s.v. "Spiritualism."

5 The 2001 Brazil census puts the precise number at 2,262,401.

6 Umbanda and Candomblé are sometimes referred to collectively as *macumba* or *quimbanda*, which suggests that black magic is involved, but there are differences between the two cults. Umbanda is practiced by Brazilians of all races and social classes. Candomblé is a very old cult that is practiced exclusively by Brazilians of African descent. Both cults practice rites that resemble those of African voodoo.

7 Playfair points out that Brazilian Spiritists make a clear distinction in Portuguese between *escrita automática* and *psicografia*; the former is a manifestation of one's unconscious (inspiration), the latter a manifestation of a separate entity such as a spirit (revelation). Although we make a similar distinction between "inspired writing" and "spirit writing" in English, both are referred to generically as automatic writing.

8 Many psychically gifted people believe that using their powers for gain will dilute or possibly even destroy their gifts. Paramount among these believers was Edgar Cayce.

9 Although he was a philanthropist and generous to those in need, Mirabelli reportedly charged high fees for his services.

10 Camille Flammarion (1842–1925), a French astronomer and skilled automatic writer, was president of the SPR in 1922–1923. Although he had gone through a number of years of doubt as to whether automatic writing and other phenomena were proof of life beyond or simply proceeded from the minds of the sitters, in his final address to the SPR in 1923 he stated, "telepathy exists just as much between the dead and the living as between the living" (Fodor 1966, 141).

11 Hans Driesch was professor of philosophy at the University of Leipzig and an influential psychical researcher in Germany. President of the SPR in 1926–1927, he maintained that there may be truth behind psychic phenomena and that those who declared such things impossible had given up the right to be heard by serious people. In a 1924 lecture before an audience at London University, he declared, "the actuality of psychic phenomena is doubted today only by the incorrigible dogmatist" (Fodor 1966, 109).

12 Among the feats he performed at various times in public were escaping from handcuffs after levitating several feet into the air, appearing to glow from within in a dark room, and, perhaps his most astonishing feat in a controlled challenge before multiple witnesses, teleporting himself across 50 miles, from the São Paulo railroad station of da Luz to São Vicenti, in 2 minutes.

13 www.lighthousespiritualcentre.ca

14 For the complete summary of results, go to http://survey.worldwidemediums.co.uk.

15 Stanley Krippner, "Shamans: The First Healers," *ASPR Newsletter* 1993;17(4):1–4.

16 At the time, Playfair was in Brazil doing research for his book *The Flying Cow* (Souvenir Press, 1975).

17 Magnetic healing is the use of magnets to improve the body's circulation, thus promoting healing.

18 "Bhagavan" is a Sanskrit word meaning "glorious, divine, venerable, or holy"; "Sri" is an Eastern honorific; "Sathya" means "truth"; "Sai" is a Muslim word for "saint"; and "Baba" is a Hindu word for "father." "Narayana," part of Sai Baba's name allegedly given at birth, is a name for God.

19 School records apparently indicate that Sai Baba was born in 1929. Detractors claim the 1926 date was a fabrication to have Sai Baba's birth coincide with a prophecy, the fulfillment of which would be proof of Sai Baba's divinity.

20 Haraldsson is an emeritus psychology professor at the University of Iceland and a psychic researcher.

21 Sai Baba refused to permit formal experimentation of his skills, which he terms "small items," with the reason that he would never use his paranormal powers for demonstration but for religious purposes only, such as helping his followers when they are in need. He did, however,

produce various items through teleportation in the presence of the investigators.

22 Erlendur Haraldsson and Karlis Osis, "The Appearance and Disappearance of Objects in the Presence of Sri Sathya Baba," *Journal of the American Society for Psychical Research* 1977;71:33–43.

23 James van Praagh, "Early Life," http://vanpraagh.com/index. php?p=EarlyLife.

24 Michael Shermer, "Does James Van Praagh Talk to the Dead? Nope! Fraud! Part 5," *Skeptic Mag Online*, http://www.holysmoke.org/praagh5.htm.

25 Please see www.drgaryschwartz.com/media_place/media_place.htm for Gary Schwartz's response to "what can be described as a character assassination segment [broadcast] on *Geraldo at Large* on Saturday, October 6th, 2007, [in which] explicit defamatory claims were made against Dr. Gary E. Schwartz concerning his ethics regarding fundraising for afterlife research."

26 In fact, Sir Winston Churchill died just before 8:00 a.m. on Sunday, January 24, 1965. He had been on the brink of death for 10 days after suffering a stroke. The *New York Times* reported that he died "in peace and without pain."

27 Spirits who manifested at the Aykroyd circles and in other locations did not typically identify themselves by name. Spirits responded with their first names if one of the sitters asked directly, but in general they made it appear as though names were of no consequence in the next world.

28 Instrumental transcommunication is the term used for two-way electronic communication across different planes of existence.

CHAPTER 4

1 Rhea A. White is the founder and former editor of the journal *Exceptional Human Experience*. The quote is from her lecture presented at the Exceptional Human Experiences Conference held in New York City, June 13, 1993, and reprinted in the ASPR Newsletter 18(3):1–6.

2 James E. Alcock, "Channeling," *Skeptical Inquirer* 1989;13(4):380–4.

3 It is presumed that "clairessence" is another word for "clairalience," although no reference to the former word could be found in either Buckland (2006) or Guiley (1991).

4 William Jackson Crawford (1880–1920) was an Irish mechanical engineer who lectured in engineering at Queen's University Belfast. *The Reality of Psychic Phenomena* (1916), *Experiments in Psychical Science* (1919), and *The Psychic Structures at the Goligher Circle* (1921) are Crawford's three important books on the Goligher circle experiments.

5   James H. Hyslop, "Review of Experiments in Physical Phenomena," *Journal of the American Society for Psychical Research* 1917; 11:728–37.

6   Harry adopted the name of his idol, the conjurer Jean Eugène Robert-Houdin, who maintained that a magician was not merely a juggler or a trickster, but "an actor playing the part of a man with supernatural powers" (Kalush and Sloman 2006, 21).

7   The precise year is unknown. Estimates suggest that Muhammad received his first message in 610.

8   *Vox divina* is the collective voice of the spirits that is said to have been heard, speaking articulately and repeating the same words in different places, since ancient times.

9   James Arthur Findlay (1883–1964), spiritualist and vice president of the Glasgow Society for Psychical Research, made extensive investigation of direct-voice medium John Campbell Sloan, which he detailed in his 1931 book *On the Edge of the Etheric*.

10 Mrs. Thomas Everitt (1825–1915) was one of the earliest British mediums.

11 Reverend Francis Ward Monck was a 19th-century English clergyman turned professional medium who excelled at slate writing. It was said he refused to sleep without a night-light for fear of the phantoms that he claimed he could see in the dark.

12 Harry Bastian was a lesser-known American materialization medium whose powers waned after 1882.

13 Gerald Davison and John Neale, quoted from their text *Abnormal Psychology* (John Wiley, 1996) at www.essays.cc/free_essays/f2/csk144.shtml. (See the section on Mrs. Garrett further on in this chapter for more on the disorder.)

14 There are also examples of glossolalia from primitive times and from primitive cultures in modern times, although there appears to be "no evidence of intelligent conversation being carried out in a recognized language unknown to the speaker in any native culture studied by anthropologists" (Christie-Murray 1978, 167).

15 Christie-Murray refers to tape recordings of schizophrenic patients whose utterings sounded similar to glossolalia (1978, 176).

16 *Out of Africa,* directed by Sidney Pollack, Mirage Enterprises, 1985.

17 *Jurassic Park* (and its sequels), directed by Steven Spielberg, Universal Pictures, 1993.

18 *The Ladykillers,* directed by Joel and Ethan Coen, Touchstone Pictures, 2004.

19 Emma Hardinge Britten (1823–1899), a British medium known among spiritualists as the Silver-Tongued Lecturer, was adept at automatic writing, healing, prophesy, and inspirational speaking. Jenny Keyes was one of her protégées.

20 This effect is known as paraeidolia, the sensation of seeing a particular image or identifiable object in something quite random, such as the "man in the moon," sheep among the cumulus clouds, or the devil's face in Queen Elizabeth II's hairdo on the old Canadian dollar bill. From the Greek *para* ("faulty" or "wrong") and *eidon* ("image"), *paraeidolia* is presumably the basis upon which the Rorschach Ink Blot Test functions.

21 Among others, Mumler photographed Mary Todd Lincoln, widow of slain US president Abraham Lincoln. The president's image appeared in the photo behind his widow.

22 The term "thoughtography" was coined in the early 20th century by Tokyo psychology professor Tomokichi Fukurai, who reproduced images that had been transferred psychically onto glass plates by his subject.

23 Harry Price (1881–1930) was at one time the director of the National Laboratory of Psychical Research in London. He was also a well-known conjurer.

24 Another of the ubiquitous Walters. See Comments, Chapter 4, ii.

25 *Cartes de visite* were small (usually 2½ by 4 inches) visiting card portraits widely used around the world from the mid-19th to the early 20th century.

26 Joe Nickell, "Spirit Painting. Part II: The Bangs Sisters," *Skeptical Briefs* 2000;10(2), http://www.csicop.org/sb/2000-06/i-files.html.

27 Joe Nickell, "Spirit Painting. Part I: The Campbell Brothers," *Skeptical Briefs* 2000;10(1), http://www.csicop.org/sb/2000-03/i-files.html.

28 Nickell, "Spirit Painting. Part I."

29 Uncle Andrew Aykroyd was my great-grandfather Daniel's brother, Dr. A.'s uncle.

30 In one test by dynamometer conducted in Warsaw, Eusapia Palladino was reported to have exerted telekinetic pressure on a table three times greater than she would normally be able to exert. The table's mass, however, was not mentioned (Buckland 2006, 295).

31 Associated Press, "Elisabeth Kubler-Ross, 78." *Globe and Mail* August 25, 2004.

32 The "season" lasts from March to October every year, although special visits to the holy water springs can be arranged during the winter months.

33 A theophany, from the Greek *theophania,* is an appearance made by God or a deity in a form visible to humans.

34 Answers.com, "Materialization," http://www.answers.com/topic/materialization-wordnet (accessed March 26, 2009).

35 Translated by J. A. Lacey and published by Fathers of the Church in 1955, as reported in Wiebe (1997, 23).

36 Pseudo-Dionysius, *The Complete Works,* trans. Colm Luibheid, New York: Paulist Press, 1987, 137B.

37 Previous experimenters had unsuccessfully attempted to take molds of materializations using lampblack paper, which produced only partial imprints, and plaster, which set much too slowly for the few moments during which a materialized entity was typically available.

38 *Light* was the official publication of the London Spiritualist Alliance.

39 Nikos K. Logothetis, "Vision: A Window on Consciousness," *Scientific American* 1999;281:44-51.

CHAPTER 5

1 The one exception to this is when table tipping occurs. If sitters lose digital contact with the table, spirit communication cannot be maintained. When the table begins to travel around the room, as it often does, sitters have to be prepared to vacate their seats and follow it.

2 The same bedroom is today referred to as "the ghost room" because of the phenomena that have occurred there. In addition to the accounts told here, the small door of the closet is often found open in the morning after it was left firmly latched the previous night.

3 Psi, the 23rd letter of the Greek alphabet, is a term used by the OSIR to refer to the "unknown element" in any phenomenological equation.

COMMENTS

1 The Royal Society, founded in 1660, is the oldest and most prestigious scientific society in Britain.

2 It seems in this context that Eglinton was pure performer, reinforcing our thesis that much of the psychic phenomena of recorded history is performance. For further elaboration, see Chapter 5.

3 Leonora Evelina Simonds Piper Biography, 2001, http://www. spiritwritings.com/leonorapiper.html.

4 Yeats, an Irish poet and recipient of the Nobel Prize for Literature in 1923, joined the Golden Dawn in 1887. He helped to write some of the order's rituals.

5 Blackwood was the author of popular occult fiction works.

6 Wiebe is author of *Visions of Jesus: Direct Encounters from the New Testament to Today,* published by Oxford University Press in 1997.

SOURCES

$\mathbf{A}$t the headquarters of the American Society for Psychical Research at 5 West 73rd Street in New York City, the library takes up one room with 20-foot ceilings. All four walls are covered, floor to ceiling, with references concerning the subject of spiritualism, constituting what is probably the most extensive collection on the subject in North America. The works included in this bibliography are but a fraction of the references that exist, but they are the ones I found particularly useful in completing this work. While I have followed the standard practice of listing these alphabetically by author, I must say that my four favorite books are *Harper's Encyclopedia of Mystical and Paranormal Experience,* by Rosemary Ellen Guiley; *The Spirit Book: The Encyclopedia of Clairvoyance, Channeling, and Spirit Communication,* by Raymond Buckland; the *Encyclopaedia of Psychic Science,* by Nándor Fodor; and *The History of Spiritualism,* by Sir Arthur Conan Doyle, which happens to be the first book I read on the subject and one that stands up admirably. All of the books are available from AbeBooks (www.abebooks.com) at a reasonable price.

TEXT SOURCES

Adler, Mortimer J. 1982. *The Angels and Us.* New York: Macmillan.

Allain, Paul, and Jen Harvie, editors. 2006. *The Routledge Companion to Theatre and Performance.* London: Routledge.

Anastasi, Anne. 1988. *Psychological Testing.* 6th ed. New York: Collier Macmillan.

Anonymous. 1970. *Encyclopedia of World Mythology*. Foreword by Rex Warner. London: Peerage Books.

Apuleius. 1950. *The Transformations of Lucius, Otherwise Known as the Golden Ass*. Robert Graves, translator. Victoria, Australia: Penguin Books.

Armstrong, Karen. 1993. *A History of God*. New York: Ballantine Books.

Arnold, Guy. 1983. *Datelines of World History*. New York: Warwick Press.

Aykroyd, Peter H. 2002. *A Sense of Place*. Kingston, ON: Quarry Press.

Baird, Alexander T., editor. 1944. *One Hundred Cases for Survival After Death*. New York: Bernard Ackerman.

Barrow, John D., and Frank J. Tipler. 1986. *The Anthropic Cosmological Principle*. Oxford, UK: Oxford University Press.

Bord, Janet, and Colin Bord. 1998. *The World of the Unexplained*. London: Blandford.

Boyer, Pascal. Why Is Religion Natural? *Skeptical Inquirer* 2004;28(2):25–31.

Bragdon, Emma. 2004. *Kardec's Spiritism*. Woodstock, VT: Lightening Up Press.

Brandon, Ruth. 1983. *The Spiritualists—The Passion for the Occult in the Nineteenth and Twentieth Centuries*. New York: Alfred A. Knopf.

Bro, Harmon Hartzell. 1989. *A Seer Out of Season: The Life of Edgar Cayce*. New York: New American Library.

Buckland, Raymond. 2006. *The Spirit Book: The Encyclopedia of Clairvoyance, Channeling, and Spirit Communication*. Canton, MI: Visible Ink Press.

———. 1995. *The Truth about Spirit Communication*. St. Paul, MN: Llewellyn Publications.

Carrington, Hereward. 1957. *The Case for Psychic Survival*. New York: Citadel Press.

———. 1930. *The Story of Psychic Science*. London: Rider.

———. 1920. *The Physical Phenomena of Spiritualism, Fraudulent and Genuine*. 3rd ed. New York: Dodd, Mead.

Cayce, Edgar. 1999. *My Life as a Seer: The Lost Memoirs*. A. Robert Smith, editor. New York: St. Martin's Press.

Chéroux, Clément, Andreas Fischer, and Pierre Apraxine. 2005. *The Perfect Medium: Photography and the Occult*. New Haven, CT: Yale University Press.

Chopra, Deepak. 2003. *The Spontaneous Fulfillment of Desire*. New York: Harmony Books.

Christie-Murray, David. 1978. *Voices from the Gods*. London: Routledge & Kegan Paul.

Colombo, John Robert. 2000. *Ghost Stories of Canada*. Toronto: Dundurn Group.

Cowan, Tom. 1994. *The Book of Séance*. Chicago: Contemporary Books.

Crookall, Robert. 1961. *The Supreme Adventure*. Cambridge, England: James Clarke.

De Morgan, Sophia Elizabeth. 1863. *From Matter to Spirit: The Result of Ten Years' Experience in Spirit Manifestations*. London: Longman, Green, Longman, Roberts & Green.

De Swarte, Lyn G. 1999. *Principles of Spiritualism*. London: Harper Collins.

Doyle, Arthur Conan. 1926. *The History of Spiritualism*. 2 volumes. New York: Arno Press.

Dufresne, Chris. 2000. *My Life with Sylvia Browne*. Carlsbad, CA: Hay House.

Flammarion, Camille, 1907. *Mysterious Psychic Sources*. Massachusetts: Boston Company.

Flint, Leslie. 1971. *Voices in the Dark*. London: Two Worlds Publishing.

Fodor, Nándor. 1966. *Encyclopaedia of Psychic Science*. Hyde Park, NY: University Books.

Frazer, James George. 1922. *The Golden Bough*. London: MacMillan Press.

Frye, Northrop. 1990. *Words with Power: Being a Second Study of "The Bible and Literature."* Toronto: Penguin Books.

———. 1982. *The Great Code: The Bible and Literature*. Toronto: Academia Press Canada.

Géley, Gustave. 1975a. *Perspectives in Psychical Research*. New York: Arno Press.

———. 1975b. *Clairvoyance and Materialization*. New York: Arno Press.

Guiley, Rosemary Ellen. 2000. *The Encyclopedia of Ghosts and Spirits*. New York: Checkmark Books.

———. 1991. *Harper's Encyclopedia of Mystical and Paranormal Experience*. New York: Harper Collins.

Hamer, Dean. 2004. *The God Gene: How Faith Is Hardwired into Our Genes*. New York: Doubleday.

Hamilton, T. Glen. 1942. *Intention and Survival*. Toronto: Macmillan.

Hancock, Graham. 2006. *Supernatural: Meetings with the Ancient Teachers of Mankind*. Toronto: Anchor Canada.

Harvie, Jen. 2005. *Staging the UK*. Manchester, UK: Manchester University Press.

Home, D. D. 1878. *Lights and Shadows of Spiritualism*. London: Virtue.

Hudson, Thompson Jay. 1977. *The Law of Psychic Phenomena*. Salinas, CA: Hudson-Cohan Publishing.

Jolly, Martyn. 2006. *Faces of the Living Dead: The Belief in Spirit Photography*. London: British Library.

Kalush, William, and Larry Sloman. 2006. *The Secret Life of Houdini: The Making of America's First Superhero*. New York: Atria Books.

Klemp, Harold. 1998. *A Modern Prophet Answers Your Key Questions about Life*. Minneapolis: Eckankar.

———. 1994. *Ask the Master*. Volume 2. Minneapolis: Eckankar.

Koestler, Arthur. 1972. *The Roots of Coincidence*. New York: Random House.

LeShan, Lawrence. 2003. *The Medium, the Mystic, and the Physicist*. New York: Helios Press.

Lewis, C. S. 1952. *Mere Christianity*. London: G. Bles.

Lodge, Sir Oliver. 1924. *Making of Man*. London: Hodder and Stoughton.

Logothetis, Nikos K. 1999. Vision: A Window on Consciousness. *Scientific American* 281:44–51.

Luckhurst, Roger. 2002. *The Invention of Telepathy, 1870-1901*. Oxford, UK: Oxford University Press.

Lynne, Carole. 2003. *How to Get a Good Reading from a Psychic Medium*. Boston: Weiser Books.

Markides, Kyriacos C. 2005. *Gifts of the Desert*. New York: Doubleday.

———. 1994. *Riding with the Lion*. London: Viking.

———. 1989. *The Magus of Strovolos*. Toronto: Penguin Books.

McDannell, Colleen, and Bernhard Lang. 2001. *Heaven: A History*. 2nd ed. New Haven, CT: Yale University Press.

McMullin, Stan. 2004. *Anatomy of a Séance: A History of Spirit Communication in Central Canada*. Kingston, ON: McGill-Queen's University Press.

Meyer, Marvin W., translator. 1984. *The Secret Teachings of Jesus: Four Gnostic Gospels*. New York: Random House.

Michell, John, and Robert J. M. Rickard. 1977. *Phenomena: A Book of Wonders*. New York: Pantheon Books.

Moore, W. Usborne. 1913. *The Voices*. London: Watts.

Murchison, Carl Allanmore. 1927. *The Case for and against Psychical Belief*. Worcester, MA: Clark University.

Murphy, Kevin R., and Charles O. Davidshofer. 1991. *Psychological Testing: Principles and Applications*. 2nd ed. Englewood Cliffs, NJ: Prentice-Hall.

Myers, Frederic William Henry. 1903. *Human Personality and Its Survival of Bodily Death*. 2 volumes. London: Longmans, Green.

Nagy, Ron. 2006. *Precipitated Spirit Paintings*. Lakeville, MN: Galde Press.

Naisbitt, John, and Patricia Aburdene. 1990. *Megatrends 2000*. New York: William Morrow.

Nickell, Joe. 2001. *Real-Life X-Files: Investigating the Paranormal*. Lexington, KY: University Press of Kentucky.

———. 1988. *Secrets of the Supernatural: Investigating the World's Occult Mysteries*. Buffalo: Prometheus Books.

Ostrander, Sheila, and Lynn Schroeder. 1970. *Psychic Discoveries behind the Iron Curtain*. Englewood Cliffs, NJ: Prentice-Hall.

Owens, Elizabeth. 2003. *How to Communicate with Spirits*. St. Paul, MN: Llewellyn Publications.

Playfair, Guy Lyon. 1975. *The Flying Cow*. Toronto: Souvenir Press.

Pleasants, Helen, editor. 1964. *Biographical Dictionary of Parapsychology*. New York: Helix Press.

Porche, Jean, and Deborah Vaughan. 2005. *Psychics and Mediums in Canada*. Toronto: Dundurn Press.

Proudfoot, Wayne, editor. 2004. *William James and a Science of Religions*. New York: Columbia University Press.

Ramachandran, V. S. Creativity versus Skepticism within Science. *Skeptical Inquirer* 2006;30(6):48–51.

Reader's Digest. 1992. *Life Beyond Death*. Pleasant Villa, NY: Reader's Digest.

Richet, Charles. 1923. *Thirty Years of Psychical Research*. Stanley De Brath, translator. New York: Macmillan.

Rider, Freemont. 1909. *Are the Dead Alive?* New York: B. W. Dodge.

Roach, Mary. 2005. *Spook: Science Tackles the Afterlife*. New York: W. W. Norton.

Russell, Jeffrey Burton. 1997. *A History of Heaven*. Princeton, NJ: Princeton University Press.

Schoemperlen, Diane. 2001. *Our Lady of Lost and Found: A Novel*. Toronto: Harper Flamingo.

Schrenck-Notzing, Baron Albert von. 1920. *Phenomena of Materialisation: A Contribution to the Investigation of Mediumistic Teleplastics*. London: Kegan, Paul, Trench, Tubner.

Shepard, Leslie, editor. 2002. *Encyclopedia of Occultism and Parapsychology*. Volume 1. Detroit: Gale Group.

Sitwell, Sacheverell. 1988. *Poltergeists: Fact or Fancy*. London: Dorset Press.

Smith, Barbara. 1998. *Ghost Stories of Manitoba*. Edmonton, AB: Lone Pine.

Smith, David V., and Robert F. Margolskee. 2006. Making Sense of Taste. *Scientific American* 16(3):84–90.

Smith, Susy. 1978. *The Conversion of a Psychic*. Garden City, NY: Doubleday.

———. 1964. *The Mediumship of Mrs. Leonard*. New Hyde Park, NY: University Books.

Swann, Ingo. 1996. *The Great Apparitions of Mary*. New York: Crossroad.

Talbot, Margaret. 2005. Darwin in the Dock. *New Yorker* 81(39):66–77.

Time-Life Books. 1992. *The Psychics*. Mysteries of the Unknown. Alexandria, VA: Time-Life Books.

———. 1989a. *Ancient Wisdom and Secret Sects*. Mysteries of the Unknown. Alexandria, VA: Time-Life Books.

———. 1989b. *Search for the Soul*. Mysteries of the Unknown. Alexandria, VA: Time-Life Books.

———. 1989c. *Spirit Summonings*. Mysteries of the Unknown. Alexandria, VA: Time-Life Books.

———. 1988. *Phantom Encounters*. Mysteries of the Unknown. Alexandria, VA: Time-Life Books.

———. 1987. *Psychic Voyages*. Mysteries of the Unknown. Alexandria, VA: Time-Life Books.

Tipler, Frank J. 1994. *The Physics of Immortality*. New York: Doubleday.

Van de Castle, Robert L. 1994. *Our Dreaming Mind*. New York: Ballantine Books.

Weisberg, Barbara. 2004. *Talking to the Dead: Kate and Maggie Fox and the Rise of Spiritualism*. New York: Harper Collins.

White, Stephen R. 2006. Spirituality and the Intellectual Development of College Students. *International Electronic Journal for Leadership in Learning* 10(13), June 30. http://www.ucalgary.ca/iejll/vol10/white.

Wicker, Christine. 2003. *Lily Dale: The True Story of the Town That Talks to the Dead*. New York: Harper Collins.

Wiebe, Phillip H. 1997. *Visions of Jesus*. New York: Oxford University Press.

Wilson, A. N. 1990. *C. S. Lewis: A Biography*. New York: W.W. Norton.

Wilson, Colin. 1975. *Mysterious Powers*. London: Aldus Books.

Youngblood, Ronald, F. F. Bruce, and R. K. Harrison. 2004. *Compact Bible Dictionary*. Nashville: Nelson.

Zimdars-Swartz, Sandra L. 1991. *Encountering Mary*. New York: Avon Books.

Zukav, Gary. 1989. *The Seat of the Soul*. New York: Simon & Schuster.

SOURCES

WEB SOURCES

Department of Electrical Engineering and Computer Sciences, College of Engineering, University of California at Berkeley: www.eecs.berkeley.edu

Essays.cc: www.essays.cc

Holysmoke.org: www.holysmoke.org

International Raelian Movement: www.rael.org

James Van Praagh: www.vanpraagh.com

Lighthouse Spiritual Centre: www.lighthousespiritualcentre.ca

Ontario Consultants on Religious Tolerance: www.religioustolerance.org

ParaResearchers of Ontario: www.pararesearchers.org

RealEstate.com: www.realestate.com

Ross Institute Internet Archives for the Study of Destructive Cults, Controversial Groups and Movements: www.rickross.com

Survival Research Institute of Canada: www.islandnet.com/sric

INDEX

Underscored page references indicate boxed text.

Dionysius Exiguus, 174
Direct-voice mediums
    Crandon (Margery) and, 131
    defined, <u>68</u>, 130
    Doyle and, 130–31
    fraud and, <u>68</u>
    glossolalia and, 134–38
    theories about, 131–32, 137–38
    ventriloquism, <u>68</u>, 132–34
Dissociative identity disorder (DID), 175
Dixon, Donna, 107–8, 110–11
Doppelgängers, 177–79
Dowding, Lord, 169
Doyle, Sir Arthur Conan
    Crandon (Margery) and, 147, 149
    Davis and, 9
    direct-voice mediums and, 130–31
    Hamilton (Glen) and, 31
    History of Spiritualism, The, 50, 221
    Houdini and, 125
    Lacey séances and, 37–38
    Leonard and, 68
    Palladino and, 55
    Piper and, 204
    Richet and, 58
    spirit of, 198
    spiritualism and, 50, 124, 203, 221
Dr. A. See Aykroyd, Samuel Augustus
Driesch, Hans, 94
Dudley, E. E., 150
Duguid, David, 158

Ectoplasm, 28–29, <u>30</u>, 34, <u>36</u>, 39, 57–58, 60–61, 63, 65, 177
Edison, Thomas Alva, 37, 113, 131
Edmonds, John Worth, 135
Edmonds, Laura, 135
Eglinton, William, 199–200
Electronic voice phenomenon (EVP), 113–17
Elizabeth M. (medium), 31–33
Ellis, D. J., 116
Emmanuel (spirit), 92
EPIs, 197

ESP, 131
Eva C. See Béraud, Marthe
EVP, 113–17
Extraordinary phenomenon, 208–9. See also specific type
Extraordinary psychic instruments (EPIs), 197
Extraordinary skills, 118–20. See also specific type
Extrasensory perception (ESP), 131

Faraday, Michael, 163–64
Feda (spirit), 67
Findlay, J. Arthur, 131–32
Finney, Charles Grandison, 16
Flammarion, Camille, 161
Fleming, Alexander, 31
Flint, Leslie, <u>68</u>, 77–83, 98, 130
Fodor, Nándor, 88, 93, 131, 134, 151, 154–55, 159, 221
Foreign languages, speaking, 134–38
Fort, Charles, 208–9
Fourierist utopian socialist movement, 16
Fox, Kate, 12, 14–17, 40, 47
Fox, Leah, 14–15, 40
Fox, Maggie, 12, 14–17, 40, 47
Fraud and trickery. See also Investigations
    automatic writing and, 125–26, 129–30
    of Béraud, 59
    of Crandon (Margery), 148–51
    direct-voice mediums and, <u>68</u>
    ectoplasm and, <u>36</u>
    of Fox sisters, 17, 47
    materialization and, 178–79
    of Palladino, 54–56, 63
    physical mediums and, 61–62
    slate writing and, 161
    "white crow" lecture and, 122–24
Frye, Northrop, 173–74
FYM (spirit), 33, 36, 38

Gallife, Marian, 207–8
Garrett, Eileen Jeanette Vancho Lyttle, 69–70, 72–76, <u>73</u>, 130, 175–77

BIOGRAPHICAL NOTES

ABOUT THE AUTHOR

Peter H. Aykroyd is a retired Government of Canada senior executive. He holds a Bachelor of Applied Science Degree from the University of Toronto. He is the author of two previous books, *The Anniversary Compulsion,* the chronicle of Canada's centennial celebrations in 1967, and *A Sense of Place,* the story of his family in Yorkshire , dating back to 1350. He lives with his wife of 57 years, the former Lorraine Gougeon, on a plot of land 20 miles north of Kingston, Ontario, that has been in the family for 180 years. Their two sons, Dan and Peter Jonathon, are both featured in *A History of Ghosts.*

ABOUT THE COLLABORATOR

Angela Narth is a full-time writer with seven books currently in print. She holds a Bachelor's Degree in Anthropology from the University of British Columbia and a Master's Degree in Educational Psychology from the University of Ottawa. A writer of both fiction and nonfiction, she has a dedicated readership under her own name, and as Angela Murphy, her alter ego. She lives with her husband, Peter, and their cat, Bentley, on the banks of the mighty Red River, a few minutes south of Winnipeg, Manitoba. They have two grown daughters.